Citizen Participation in Environmental Affairs
1970 - 1986:
A Bibliography

AMS STUDIES IN SOCIAL HISTORY, NO. 8
ISSN 0270-6253
Other Titles in This Series:

1. Esmond Wright, ed. *Red, White & True Blue: The Loyalists in the Revolution.* 1976.
2. Richard V. Francaviglia. *The Mormon Landscape.* 1978.
3. Taylor Stoehr. *Free Love In America.* 1979.
4. Cynthia Huff. *British Women's Diaries: A Descriptive Bibliography of Selected Nineteenth-Century Women's Manuscript Diaries.* 1985
5. Nan Hackett. *XIX Century British Working-Class Autobiographies: An Annotated Bibliography.* 1985.
6. Elizabeth Benson-von der Ohe and Valmari M. Mason. *An Annotated Bibliography of U.S. Scholarship on the History of the Family.* 1986.
7. Barbara E. Nolan. *The Political Theory of Beatrice Webb.* 1988.

CITIZEN PARTICIPATION IN ENVIRONMENTAL AFFAIRS, 1970-1986: A BIBLIOGRAPHY

by

Frederick Frankena

Joann Koelln Frankena

AMS Press
New York

Library of Congress Cataloging-in-Publication Data

Frankena, Frederick.
   Citizen participation in environmental affairs, 1970—1986.

   (AMS studies in social history; no. 8)
   Bibliography: p.
   1. Environmental policy—Citizen participation—
Bibliography. I. Frankena, Joann Koelln.
II. Title.   III. Series.
25863.P6F73   1988   016.3637'058   87-45800
[HC79.E5]
ISBN 0-404-61608-9

AMS PRESS, INC.
56 East 13th Street
New York, N.Y. 10583

Printed in the United States of America

Contents

Contents (cont.)

Preface

The year 1970 is well remembered for Earth Day but its importance goes well beyond that effort at consciousness-raising. It was a watershed for the environmental movement, ushering in a period of effective action by environmental groups in American administrative politics.[1] Expanded opportunity for citizen participation has been a significant result of this political activity. Public opinion polls continue to show widespread support for environmental quality, a fact that underlines the relevance of citizen participation in environmental decision making today. We undertook this project in full view of these developments. Indeed, our motive was to fill a gap in the reporting of this important literature.

This bibliography is the serendipitous result of a more modest project -- to create a personal research database on citizen participation in environmental affairs. Work on the database made us acutely aware of the perils and pitfalls awaiting anyone desiring to access this literature.

At the same time, it became clear that the multifaceted activity of compiling references on a salient topic can produce a work of special value. Bibliography imparts a quality that transcends the works cited. A topical bibliography is like a fabric woven from the individual works that it cites and that in turn cite each other. The juxtaposition of interrelated references in itself serves to illuminate the topic. But there is a more significant value. A bibliography on relatively recent change that by nature cuts across disciplinary boundaries can yield an immense savings of time for the interested researcher. A good bibliography achieves an economy of effort. It obviates the need for everyone to plod through the same perilous search procedures which often yield mixed results due to limitations of time and library resources. This value, in conjunction with the timeliness of such areas as radioactive waste disposal, management and disposal of toxic and hazardous materials, and development of the national forests, led directly to consideration of a book compiling this database.

The organization of the bibliography was not prejudged. Rather, the distribution of topics among references served as a guide to the creation of content categories. In effect, the references were collected and added to the database before any attempt to organize the information. Consequently, the organizational structure evolved from familiarity with the literature. The five major sections and their various subcategories evolved from interaction with the database. Of course, our method is not the only conceivable way of organizing this literature. Nevertheless, we hope it proves useful both for gaining a sense of the subject and for efficiently locating materials on specific topics.

---

[1] Samuel P. Hays, "The Structure of Environmental Politics Since World War II," Journal of Social History, 14, 4 (1981): 719-738.

Some of the materials cited here are either not specifically on citizen participation or not directly related to environmental issues. There are several reasons for this. We assumed that references on the general topic are relevant to its environmental facets. Works on citizen participation in traffic planning or transportation decisions regarding neighborhood displacement, for example, might well suggest something about participation in the environmental aspects of transportation. Similarly, works on citizen participation in utility rate-making can serve to illuminate utility decisions on such environmental issues as power plant development and siting. In general, citation in a research review or a bibliography on citizen participation in a specific environmental issue was taken as an indication of relevance for purposes of this bibliography. We also thought it would be useful to include examples of reports produced by citizen organizations. Consistent with this spirit of inclusiveness, we chose to cite a variety of published and unpublished materials.[2] Our purpose was to cater to the widest possible range of informational needs while maintaining a commitment to the general topic.

In this connection two special categories included in the bibliography are worthy of mention. Environmental mediation is a relatively recent method for resolving disputes. It is a direct response to environmental conflict and the public's demand for a role in decision making. In recognition of its importance to citizen participation in environmental decision making, we included environmental mediation as Part IV of the bibliography. The driving force for social, political, economic, and environmental change is science and technology. Accordingly, Part V covers citizen participation in decision making about science and technology in general.

Two features of the bibliography are handled differently than usual -- cross-references and the index. Each is discussed in turn.

It is annoying to have to page through a bibliography to find all the cross-references. To help alleviate this problem, we duplicated references and included them under other relevant categories. A given reference may be cited under two or three subtopics, although most are cited in only one place. What is true for individual citations may not be true for the organizing categories of the bibliography. The reader would therefore do well to exercise judgment in deciding which categories to use. For example, one should look under both water pollution and water resources to find all relevant works on citizen participation in water quality decisions.

---

[2] Two sources are useful for finding addresses of authors of unpublished works and papers in hard-to-locate proceedings -- the National Faculty Directory (Detroit, MI: Gale Research Co.) and the "source" volume of the Social Science Citation Index (Philadelphia, PA: Institute for Scientific Information), which lists authors' addresses with their publications. You may need to check several volumes of the SSCI to find one in which the author's work is cited.

The most difficult decision was whether or not to include an index. Based on considerations of organization of the bibliography, the duplication of cross-references, and the relative brevity of the work as a whole, we decided not to do an index. References for a given subtopic are already conveniently concentrated in one place. The additional effort required to peruse the category is relatively modest. Moreover, this approach is recommended for locating other references that might be relevant. On the other hand, looking up a list of accession numbers from an index can be a tedious and time-consuming task that might not convey this sense of content.

For reasons implicit in the initial statement, this bibliography covers the period from approximately 1970 through 1986. Some items dated prior to 1970 have been selected for inclusion. A number of retrospective bibliographies; references in books, reports, and academic articles; and indexes or databases were utilized in the search. The latter included Environment Index / Environment Abstracts, Environmental Periodicals Bibliography, Index to Legal Periodicals, and Social Sciences Citation Index.

A wide variety of theoretical and practical materials on topics related to citizen participation and the environment are cited here. The bibliography should therefore be of interest both to scholars and practitioners. It should assist both groups in moving beyond the disciplinary and topical boundaries of this emergent speciality. We hope that this modest effort thereby serves to improve knowledge and practice.

The rapid development of the personal computer has had an impact on compilation of this bibliography, significantly increasing our speed, accuracy, and efficiency. The manuscript was created on the Apple Macintosh with the help of *DB Master* for database management and *MacWrite* for word processing.

Finally, we gratefully acknowledge the information resources provided by the Library of Michigan and the Michigan State University Library. We sincerely hope that the bibliography helps librarians, practitioners, and citizen groups to meet the information needs of citizens involved in environmental affairs.

Part I
Environmental Decision Making

General

Blowers, A. "Environmental Politics and Policy in the 1980s: A Changing Challenge." Policy and Politics, 14, 1 (1986): 1-8.

Bolle, A. W. "Public Participation and Environmental Quality." Natural Resources Journal, 11, 3 (1971): 497-505.

Bridgeland, W. and A. J. Sofranko. Community Structure and Citizen Mobilization: The Case of Environmental Quality. Department of Agricultural Economics and Rural Sociology, University of Illinois, Urbana, IL, 1972.

Brooks, H. "Environmental Decision Making: Analysis and Values." In L. Tribe et al. (eds.). When Values Conflict: Essays on Environmental Analysis, Discourse, and Decision. Cambridge, MA: Ballinger Publishing Co., 1976.

Buchan, G. "Institutional Design for Energy Systems/Environmental Decision Making." In MIT Symposium, Cambridge, MA, February 12-14, 1973: Proceedings, pp. 261-271.

Burton, T. L. "A Review and Analysis of Canadian Cases in Public Participation." In B. Sadler (ed.), Involvement and Environment: Proceedings of the Canadian Conference on Public Participation. Vol. 2: Working Papers and Case Studies. Edmonton, Alberta: Environment Council of Alberta, 1979, pp. 3-16.

Buskirk, E. D. Public Participation: Instructor Guide. U. S. Environmental Protection Agency, Washington, DC, 1980. 31 p.

Carpenter, R. "Information for Decisions in Environmental Policy." Science, 168 (1970): 1316-1322.

Clemente, F. et al. Public Participation in Energy-Related Decisionmaking: Six Case Studies. Report No. M76-53. Mitre Corporation and National Academy of Public Administration, McLean, VA, December 1977.

Conservation Foundation. "Public Participation in Environmental Decisions: As Opportunities for Public Participation in Environmental Decisions Increase, So Do the Challenges and Burdens." CF Letter, 3 (March 1973): 1-12.

Craig, D. "Citizen Participation in Australian Environmental Decisions." Northwest Environmental Journal, 2, 2 (1986): 115-140.

Daneke, G. A. "Public Involvement: What, Why, How -- Introduction." In G. A. Daneke et al. (eds.), Public Involvement and Social Impact Assessment. Boulder, CO: Westview Press, 1983, pp. 11-33.

DeBell, G. (ed.). The Voter's Guide to Environmental Politics Before, During, and After the Election. New York: Ballantine Books, 1970.

Draper, J. A. "Evolution of Citizen Participation in Canada." In B. Sadler (ed.), Involvement and Environment: Proceedings of the Canadian Conference on Public Participation. Vol. 1: A Review of Issues and Approaches. Edmonton, Alberta: Environment Council of Alberta, 1978, pp. 26-41.

Environmental Policy Institute. The Strip Mine Handbook: A Citizens Guide to the New Federal Surface Mine Law: How to Use It to Protect Your Community and Yourself. Washington, DC, 1978. 107 p.

Farrell, G. M., Melin, J. P., and S. R. Stacey. Involvement: A Saskatchewan Perspective. Department of the Environment, Government of Saskatchewan, Regina, Canada, 1976.

Freudenberg, Nicholas. Not In Our Backyards: Community Action for Health and the Environment. New York: Monthly Review Press, 1984. 304 p.

"Gaining Environmental Success." EPA Journal 6, 4 (1980): 10-11.

Gale, R. P. "The Consciousness Raising Potential of Social Impact Assessment." Paper presented at the Research Conference on Public Involvement and Social Impact Assessment, University of Arizona, Tucson, February 1981. 16 p.

Galloway, L. T. and T. FitzGerald. "The Surface Mining Control and Reclamation Act of 1977: The Citizen's 'Ace in the Hole.'" Northern Kentucky Law Review, 8, 2 (1981): 259-276.

Goldstein, J. Environmental Decision Making in Rural Locales: The Pine Barrens. New York: Praeger, 1981.

Graham, L. R. "Comparing United States and Soviet Experiences: Science, Citizens, and the Policy-Making Process." Environment, 26, 7, (1984): 6-9+.

Gresser, J. "A Japan Center for Human Environmental Problems: The Beginning of International Public Interest Cooperation." Ecology Law Quarterly, 3, 4 (1973): 759-797.

Haefele, E. T. "Social Choices and Environmental Quality." In Resources for the Future Annual Report, Washington, DC, 1970, pp. 23-31.

Hays, S. P. Beauty, Health, and Permanence: Environmental Politics in the United States, 1955-1985. New York: Cambridge University Press, 1987. 630 p.

Henderson, H. "Citizen Power in the Overdeveloped Countries." World Issues, 1, 2 (1977): 9-11.

Hunt, C. D. "Environmental Protection and the Public in the 1970s." Alternatives, 8, 1 (1978): 37-43.

League of Women Voters. Protecting the California Environment: A Citizen's Guide. San Francisco, CA, 1980.

Lucas, A. R. "Fundamental Prerequisites for Citizen Participation." In B. Sadler (ed.), Involvement and Environment: Proceedings of the Canadian Conference on Public Participation. Vol. 1: A Review of Issues and Approaches. Edmonton, Alberta: Environment Council of Alberta, 1978, pp. 58-76.

Manheim, M. et al. Transportation Decision-Making: A Guide to Social and Environmental Considerations. NCHRP Report No. 156. Transportation Research Board, Washington, DC, 1975.

Mattison, B. F. "The Role of Professional Organizations in Environmental Health." Archives of Environmental Health, 16 (January 1968): 116-120.

Maurice, R. "Citizen Utilization of Networking Technology." Journal of Environmental Systems, 1, 1 (1971): 37-46.

Mumme, S. P. "The Cananea Copper Controversy: Lessons for Environmental Diplomacy." Inter-American Economic Affairs, 38 (Summer 1984): 3-22.

Nelkin, D. (ed.). Controversy: The Politics of Technical Decisions. Beverly Hills, CA: Sage, 1979. 256 p.

Nelson, J. G. "Setting the Stage." In B. Sadler (ed.), Involvement and Environment: Proceedings of the Canadian Conference on Public Participation. Vol. 1: A Review of Issues and Approaches. Edmonton, Alberta: Environment Council of Alberta, 1978, pp. 13-25.

Nicholson, J. M. "Citizens Can Have a Voice in Environmental Decision-Making." Catalyst for Environmental Energy, 7, 2 (1980): 28-31.

Nicholson, J. M. "Public Participation and Environmental Protection." Environmental Impact Assessment Review, 1 (March 1980): 5-7.

Organization for Economic Cooperation and Development. Public Participation and Environmental Matters. Report ENV/Min(79)7. OECD Environmental Committee, Paris, April 1979. 30 p.

O'Riordan, T. "Public Opinion and Environmental Quality." Environment and Behavior, 3 (June 1971): 191-194.

Orton, B. M. "Mass Media Balloting on Regional Issues: Public Participation or Public Relations." Environmental Impact Assessment Review, 1 (June 1980): 125-153.

Peterson, R. W. "The Citizen: Power and/or Powerlessness?" CEQ Monitor 102, 4, 2 (1974): 1-23.

Portney, P., Sonstelie, J., and A. Kneese. "Environmental Quality, Household Migration, and Collective Choice." In E. T. Haefele (ed.), The Governance of Common Property Resources. Baltimore, MD: Johns Hopkins University Press, 1974, pp. 65-93.

Potter, F. M. "Everyone Wants to Save the Environment But No One Knows Quite What to Do." In R. Disch (ed.), Ecological Conscience: Values for Survival. Englewood Cliffs, NJ: Prentice-Hall, 1970, pp. 130-140.

Potter, H. R. and H. J. Norville. "Citizens' Participation and Effectiveness in Environmental Issues." In G. A. Daneke et al. (eds.), Public Involvement and Social Impact Assessment. Boulder, CO: Westview Press, 1983, pp. 35-44.

Sadler, B. "Basic Issues in Public Participation: A Background Perspective." In B. Sadler (ed.), Involvement and Environment: Proceedings of the Canadian Conference on Public Participation. Vol. 1: A Review of Issues and Approaches. Edmonton, Alberta: Environment Council of Alberta, 1978, pp. 1-12.

Sadler, B. (ed.), Involvement and Environment: Proceedings of the Canadian Conference on Public Participation. Vol. 1: A Review of Issues and Approaches. Edmonton, Alberta: Environment Council of Alberta, 1978.

Sadler, B. (ed.), Involvement and Environment: Proceedings of the Canadian Conference on Public Participation. Vol. 2: Working Papers and Case Studies. Edmonton, Alberta: Environment Council of Alberta, 1979.

Saltonstall, R. Jr. Your Environment and What You Can Do About It. New York: Walker and Co., 1970.

Schoenfeld, C. Interpreting Environmental Issues. Dembar Educational Research Service, Madison, WI, 1972. 200 p.

Schroth, P. W. "Public Participation in Environmental Decision-Making: A Comparative Perspective." Forum: American Bar Association, 14, 2 (1978): 352-368.

Seltzer, E. P. Citizen Participation in Environmental Planning: Context and Consequences. Unpublished Ph.D. dissertation. University of Pennsylvania, Philadelphia, PA, 1983. 238 p.

Sewell, W. R. D. and T. O'Riordan. "The Culture of Participation in Environmental Decision-making." Natural Resources Journal, 16 (January 1976): 1-21.

Stokes, B. "Helping Ourselves." Futurist, 15 (August 1981): 44-51.

Stokes, B. Helping Ourselves: Local Solutions to Global Problems. New York: Norton, 1981. 160 p.

Thomas, L. M. et al. "The Challenge of Community Involvement." EPA Journal, 11, 10 (1985): 2-20.

Thompson, G. P. "The Environmental Movement Goes to Business School." Environment, 27, 4 (1985): 6-12.

Train, R. E. "In Defense on the Environment." Living Wilderness, 37 (Autumn 1973): 9-13.

Tribe, L. H., Schelling, C. S., and J. Voss (eds.). When Values Conflict: Essays on Environmental Analysis, Discourse, and Decision. Cambridge, MA: Ballinger Publishing Co., 1976. 178 p.

Van Reijen, L. G. "Citizen Participation in Decision-Making on Environment." IULA Newsletter, 5, 10-11 (1971): 7-8.

Wandersman, A. "User Participation: A Study of Types of Participation, Effects, Mediators, and Individual Differences." Environment and Behavior, 11, 2 (1979): 185-208.

Weiner, P. and E. J. Deak. Environmental Factors in Transportation Planning. Lexington, MA: Lexington Books, 1972. 283 p.

Wilkinson, P. "The Role of the Public in Environmental Decision Making." In O. P. Dwivedi (ed.), Protecting the Environment: Issues and Choices -- Canadian Perspectives. Toronto, Ontario: Copp Clark Publishing, 1974, pp. 232-250.

Wilson, J. "When the Public and the Company Face Off." Environmental Views, 7, 6 (1984): 23-27.

Wilson, R. "Public Participation: An Industrial Perspective." In B. Sadler (ed.), Involvement and Environment: Proceedings of the Canadian Conference on Public Participation. Vol. 2: Working Papers and Case Studies. Edmonton, Alberta: Environment Council of Alberta, 1979, pp. 189-202.

Air Pollution

Ayres, R. et al. Action for Clean Air. Natural Resources Defense Council, Washington, DC, September 1971. 77 p.

Bates, D. V. A Citizen's Guide to Air Pollution. Montreal, Canada: McGill-Queen's University Press, 1972.

Burwell, D. G. A Citizen's Guide to Clean Air and Transportation: Implications for Urban Revitalization. U. S. Environmental Protection Agency, Washington, DC, 1980.

Call, G. D. "Arsenic, ASARCO, and EPA-Cost-Benefit Analysis, Public Participation, and Polluter Games in the Regulation of Hazardous Air Pollutants." Ecology Law Quarterly, 12, 3 (1985):567-618.

Cannon, J. S. A Clear View: Guide to Industrial Pollution Control. Emmaus, PA: Rodale Press, 1976. 246 p.

Chalupnik, J. C. and M. G. Ruby. "Public Participation in Air Pollution Control Programs." Journal of the Air Pollution Control Association, 29, 3 (1979): 226-229.

Crenson, M. A. The Un-Politics of Air Pollution: A Study of Non-Decision Making in the Cities. Baltimore, MD: Johns Hopkins University Press, 1971.

Holtz, S. "Public Concerns over the Combustion of Coal." In APCA 6th Annual Symposium, New Brunswick, Canada, September 1982: Proceedings, pp. 105-107.

Jones, C. O. "The Limits of Public Support: Air Pollution Agency Development." Public Administration Review, 32 (September-October 1972): 502-508.

Manning, R. C. "Air Pollution: Group and Individual Obligations." Environmental Ethics, 6, 3 (1984): 211-225.

McCarty, B. "Participation in Transportation-Air Quality Plans." In Transportation and the 1977 Clean Air Act Amendments Conference, San Francisco, November 12-14, 1979: Proceedings, pp. 375-381.

Medalia, N. Z. "Citizen Participation and Environmental Health Action: The Case of Air Pollution Control." Journal of Public Health, 59, 8 (1969): 1385-1391.

Stewart, T. R. and R. L. Dennis. "Citizen Participation and Judgment in Policy Analysis: A Case Study of the Urban Air Quality Policy." Policy Sciences, 17, 1 (1984): 67-87.

Swan, J. A. "Public Response to Air Pollution." In J. F. Wohlwill and D. H. Carson (eds.), Environment and the Social Sciences: Perspectives and Application. Washington, DC: American Psychological Association, Inc., 1972, pp. 66-74.

Education

Allen, R. F. "Suggestions for Community Participation in Environmental Studies." Journal of Geography, 73 (October 1974): 54-59.

Breakell, M. "Participatory Environmental Education for Planners." Environmental Education and Information, 2, 1 (1982): 41-.

Disinger, J. F. "Environmental Education Research News." Environmentalist, 4, 3 (1984): 181-.

Fortner, R. W. "Public Information Conferences as Tools for Environmental Communication Training." Journal of Environmental Education, 17, 2 (1985-86): 14-19.

Lingwood, D. A. "Environmental Education Through Information-Seeking: The Case of an 'Environmental Teach-In.'" Environment and Behavior, 3, 3 (1971): 230-262.

Matthews, J. "Environmental Education and Community Action." Journal of Environmental Education, 6, 2 (1974): 45-49.

Swan, J. "Environmental Education: One Approach to Resolving the Environmental Crisis." Environment and Behavior, 3, 3 (1971): 223-229.

Swan, J. A. "Some Human Objectives for Environmental Education." In J. A. Swan and W. B. Stapp (eds.), Environmental Education: Strategies Toward a More Livable Future. New York: John Wiley and Sons, 1974, pp. 25-41.

Ward, C. "Environmental Education: The City on the Wall." Town and Country Planning, 40, 6 (1972): 327-330.

Westphal, J. M. and W. F. Halverson. "Assessing the Long-Term Effects of an Environmental Education Program: A Pragmatic Approach." Journal of Environmental Education, 17, 2 (1985-86): 26-30.

Environmental Action

Alderson, G. and E. Sentman. "How to Win Friends and Pass Legislation." Environmental Action, 11, 7 (1980): 14-17.

Allaby, M. The Eco-Activists: Youth Fights for a Human Environment. London: Charles Knight and Co., 1971.

Andrews, E. "Community Appearance -- An Environmental Issue: Organizing Resources for Local Action." In National Association for Environmental Education 12th Annual Conference, Ypsilanti, MI, 1983: Proceedings, pp. 39-47.

Bromenshenk, J. J. and E. M. Preston. "Public Participation in Environmental Monitoring: A Means of Attaining Network Capability." Environmental Monitoring and Assessment, 6, 1 (1986): 35-47.

Bryan, W. L. An Identification and Analysis of Power-Coercive Change and Techniques Utilized by Selected Environmental Change Agents. Unpublished Ph. D. dissertation. University of Michigan, Ann Arbor, MI 1971.

Caldwell, L. K., Hayes, R., and I. M. MacWhirter. Citizens and the Environment: Case Studies in Popular Action. Bloomington, IN: Indiana University Press, 1976. 449 p.

Coan, G. (ed.). Sierra Club Political Handbook: Tools for Action. 5th ed. San Francisco: Sierra Club, 1979. 76 p.

Connor, D. M. "Models and Techniques of Citizen Participation." In B. Sadler (ed.), Involvement and Environment: Proceedings of the Canadian Conference on Public Participation. Vol. 1: A Review of Issues and Approaches. Edmonton, Alberta: Environment Council of Alberta, 1978, pp. 58-76.

Crowfoot, J. E. and B. I. Bryant. "Environmental Advocacy: An Action Strategy for Dealing with Environmental Problems." Journal of Environmental Education, 11, 3 (1980): 36-41.

DeBell, G. (comp.). Environmental Handbook. New York: Ballantine Books, 1970. 365 p.

Dunlap, R. E. and R. P. Gale. "Politics and Ecology: A Political Profile of Student Eco-Activists." Youth and Society, 3, 4 (1972): 379-397.

Fanning, O. Man and His Environment: Citizen Action. New York: Harper and Row, 1975.

Ford Foundation Staff. Grass-Roots Environmentalists. Ford Foundation, New York, 1977. 32 p.

Frankena, F. "The Emergent Social Role and Political Impact of the Voluntary Technical Expert." Environmental Impact Assessment Review, forthcoming.

Freudenberg, N. "Citizen Action for Environmental Health: Report on a Survey of Community Organizations." American Journal of Public Health, 74, 5 (1984): 444-448.

Gerlach, L. P. and V. Hine. "You and the Ecology Movement." Natural History, 79 (June-July 1970): 27-29.

Goetz, C. J. and G. Brady. "Environmental Policy Formation and the Tax Treatment of Citizen Interest Groups." Law and Contemporary Problems, 39, 4 (1975): 211-231.

Goldrich, D. et al. "Community-Controlled Economic Development and Environmental Enhancement: The Case of the Whiteaker Neighborhood, Eugene, Oregon." In G. J. Coates (ed.), Resettling America: Energy, Ecology, and Community. Andover, MA: Brick House Publishing, 1981.

Harnik, P. "In Search of Eco-Activists." Journal of Environmental Education, 5, 1 (1973): 18-20.

Hays, S. P. Beauty, Health, and Permanence: Environmental Politics in the United States, 1955-1985. New York: Cambridge University Press, 1987. 630 p.

Hays, S. P. "The Structure of Environmental Politics Since World War II." Journal of Social History, 14, 4 (1981): 719-738.

Hodge, B. J. "Write for Your Life." Parents' Magazine, 47 (February 1972): 50+.

Kennedy, K. and J. Spearman. "The People's Turn at Bat: Environmental Activism." Environmental Views, 1, 6 (1979): 3-12.

Klain, A. and D. M. Phelan. A Practical Guide to Urban and Environmental Movies. No. 780. Council of Planning Librarians, Monticello, IL, April 1975.

Langton, S. (ed.). Environmental Leadership: A Sourcebook for Staff and Volunteer Leaders of Environmental Organizations. Lexington, MA: Lexington Books, 1984. 138 p.

Larson, M. A. "Participation in Pro-Environmental Behavior." Journal of Environmental Education, 12, 3 (1981): 21-24.

Larson, M. A. et al. "Communication Behavior by Environmental Activists Compared to Non-Active Persons." Journal of Environmental Education, 14, 1 (1982): 11-20.

League of Women Voters. How ti Plan an Environmental Conference. Publication No. 695. Education Fund, Washington, DC, 1971. 48 p.

Love, S. Earth Tool Kit: A Field Manual for Citizen Activists. New York: Pocket Books, 1971.

Love, S. and D. Obst (eds.). Ecotage! New York: Pocket Books, 1972.

McKean, M. Environmental Protest and Citizen Politics in Japan. Berkeley, CA: University of California Press, 1981.

Mitchell, J. G. (ed.). Eco-Tactics: The Sierra Club Handbook for Environmental Activists. New York: Trident Press, 1970. 288 p.

O'Riordan, T. "Public Interest Environmental Groups in the United States and Britain." Journal of American Studies, 13 (December 1979): 409-438.

Robertson, J. and J. Lewallen. The Grass Roots Primer. San Francisco: Sierra Club, 1975.

Robinson, G. "The Best Little Citizens Groups in Texas." Environmental Action,11 (May 1980): 4-11.

Sager, L. B. "The Intentional Community." Cry California, 8, 2 (1973): 28-35.

Sanders, N. K. Stop It! A Guide to Defense of Environment. San Francisco: Rinehart Press, 1972. 160 p.

Sandman, P. "Making Yourself Heard." Environmental Action, 9 (May 7, 1977): 3-7.

Scott, D. W. "Student Activism on Environmental Crisis." Living Wilderness, 34 (Spring 1970): 8-9.

"State Bottle Bills: Taking the Initiative." Environmental Action, 8, 6 (1976): 8-12.

Stevenson, D. et al. 50 Million Volunteers: A Report on the Role of Voluntary Organizations and Youth in the Environment. London: Her Majesty's Stationary Office, 1972.

Templeton, C. C. A Guide to Citizen Participation in Environmental Action: A Manual and Roster for Citizen Groups in Southern California. Regional Plan Association of Southern California, Los Angeles, 1972. 122 p.

U. S. Citizens' Advisory Committee on Environmental Quality. Citizens Make the Difference: Case Studies of Environmental Action. Washington, DC: U. S. Government Printing Office, 1973. 71 p.

U. S. Citizens' Advisory Committee on Environmental Quality. Community Action for Environmental Quality. Washington, DC: U. S. Government Printing Office, 1970. 42 p.

U. S. Department of Housing and Urban Development. Environment and the Community: An Annotated Bibliography. Washington, DC, April 1971. 66 p.

U. S. Environmental Protection Agency. "Citizen Action Can Get Results." Environmental Protection Agency Citizens' Bulletin, (March 1972): 1-7.

U. S. Environmental Protection Agency. Don't Leave It All to the Experts: The Citizens' Role in Environmental Decision-Making. Washington, DC: U. S. Government Printing Office, 1972. 20 p.

U. S. Environmental Protection Agency. Groups That Can Help: A Directory of Environmental Organizations. Washington, DC, 1972. 12 p.

Zinger, C. L., Dalsemer, R. and H. Magargle. Environmental Volunteers in American. EPA Project Report R801243. National Center for Voluntary Action, Washington, DC, October 1972. 614 p.

Environmental Management

Brown, K. F. "Involving the Public in Environmental Decision-Making." In Ford Foundation Experiments in Regional Environmental Management, 1974, pp. 15-23.

DeFalco, P. "Regional Environmental Management in the San Francisco Bay Area." In Ford Foundation Experiments in Regional Environmental Management, 1974, pp. 39-48.

Dodson, E. N. "Citizen Action in Environmental Management." Public Management, 56, 3 (1974): 22-23.

Elder, P. S. (ed.). Environmental Management and Public Participation. Report No. 40-83. Canadian Environmental Law Association, Toronto, Canada.

Ford Foundation. The Art of Managing the Environment. Report. September 1974.

Godschalk, D. R. Evaluating Public Participation in Environment/Land Use Management: Strategies and Lessons. Department of City and Regional Planning, University of North Carolina, Chapel Hill, NC, January 1980.

Goodman, J. et al. "Implementation of Citizen Participation." In U. S. Environmental Protection Agency, Managing the Environment. EPA 600-5-73-010. Environmental Studies Division, Washington Environmental Research Center, Office of Research and Development, Washington, DC, 1973, pp. 168-171.

Haefele, E. T. Representative Government and Environmental Management. Baltimore, MD: Johns Hopkins University Press, 1973. 188 p.

Johnston, W. D., Donovan, J. F., and H. O. Wilson. "Nurturing Public Participation in Environmental Management -- Social Function for Academia: Translating for Layman, Enabling Activist, and Verifying Official, with Examples." Bulletin of the American Physical Society, 22, 4 (1977): 524.

Judge, R. M. and J. E. Podgor. "Use of the Delphi in a Citizen Participation Project." Environmental Management, 7, 5 (1983): 399-400.

Kalikow, B. N. "Environmental Risk: Power to the People." Technology Review, 87, 7 (1984): 54-61.

LaBreche, R. A. et al. "Inexpensive Community Noise Assessments for Medium and Small Cities." Sound and Vibration, 10, 12 (1976): 12-14.

McInnis, M. "Regional Environmental Quality Councils." Paper presented at the AAAS Meeting, New York City, January 1975. 11 p.

Nelson, J. G. "Public Participation in Comprehensive Resource and Environmental Management." Science and Public Policy, 9, 5 (1982): 240-250.

O'Riordan, T. "Policy Making and Environmental Management: Some Thoughts on Processes and Research Issues." Natural Resources Journal, 16, 1 (1976): 55-72.

Rowe, P. Principles for Local Environmental Management. Cambridge, MA: Ballinger, 1978.

Werner, J. "Citizen Participation in Environmental Management." In U. S. Environmental Protection Agency, Managing the Environment. EPA 600-5-73-010. Environmental Studies Division, Washington Environmental Research Center, Office of Research and Development, Washington, DC, 1973, pp. 153-161.

Wilkinson, P. "Public Participation in Environmental Management: A Case Study." Natural Resources Journal, 16, 1 (1976): 117-135.

Environmentalism

Andrews, R. N. L. "Class Politics or Democratic Reform: Environmentalism and American Political Institutions." Natural Resources Journal, 20, 2 (1980): 221-241.

Bair, H. A. "Greening of the Gray Panthers." EPA Journal, 7 (January 1981): 32.

Betten, N. and M. Austin. "The Unwanted Helping Hand." Environment, 19, 1 (1977): 13-20+.

Bowling, K. R. "The New Conservationists." Journal of Environmental Education, 1 (Spring 1970): 78-79.

Bowman, J. S. "Attitudes and Orientations of Environmentally-Concerned Citizens." Environmental Conservation, 4 (1977): 259-269.

Bryan, W. L. Jr. "Toward a Viable Environmental Movement." Journal of Applied Behavioral Science, 10, 3 (1974): 387-401.

Coates, G. J. (ed.). Resettling America: Energy, Ecology, and Community. Andover, MA: Brick House Publishing, 1981. 560 p.

Conservation Foundation. "Environmentalists Savor Past, Look Anxiously Ahead." Conservation Foundation Letter, (January-February 1980): 1-16.

Conservation Foundation. "Ideological Roots Nurture Growth of Environmentalism." Conservation Foundation Letter, (December 1979): 1-8.

DeLong, E. K. "Environmentalism in Our Age." Ecolibrium, 8, 1 (1979): 17-21.

Downs, A. "Up and Down with Ecology: The Issue Attention Cycle." Public Interest, 29 (Summer 1972): 38-50.

Faich, R. G. and R. P. Gale. "The Environmental Movement: From Recreation to Politics." Pacific Sociological Review, 14 (July 1971): 270-287.

Hays, S. P. Beauty, Health, and Permanence: Environmental Politics in the United States, 1955-1985. New York: Cambridge University Press, 1987. 630 p.

Hays, S. P. "The Structure of Environmental Politics Since World War II." Journal of Social History, 14, 4 (1981): 719-738.

Hine, V. and L. P. Gerlach. "Many Concerned, Few Committed." Natural History, 79, 10 (1970): 16-17+.

Jackson, A. and A. Wright. "Nature's Banner: Environmentalists Have Just Begun to Fight." Progressive, 45, 10 (1981): 26-31.

Lake, L. M. "The Environmental Mandate: Activists and the Electorate." Political Science Quarterly, 98, 2 (1983): 215-234.

Lowe, G. D. and T. K. Pinhey. "Rural-Urban Differences in Support for Environmental Protection." Rural Sociology, 47 (Spring 1982): 114-128.

Mayer, R. N. "Environmental Consciousness and Class Consciousness: Two Case Studies." Social Science Journal, 19 (January 1982): 105-119.

Miller, A. "Ideology and Environmental Risk Management." Environmentalist, 5, 1 (1985): 21-30.

Mitchell, R. C. "From Elite Quarrel to Mass Movement." Society, 18, 5 (1981): 76-84.

Mitchell, R. C. "Since Silent Spring: Science, Technology and the Environmental Movement in the United States." In H. Skoie (ed.), Scientific Expertise and the Public: Conference Proceedings. Oslo: Institute for Studies in Research and Higher Education, Norwegian Research Council for Science and the Humanities, 1979, pp. 171-207.

Mohai, P. "Public Concern and Elite Involvement in Environmental-Conservation Issues." Social Science Quarterly, 66, 4 (1985): 820-838.

Neiman, M. and R. O. Loveridge. "Environmentalism and Local Growth Control: A Probe into the Class Bias Thesis." Environment and Behavior, 13 (November 1981):759-772.

"Paler Shade of Green; West Germany." Economist, 274 (March 15, 1980): 44-45.

Pierce, J. C. et al. "Vanguards and Rearguards in Environmental Politics: A Comparison of Activists in Japan and the United States." Comparative Political Studies, 18, 4 (1986): 419-448.

Shepard, P. "Establishment and Radicals on the Environmental Crisis." Ecology, 51 (1970): 941-942.

St. George, A. The Sierra Club, Organizational Commitment and the Conservation Movement in the United States. Unpublished Ph. D. dissertation. University of California, Davis, CA, 1973.

St. George, A. and J. McEvoy. The Sierra Club, A Sociological Portrait. Department of Sociology, University of California, Davis, CA, 1972.

Sofranko, A. J. and W. M. Bridgeland. "Community Structure and Issue-Specific Influences: Community Mobilization Over Environmental Quality." Urban Affairs Quarterly, 11 (December 1975): 186-214.

Stokey, S. R. "Citizen Participation and the New Environmentalism." Journal of the Urban Planning Development Division ASCE, 99, 1 (1973): 69-75.

Warne, W. E. "An Editorial: Virulent Environmentalism." Public Administration Review, 30, 3 (1970): 327-238.

Government

Anand, R. and I. G. Scott. "Financing Public Participation in Environmental Decision-Making." Canadian Bar Review, 60, 1 (1982): 81-120.

Buckley, J. L. "The Environmental Quality Council and the Citizens' Advisory Committee on Environmental Quality." In Argonne Universities Association Conference, Chicago, July 1969: Proceedings, p. 43-51.

Clary, B. B. and R. F. Goodman. "What Are Our Most Important Environmental Problems?" Popular Government, 42, 2 (1976): 10-13+.

Cohen, S. Citizen Participation in Bureaucratic Decision Making: With Special Emphasis on Environmental Policy Making. Unpublished Ph.D. dissertation. State University of New York, Buffalo, NY, 1979.

Council on the Environment of New York City. A Citizen's Policy Guide to Environmental Priorities for New York City, 1974-1984: Interim Report. New York, NY, December 1973. 60 p.

Cuthbertson, I. D. "Evaluating Public Participation: An Approach for Government Practitioners." In G. A. Daneke et al. (eds.), Public Involvement and Social Impact Assessment. Boulder, CO: Westview Press, 1983, pp. 101-109.

Cutler, M. R. and D. A. Bronstein. "Public Involvement in Government Decisions." Alternatives, 4 (Autumn 1974): 11-13.

Davos, C. A. "Evaluation of Collective Choices: A New Challenge and the Priority-Tradeoff-Scanning Approach." Paper presented at the Research Conference on Public Involvement and Social Impact Assessment, University of Arizona, Tucson, AZ, February 1981.

Edelstein, M. R. "Disabling Communities: The Impact of Regulatory Proceedings." Journal of Environmental Systems, 16, 2 (1986): 87-110.

Environment Council of Alberta. Public Participation in Environmental Decision Making, Edmonton, Alberta, 1980. 177 p.

Estrin, D. "The Public Is Still Voiceless: Some Negative Aspects of Public Hearings." In B. Sadler (ed.), Involvement and Environment: Proceedings of the Canadian Conference on Public Participation. Vol. 2: Working Papers and Case Studies. Edmonton, Alberta: Environment Council of Alberta, 1979.

Forkosch, M. D. "Administrative Conduct in Environmental Areas: A Suggested Degree of Public Control." Southern Texas Law Journal, 12, 1 (1970): 1-23.

Frauenglass, H. "Environmental Policy; Public Participation and the Open Information System." Natural Resources Journal, 11, 3 (1971): 489-496.

Freeman, M. "Advocacy and Resource Allocation Decisions in the Public Sector." Natural Resources Journal, 9 (April 1969): 166-175.

Frieden, B. J. "Consumer's Stake in Environmental Regulation." Annals of the American Academy of Political and Social Science, 451 (1980): 36-44.

Gage, K. and S. Epstein. "The Federal Advisory Committee System: An Assessment." Environmental Law Reporter, 7, 2 (1977):

Gershinowitz, H. Citizen's Policy Guide to Environmental Priorities for New York City, 1974-1984: Part I -- Energy and the New York City Environment. Council of the Environment of New York City, NY, February 1974. 59 p.

Gurchin, M. H. et al. "Proposals for Improving Transportation and Environmental Planning at the State and Local Level." Harvard Environmental Law Review, 2 (1978): 542-561.

Hartner, P. J. "EPA's Regulatory Negotiation Will Provide Opportunity for Direct Participation in Development of a Regulation." Environmental Law Reporter, 13, 7 (1983): 10202-.

Henning, D. H. Environmental Policy and Administration. New York: American Elsevier Pub. Co., 1974. 205 p.

Henning, D. H. "Environmental Policy and Politics: Value and Power Context." Natural Resources Journal, 11, 3 (1971): 447-454.

Homenuck, P., Durlak, J., and J. Morgenstern. "Evaluation of Public Participation Programs." In B. Sadler (ed.), Involvement and Environment: Proceedings of the Canadian Conference on Public Participation. Vol. 1: A Review of Issues and Approaches. Edmonton, Alberta: Environment Council of Alberta, 1978, pp. 103-119.

Hornback, K. E. "Overcoming Obstacles to Agency and Public Involvement: A Program and Its Methods." In K. Finsterbusch and C. P. Wolf (eds.), Methodology of Social Impact Assessment. Stroudsburg, PA: Dowden, Hutchinson, and Ross, 1977, pp. 355-363.

Hughes, E. M. "Representative Public Involvement." In Western Water and Energy Conference, Fort Collins, CO, June 1982: Proceedings, American Society of Civil Engineers, pp. 616-611.

Ingram, H. M. and S. J. Ullery. "Public Participation in Environmental Decision-Making: Substance or Illusion?" In W. R. Sewell and J. T. Coppock (eds.), Public Participation in Planning. New York: John Wiley and Sons, 1977, pp. 123-139.

Inguartsen, O. et al. Democracy and the Environment. National Association of Local Authorities in Denmark, 1973.

Kasperson, R. E. "Citizen Participation in Environmental Policy Making: The U.S.A. Experience." In B. Sadler (ed.), Involvement and Environment: Proceedings of the Canadian Conference on Public Participation. Vol. 1: A Review of Issues and Approaches. Edmonton, Alberta: Environment Council of Alberta, 1978, pp. 128-137.

Klessig, L. L. and V. L. Strite. The ELF Odyssey: National Security Versus Environmental Protection. Boulder, CO: Westview Press, 1980. 310 p.

Krier, J. E. "Environmental Watchdogs: Some Lessons from a 'Study' Council." Stanford Law Review, 23 (1971): 623-675.

Like, I. "Multi-Media Confrontation -- The Environmentalists' Strategy for a 'No-Win' Agency Proceeding." Ecology Law Quarterly, 1, 3 (1971): 495-518.

Lindaman, E. B. Alternatives for Washington, Vol. I; Pathways to Washington 1985, A Beginning; Citizens' Recommendations for the Future. Report No. 1. Alternatives for Washington, Statewide Citizen Task Force, May 1975.

Murphy, E. F. "Environmental Bureaucracies Appraised." Ekistics, 44 (September1977): 156-164.

Pogell, S. M. "Government-Initiated Public Participation in Environmental Decisions." Environmental Comment, (April 1979): 4-6.

Polayes, J. State Environmental Policy Acts and the Public. Working Paper No. 6. School of Forestry and Environmental Studies, Yale University, June 1977.

Rosenbaum, W. "The EPA and Public Participation." Citizen Participation, 1 (July-August 1980): 19.

Rosenbaum, W. A. "Slaying Beautiful Hypotheses with Ugly Facts: EPA and the Limits of Public Participation." Paper presented at the Meeting of the American Society for Public Administration, Chicago, IL, 1975.

Rudel, T. "Activists, Agencies, and the Division of Labor in Environmental Protection." Journal of Environmental Management, 15 (1982): 1-14.

Schatzow, S. "The Influence of the Public on Federal Environmental Decisionmaking in Canada." In W. R. Sewell and J. T. Coppock (eds.), Public Participation in Planning. New York: John Wiley and Sons, 1977, pp. 141-158.

Scoville, A. and C. E. A. Noad. Citizen Participation in State Government: A Summary Report. Environmental Planning Information Center, Montpelier, VT, 1973. 26 p.

Seeger, E. H. et al. "Public Participation in Oversight." Environmental Forum, 2, 5 (1983): 30-34.

Sewell, W. R. D. and T. O'Riordan. "The Culture of Participation in Environmental Decision-making." Natural Resources Journal, 16, 1 (1976): 1-21.

Sibbison, J. "The Agency of Illusion." Sierra, 70, 3 (1985): 18-20.

Stern, C. and M. Reynolds. "Public Participation Regulations: A New Dimension in EPA Programs." Public Works, 11, 10 (1979): 71-74.

Sugai, W. H. "The WNP 4 and 5 Participation Decision: Seattle and Tacoma -- A Tale of Two Cities." Northwest Environmental Journal, 1, 1 (1984): 45-.

Swaigen, J. "Environmental Legislation: Role of Public Interest Groups." Water and Pollution Control, 114, 4 (1976): 21-22+.

Symonds, W. "Washington in the Grip of the Green Giant." Fortune, (October 4, 1982): 136-141.

U. S. Congress. Senate. Committee on Commerce. Environmental Protection Act of 1973, S1104: Hearings, April 2 and 5, 1973. 93rd Congress, 1st Session. Washington, DC: U. S. Government Printing Office, 1973. 342 p.

U. S. General Accounting Office. Federal, State, Local, and Public Roles in Constructing Waste Water Treatment Facilities. Report RED-65-45. Washington, DC, December 1975. 51 p.

Wandesforde-Smith, G. "The Bureaucratic Response to Environmental Politics." In A. E. Utton and D. H. Henning (eds.), Environmental Policy. New York: Praeger Publishers, 1973, pp. 76-85.

Wengert, N. "Political and Social Accommodation: The Political Process and Environmental Preservation." In A. E. Utton and D. H. Henning (eds.), Environmental Policy. New York: Praeger Publishers, 1973, pp. 33-44.

Impact Assessment

Auerbach, L. "Toward Better Impact Assessments." In 17th Annual Meeting of the Canadian Society of Environmental Biologists, Ottawa, January 1976: Proceedings, pp. 76-80.

Bechmann, G. and F. Gloede. "Public Participation in the Licensing of Large-Scale Projects with Environmental Impacts." In H. A. Becker and A. L. Porter (eds.), Impact Assessment Today. Vol. 1. Utrecht, Netherlands: Utigeverij Jan van Arkel, 1986, pp. 201-226.

Bishop, A. B. "Public Participation in Environmental Impact Assessment." In M. Blissett (ed.), Environmental Impact Assessment. New York: Engineering Foundation, 1976.

Butler, L. M. and R. E. Howell. Coping with Growth: Community Needs Assessment Techniques. Cooperative Extension Service, Washington State University, Pullman, WA, 1979.

Connor, D. M. "A Community Approach to Social Impact Assessment." Paper presented at the Annual Meetings of the American Association for the Advancement of Science, Toronto, Canada, January 1981.

Connor, D. M. "The Community -- Partner or Patient in Social Impact Assessment?" Constructive Citizen Participation, 6, 3 (December 1978):

Connor, D. M. "Institutional Roles in SIA: The Community -- Partner or Patient in Social Impact Assessment." In F. J. Tester and W. Mykes (eds.), Social Impact Assessment: Theory, Method, and Practice. Calgary, Alberta, Canada: Detselig Enterprises, 1981.

Connor, D. M. "A Participative Approach to Social Impact Assessment: A Proposed Mine Near Atlin, British Columbia." In G. A. Daneke et al. (eds.), Public Involvement and Social Impact Assessment. Boulder, CO: Westview Press, 1983, pp. 185-194.

Cortner, H. J. "Navajo Environmental Protection Commission: Developing the Capabilities for Environmental Impact Assessment and Regulation." Indian History, 9 (Fall 1976): 32-37.

Cramton, R. C. and R. K. Berg. "On Leading a Horse to Water: NEPA and the Federal Bureaucracy." Michigan Law Review, 71, 3 (1973): 511-536.

Creighton, J. L. "An Overview to the Research Conference on Public Involvement and Social Impact Assessment." In G. A. Daneke et al. (eds.), Public Involvement and Social Impact Assessment. Boulder, CO: Westview Press, 1983, pp. 1-10.

Creighton, J. L., Chalmers, J. A., and K. Branch. "Integrating Planning and Assessment Through Public Involvement." In G. A. Daneke et al. (eds.), Public Involvement and Social Impact Assessment. Boulder, CO: Westview Press, 1983, pp. 177-184.

Czarnecki, J. E. "Some Initial Empirical Findings on the Use of Projective Surveys in Community Impact Assessment." Paper presented at the Research Conference on Public Involvement and Social Impact Assessment, University of Arizona, Tucson, AZ, February 1981.

Daneke, G. A., Garcia, M. W., and J. D. Priscoli (eds.). Public Involvement and Social Impact Assessment. Boulder, CO: Westview Press, 1983. 303 p.

Elder, P. S. "Project Approval, Environmental Assessment and Public Participation." Environmentalist, 2, 1 (1982): 55-61.

"Environmental Law: Public Participation in the Environmental Impact Statement Process." Minnesota Law Review, 61, 2 (1977): 363-381.

Fairfax, S. and L. Burton. "A Decade of NEPA: Milestone or Millstone?" Fisheries, 8, 6 (1983): 5-8.

Francis, M. "Urban Impact Assessment and Community Involvement: The Case of the John Fitzgerald Kennedy Library." Environment and Behavior, 7, 3 (1975): 373-404.

Freudenburg, W. R. "The Promise and Peril of Public Participation in Social Impact Assessment." In G. A. Daneke et al. (eds.), Public Involvement and Social Impact Assessment. Boulder, CO: Westview Press, 1983, pp. 227-234.

Freudenburg, W. R. and K. M. Keating. "Applying Sociology to Policy: Social Science and the Environmental Impact Statement." Rural Sociology, 50, 4 (1985): 578-605.

Freudenburg, W. R. and D. Olsen. "Public Interest and Political Abuse: Public Participation in Social Impact Assessment." Journal of the Community Development Society, 14, 2 (1983): 67-82.

Fusco, S. M. "Public Participation in Environmental Statements." Journal of Water Resource Planning and Management Division ASCE, 106, 1 (1980): 123-129.

Gale, R. P. "The Consciousness Raising Potential of Social Impact Assessment." Paper presented at the Research Conference on Public Involvement and Social Impact Assessment, University of Arizona, Tucson, AZ, February 1981.

Garcia, M. W. "The Future of Social Impact Assessment and Public Involvement." In G. A. Daneke et al. (eds.), Public Involvement and Social Impact Assessment. Boulder, CO: Westview Press, 1983, pp. 283-297.

Garcia, M. W. and G. A. Daneke. "The Role of Public Involvement in Social Impact Assessment: Problems and Prospects: Introduction." In G. A. Daneke et al. (eds.), Public Involvement and Social Impact Assessment. Boulder, CO: Westview Press, 1983, pp. 161-176.

Goldenberg, S. and J. S. Frideres. "Measuring the Effects of Public Participation Programs." Environmental Impact Assessment Review, 6, 3 (1986): 273-281.

Holland, L. "The Use of NEPA in Defense Policy Politics: Public and State Involvement in the MX Missile Project." Social Science Journal, 21, 3 (1984): 53-71.

Johnston, R. A. "The Organization of Social Impact Information for Evaluation by Decision-makers and Citizens." In J. McEvoy III and T. Dietz (eds.), Handbook for Environmental Planning: The Social Consequences of Environmental Change. New York: John Wiley and Sons, 1977, pp. 279-316.

Kuennen, D. S. Community Project Impact Check List. Rural Development Program Aid No. 2. Cooperative Extension Service, University of Delaware, Georgetown, DE, 1975. 15 p.

MacIntosh, B. "Impact on What, Reports to Whom." Equilibrium-ZPG, 1, 4 (1973): 15-17.

Mandelker, D. R. NEPA Law and Litigation: The National Environmental Protection Act. Wilmette, IL: Callaghan and Co., 1984.

Maurer, K. F. Public Participation in Environmental Assessment Hearings: An Analysis of Current Practice in Canada and the United States with Proposed Options for the Ontario Environmental Assessment Board. Institute for Environmental Studies, University of Toronto, Toronto, Canada, 1978.

McCallum, S. K. "Environmental Impact Procedures: A Critique of the Canadian Proposal." Earth Law Journal, 1, 4 (1975): 275-299.

Orloff, N. The Environmental Impact Statement Process: A Guide to Citizen Action. Washington, DC: Information Resources Press, 1978. 242 p.

Polack, S. "Reimagining NEPA: Choices for Environmentalists." Harvard Environmental Law Review, 9, 2 (1985): 359-418.

Priscoli, J. D. "Public Involvement and Social Impact Assessment: A Union Seeking Marriage." In G. A. Daneke et al. (eds.), Public Involvement and Social Impact Assessment. Boulder, CO: Westview Press, 1983, pp. 271-282.

Rock, M. J. "Colorado's Joint Review Process: The AMAX Experience." In G. A. Daneke et al. (eds.), Public Involvement and Social Impact Assessment. Boulder, CO: Westview Press, 1983, pp. 207-213.

Runyan, D. "Tools for Community-Managed Impact Assessment." Journal of the American Institute of Planners, 43, 2 (1977): 125-135.

Spiegel, H. B. C. "Citizen Participation, Public Planning, and Social Impact Assessment." Paper presented at the Annual Meeting of the Environmental Design Research Association, New York City, June 1985.

Tablot, F. "Environmental Impact Assessment: Summary and Prospects." Search, 7, 6 (1976): 273-274.

Tobin, R. J. and R. A. Carpenter. "Public Participation in the Environmental Review Process, with Special Reference to Coal-Fired Power Plant Siting." Environmental Conservation, 10, 4 (1983): 315-321.

Tweit, S. "Playing the Game: Public Input in NEPA Planning." High Country News, 14, 6 (1982): 14-.

U. S. Council on Environmental Quality. Environmental Impact Statements: An Analysis of Six Years' Experience by Seventy Federal Agencies. Washington, DC, March 1976.

U. S. Council on Environmental Quality. Regulations for Implementing the Procedural Provisions of the National Environmental Policy Act. Washington, DC: U. S. Government Printing Office, 1978.

Vance, M. A. Environmental Impact Analysis and Statements: Monographs. Public Administration Series No. 1578. Monticello, IL: Vance Bibliographies, 1984. 33 p.

Westman, W. E. "Environmental Impact Statements: Boon or Burden?" Search, 4, 11 (1973): 465-470.

Information/Communication

Carpenter, R. A. "Information for Decisions in Environmental Policy." Science,168 (June 12, 1970): 1316-1322.

Fox, I. K. and L. F. Wible. "Information Generation and Communication to Establish Environmental Quality Objectives." Natural Resources Journal, 13, 1 (1973): 134-149.

Ingram, H. M. "Information Channels and Environmental Decision Making." Natural Resources Journal, 13, 1 (1973): 150-169.

Nedelman, J. I. and G. S. Pellathy. "Quiet Usurping of the Public's Right to Know." Journal of Environmental Education, 5, 1 (1973): 37-40.

"Public Information and Participation." In Environmental Impact Assessment Symposium, Villach, Austria, September 1979: Proceedings, UN Economic Commission for Europe, pp. 277-304.

Stamm, K. R. and J. E. Bowes. "Communication During an Environmental Decision." Journal of Environmental Education, 3, 3 (1972): 49-55.

Stiftel, B. "Dialogue: Does It Increase Participant Knowledgeability and Attitude Congruence?" In G. A. Daneke et al. (eds.), Public Involvement and Social Impact Assessment. Boulder, CO: Westview Press, 1983, pp. 61-77.

Walmsley, D. J. "Public Information Flows in Rural Australia." Environment and Planning, 15, 2 (1983): 255-263.

Litigation

Bross, J. L. "Taking Design Review Beyond the Beauty Part: Aesthetics in Perspective." Environmental Law, 9 (Winter 1979): 211-240.

Butler, W. A. "The Environmental Defense Fund (EDF): Science and Law as Citizens' Weapons to Preserve the Environment." In Citizens' Advisory Committee on Environmental Quality, Citizens Make the Difference: Case Studies of Environmental Action. Washington, DC, January 1973, pp. 55-61.

"Courting Trouble Abroad: Environmentalists vs. Alcoa." Economist, 278 (March 28-April 3, 1981): 74-75.

D'Amato, A. A. "Environmental Degradation and Legal Action." Science and Public Affairs, 26, 3 (1970): 24-26.

DiMento, J. F. "Citizen Environmental Litigation and the Administrative Process: Empirical Findings, Remaining Issues and a Direction for Future Research." Duke Law Journal, 22 (1977): 409-452.

Epstein, S. Scientists in the Courtroom in Environmental Proceedings: Problems of Expert Testimony. Critical Mass Energy Project, Washington, DC, n. d. 20 p.

Estrin, D. and J. Swaigen (eds.). Environment on Trial. 2nd ed. Toronto: Canadian Environmental Law Research Foundation, 1978.

Fadil, A. "Citizen Suits Against Polluters: Picking Up the Pace." Harvard Environmental Law Review, 9, 1 (1985); 23-82.

Frankena, F. Experts and Expertise in Environmental Litigation: A Bibliography. Public Administration Series No. 1909. Monticello, IL: Vance Bibliographies, April 1986. 6 p.

Gelpe, M. R. and D. A. Tarlock. "The Uses of Scientific Evidence in Environmental Decision-Making." Southern California Law Review, 48, 1 (1974): 371-427.

Gregory, D. D. "Standing to Sue in Environmental Litigation in the U. S." Environmental Law Paper No. 3. International Union for Conservation of Nature and Natural Resources, 1972. 34 p.

Katzman, M. T. "Chemical Catastrophes and the Courts." Public Interest, 82 (Winter 1986): 91-105.

Landau, N. J. Environmental Law Handbook. New York: Ballantine, 1971. 496 p.

Lucas, A. R. "Legal Foundations for Public Participation in Environmental Decisionmaking." Natural Resources Journal, 16, 1 (1976): 73-102.

MacDonald, J. B. and J. E. Conway. Environmental Litigation. Department of Law, University of Wisconsin Extension, Madison, WI, 1972. 438 p.

Polebaum, E. E. "Preclusion of Citizen Environmental Enforcement Litigation by Agency Action." Environmental Law Reporter, 16, 1 (1986): 10013-10018.

Post, T. R. and R. B. Ravikoff. "Organizational Support to Fund Environmental Litigation." Environmental Affairs, 6, 4 (1978): 457-489.

Roisman, A. Z. "The Role of the Citizen in Enforcing Environmental Laws." Environmental Law Reporter, 16, 7 (1986): 10163-10164.

"Ruckelshaus v. Sierra Club: A Misinterpretation of the Clean Air Act's Attorney's Fees Provisions." Ecology Law Quarterly, 12, 1 (1985): 399-421.

Sax, J. Defending the Environment: A Strategy of Citizen Action. New York: Knopf, 1971. 252 p.

Sax, J. L. "Emerging Legal Strategies: Judicial Intervention." Annals of the American Academy of Political and Social Science, 389 (May 1970): 71-76.

Sax, J. L. "The Search for Environmental Quality: The Role of the Courts." In H. W. Helfrich Jr. (ed.), The Environmental Crisis. New Haven, CT: Yale University Press, 1970, pp. 99-114.

Sive, D. "Environmental Decisionmaking: Judicial and Political Review." Case Western Reserve Law Review, 28, 4 (1978): 827-841.

Slone, D. K. "The Michigan Environmental Protection Act: Bringing Citizen Initiated Environmental Suits into the 1980s." Ecology Law Quarterly, 12, 2 (1984): 271-362.

Thompson, G. P. "The Courts, the Cities, and the Environment." Public Management, 56, 3 (1974): 19-21.

Vogel, J. V. "Constitutional Malice: Protecting the Citizen's Reporting Role in Environmental Law." Virginia Journal of Natural Resources Law, 1, 2 (1981): 251-277.

Wenner, L. M. "Interest Group Litigation and Environmental Policy." Policy Studies Journal, 11 (June 1983): 671-683.

Planning

Alterman, R. "Planning for Public Participation: The Design of Implementable Strategies." Environment and Planning-B: Planning and Design, 9, 3 (1982): 295-313.

Citizen Participation in Growth Management, 2nd Conference on Planning for Growth Management, Honolulu, HI, November 1979: Proceedings. Office of Council Services, Honolulu City Council, 1980. 72 p.

Conservation Foundation. "Futurists Call for Reforms in Planning." Conservation Foundation Letter, (June 1975): 1-8.

"Ecology and the Future." EPA Journal, 6, 4 (1980): 14-17.

Felling, W. E. "Experiments in Regional Environmental Planning." Environmental Conservation, 1, 4 (1974): 271-275.

Gillespie, D. F. and R. W. Perry. "Administrative Principles in Emergency Planning." Environmental Professional, 6, 1 (1984): 41-45.

Gladwin, T. N. and M. G. Royston. "An Environmentally-Oriented Mode of Industrial Project Planning." Environmental Conservation, 2, 3 (1975): 189-198.

Godchot, J. E. "Our Future Options." In Man and His Environment, 3rd International Conference, Banff, Alberta, May 1978, Proceedings, Vol. 3, pp. 97-106.

Hahn, A. J. and C. D. Dyballa. "State Environmental Planning and Local Influence." American Planning Association Journal, 47, 3 (1981): 324-335.

Hanie, R. "Atlanta 2000." Ecologist, 5, 9 (1975): 329-330.

Hoinville, G. "Evaluating Community Preferences." Environment and Planning, 3, 1 (1971): 33-50.

Lange, T. "Boulder Smolders as Growth Struggle Continues." High Country News, 11, 17 (1979): 1-3.

Lange, T. "New Kind of 'Public Interest.'" High Country News, 12, 1 (1980): 1-3.

Little, R. L. and R. S. Krannich. "Before the Boom: Organizing for Local Control in Pre-Impact Communities." Paper presented at Coping with Rapid Growth Conference, Scottsdale, AZ, February 1980.

Lotz, J. "Community Development and Public Participation." In B. Sadler (ed.), Involvement and Environment: Proceedings of the Canadian Conference on Public Participation. Vol. 2: Working Papers and Case Studies. Edmonton, Alberta: Environment Council of Alberta, 1979, pp. 49-60.

Macor, Y. "Public Participation in Environmental Decision-Making." Plan Canada, 20 (September-December 1980): 154-165.

Milbrath, L. W. "Incorporating the Views of the Uninterested but Impacted Public in Environmental Planning." Policy Studies Journal, 8, 6 (1980): 913-920.

New York State Department of Environmental Conservation. "Citizens Speak Out on the Environmental Plan." New York State Environment, 3, 3 (1973): Supplement, 4 p.

Puls, M. "Colorado Under Seige by Developers: Enviromentalists Gearing for a Show-Down." Environmental Action Bulletin 7, 17 (1976): 4-7.

Semling, H. "Early Citizen Involvement Key to Successful Environmental Planning, City Managers Told." American City, 88 (July 1973): 18.

Sorte, G. J. "Methods for Presenting Planned Environments." Man-Environment Systems, 5 (1975): 148-154.

Susskind, L. E. "Citizen Involvement in Growth Management and Local Land Use Planning." In Land Use/Growth Management National Conference, San Francisco, CA, March 1979: Proceedings. Golden Gate University, pp. 90-102.

Wandersman, A. "User Participation in Planning Environments: A Conceptual Framework." Environment and Behavior, 11, 4 (1979): 465-482.

Woollahra Municipal Council. The Darling Point Precinct Environmental Control Plan, Vol. 1: Evaluation Through Public Participation. Sydney, Australia, 1970.

Wrobel, D. D. "Public Participation Program Regulations for Facilities Planning." In Alternative Wastewater Treatment Systems Conference, Urbana, IL, June 1979: Proceedings. University of Illinois, pp. 27-32.

Pollution

American Association of University Women. A Resource Guide on Pollution Control. Washington, DC, 1970.

Atkinson, G. A. "Pollution, Protest and Participation." Ekistics, 26, 156 (1968): 430-431.

Conservation Foundation. "Students Rally to Halt Pollution, Raise Quality of Man's Environment." CF Letter, (January 1970): 1-12.

Dorcey, A. H. J. "Effluent Changes, Information Generation and Bargaining Behavior." Natural Resources Journal, 13, 1 (1973): 118-133.

"Energy and the Environment." Energy Consumer, 3 (January 1981): entire issue (43 p.).

"Health at Risk: Citizen Participation and Pollution." CW - Canadian Welfare, 52, 5 (1976): 5.

Lovrich, N. P. et al. "Policy Relevant Information and Public Attitudes: Is Public Ignorance a Barrier to Nonpoint Pollution Management?" Water Resources Bulletin, 22, 2 (1986): 229-236.

Lucas, A. R. and P. A. Moore. "The Utah Controversy: A Case Study of Public Participation in Pollution Control." Natural Resources Journal, 13, 1 (1973): 36-75.

Mason, R. J. An Assessment of the Pollution from Land Use Activities Reference Group Public Consultation Programme. Report No. EJ-1. Institute for Environmental Studies, University of Toronto, Toronto, 1980.

Mattoon, J. "Public Affairs: An Essential Ingredient in Pollution Response." In Pollution Response Conference, St. Petersburg, FL, May 1979: Proceedings, U. S. Fish and Wildlife Service, pp. 146-150.

Schnaiberg, A. "Politics, Participation and Pollution: The 'Environmental Movement.'" In J. Walton and D. Corns (eds.), Cities in Change: A Reader in Urban Sociology. Boston, MA: Allyn and Bacon, 1972.

Sharma, N. C. "Environmental Pollution: Is There Enough Public Concern to Lead to Action." Environmental and Behavior, 7, 4 (1975): 455-471.

Toxic and Hazardous Substances/Wastes

Anderson, R. F. "Public Participation in Hazardous Waste Facility Location Decisions." Journal of Planning Literature, 1, 2 (1986): 145-161.

Anderson, R. F. and M. F. Greenberg. "Hazardous Waste Facility Siting: A Role for Planners." American Planning Association Journal, 48 (Spring 1982): 204-218.

Antunes, G. E. and G. Halter. "The Politics of Resource Recovery, Energy Conservation, and Solid Waste Management." Administration and Society, 8, 1 (1976): 55-77.

Association of New Jersey Environmental Commissions. A Citizen's Guide to the Major Hazardous Waste Facilities Siting Act (New Jersey). Mendham, NJ, 1981.

Bacow, L. S. and J. R. Milkey. "Overcoming Local Opposition to Hazardous Waste Facilities: The Massachusetts Approach." Harvard Environmental Law Review, 6 (1982): 265-305.

Bacow, L., Higgs, K., and J. Rose. Public Interest Advocates and the Siting Process. MIT Laboratory of Architecture and Planning, Cambridge, MA, 1979.

Baas, L. "Impacts of Strategy and Participation of Volunteer Organizations of Involved Inhabitants in Living-Quarters on Contaminated Soil." In H. A. Becker and A. L. Porter (eds.), Impact Assessment Today. Vol. 2. Utrecht, Netherlands: Utigeverij Jan van Arkel, 1986, pp. 835-842.

Bealer, R. C. and D. Crider. "Sociological Considerations of Siting Facilities for Solid Waste Disposal." In S. K. Majumdar and E. W. Miller (eds.), Solid and Liquid Wastes: Management, Methods and Socioeconomic Considerations. Easton, PA: Pennsylvania Academy of Science, 1984, pp. 364-376.

Bealer, R. C., Martin, K. E., and D. M. Crider. Sociological Aspects of Siting Facilities for Solid Waste Disposal: A State-of-the-Art Study and Annotated Bibliography. Department of Agricultural Economics and Rural Sociology, Pennsylvania State University, University Park, PA, 1980.

Belfiglio, J., Lippe, T., and S. Franklin. Hazardous Waste Disposal Sites: A Handbook for Public Input and Review. Stanford Environmental Law Society, Stanford, CA, 1981.

Bellman, H. S. "Siting for a Sanitary Landfill for Eau Claire, Wisconsin." Environmental Professional, 2, 1 (1980): 56-57.

Bellman, H. S., Cormick, G. W., and C. Sampson. Using Mediation When Siting Hazardous Waste Management Facilities: A Handbook. Report No. SW-944. Washington, DC: U.S. Government Printing Office, 1982.

Blanc, P. Stop Environmental Cancer: A Citizen's Guide to Organizing. Campaign for Economic Democracy, Santa Monica, CA, 1980.

Brickman, R., Jasanoff, S., and T. Ilgen. Chemical Regulation and Cancer: A Cross-National Study of Policy and Politics. Ithaca, NY: Cornell University Press, 1982.

Brown, J. L. and D. Allen. "Toxic Waste and Citizen Action." Science for the People, 15, 4 (1983): 6-12.

Brown, M. H. Laying Waste: The Poisoning of America by Toxic Chemicals. New York: Pantheon, 1979. 351 p.

Cahill, C. "Public Participation: Citizens Challenge Asbestos Pipe Use." Environment, 24, 4 (1982): 43-44.

California Governor's Office of Appropriate Technology. Alternatives to the Land Disposal of Hazardous Wastes: An Assessment for California. Toxic Waste Assessment Group, Sacramento, CA, 1981.

Call, G. D. "Arsenic, ASARCO, and the EPA: Cost-Benefit Analysis, Public Participation, and Polluter Games in the Regulation of Hazardous Air Pollutants." Ecology Law Quarterly, 12, 3 (1985): 567-617.

Canter, B. D. "Hazardous Waste Disposal and the New State Siting Programs." Natural Resources Lawyer, 14, 3 (1982): 421-456.

Centaur Associates, Inc. Siting of Hazardous Waste Management Facilities and Public Opposition. Report No. SW-809. U. S. Environmental Protection Agency, Washington, DC, 1979.

Chess, C. Winning the Right to Know: A Handbook for Toxic Activists. Delaware Valley Toxics Coalition, Philadelphia, PA, 1983.

Citizen's Clearinghouse for Hazardous Waste. Leadership Handbook. Arlington, VA, 1983.

Clark-McGlennon Associates. Criteria for Evaluating Sites for Hazardous Waste Management: A Handbook on Siting Acceptable Hazardous Waste Facilities in New England. New England Regional Commission, Boston, MA, 1980.

Clark-McGlennon Associates. A Decision Guide for Siting Acceptable Hazardous Waste Facilities in New England. New England Regional Commission, Boston, MA, 1980.

Clark-McGlennon Associates. An Introduction to Facilities for Hazardous Waste Management: A Handbook on Siting Acceptable Hazardous Waste Facilities in New England. New England Regional Commission, Boston, MA, 1980.

Cohen, S. "Superfund Community Relations Policy." EPA Journal, 7 (June 1981): 29.

Conservation Foundation. "Public Apathy Toward Chemical Risks Is Perilous." Conservation Foundation Letter, (September 1978): 1-8.

Conservation Foundation. Siting Hazardous Waste Management Facilities: A Handbook. Program for Environmental Dispute Resolution, Washington, DC, 1983. 71 p.

Cormick, G. W. "Siting New Hazardous Waste Management Facilities Using Mediated Negotiations." Paper presented to the conference Meeting the New RCRA Requirements on Hazardous Waste, Alexandria, VA, October 1985.

Danner, R. A. "Federal Regulation of Non-Nuclear Hazardous Wastes: A Research Bibliography." Law and Contemporary Problems, 46, 3 (1983): 285-305.

Davis, C. "Substance and Procedure in Hazardous Waste Facility Siting." Journal of Environmental Systems, 14, 1 (1984-85): 51-62.

Doutt, R. L. "De-Bugging the Pesticide Law." Environment, 21, 10 (1979): 32-36.

Duberg, J. A., Frankel, M. L., and C. M. Niemczewski. "Siting of Hazardous Waste Management Facilities and Public Opposition." Environmental Impact Assessment Review, 1 (March 1980): 83-84.

Duffy, C. "State Hazardous Waste Facility Siting: Easing the Process through Local Cooperation and Preemption." Boston College Environmental Affairs Law Review, 11 (October 1984): 755-804.

Dunn, J. J. Jr. "Public Participation in Landfill Siting Process Can Help Smooth the Way." Solid Wastes Management, 22, 5 (1979): 81-82.

Easton, E. R. "EPA's New Public Participation Rules: Constructive or Obstructive?" Sludge, 2, 3 (1979): 17-19.

Ellis, R. A. and R. W. Howe. "Public Participation in Hazardous Waste Site Control: Not 'If' But 'How.'" In Management of Uncontrolled Hazardous Waste Sites National Symposium, Washington, DC, November-December 1982: Proceedings. U. S. Environmental Protection Agency, pp. 340-345.

Engler, R. "The New Jersey 'Right-To-Know' Campaign: The Nation's Toughest Toxics Law." Health and Medicine, 2 (Winter 1983-84): 10-12.

Environmental Defense Fund. Dumpsite Cleanups: A Citizen's Guide to the Superfund Program. Washington, DC, 1983.

Epstein, S., Brown, L. O., and C. Pope. Hazardous Waste in America. San Francisco: Sierra Club Books, 1982. 593 p.

Ervine, H. C. Jr. "Role of Local Government in Hazardous Waste Management." Public Works, 114 (July 1983): 67-68+.

Farkas, A. "Overcoming Public Opposition to the Establishment of New Hazardous Waste Disposal Sites." Capital University Law Review, 9 (1980): 451-465.

Freudenberg, N. Not In Our Backyards: Community Action for Health and the Environment. New York: Monthly Review Press, 1984. 304 p.

Freudenthal, H. D. and J. A. Celender. "Public Involvement in Resolving Hazardous Waste Site Problems." In Management of Uncontrolled Hazardous Waste Sites National Symposium, Washington, DC, November-December 1982: Proceedings. U. S. Environmental Protection Agency, pp. 346-349.

Frost, J. L. et al. "Choosing Sewage Sludge Ash Disposal Sites in the Twin Cities Metropolitan Area." In 5th Municipal and Industrial Waste Research and Practice Conference, Madison, WI, September 1982: Proceedings. University of Wisconsin, pp. 59-78.

Gamm, L. "Citizen Involvement in Sanitary Landfill Siting." Paper presented to the International Voluntary Association and Voluntary Action Research Association, Grenoble, France, June 1979.

Glodshore, L. "Hazardous Waste Facility Siting." New Jersey Law Journal, 108 (November 29, 1981): 453.

Gordon, W. A Citizen's Handbook on Groundwater Protection. Natural Resources Defense Council, New York, 1984.

Grad, F. P. "Siting of Hazardous Waste Disposal Facilities -- Problem or Solution." In Environmental Law: ALI-ABA Course of Study Materials. Philadelphia, PA: American Law Institute, 1985, pp. 227-240.

Great Lakes Basin Commission. PCB Information Packet. Ann Arbor, MI, September1980. 68 p.

Greenberg, M. R. and R. F. Anderson. Hazardous Waste Sites: The Credibility Gap. New Brunswick, NJ: Center for Urban Policy Research, 1984. 276 p.

Gregerman, S. Waste Alert Spotlight on Hazardous Waste Technologies. Environmental Action Foundation, Washington, DC, September 1981.

Hadden, S. G., Veillette, J., and T. Brandt. "State Roles in Siting Hazardous Waste Disposal Facilities: From State Preemption to Local Veto." In J. P. Lester and A. O. Bowman (eds.), The Politics of Hazardous Waste Management. Durham, NC: Duke University Press, 1983, pp. 196-211.

Harley, M. Social and Economic Issues in Siting a Hazardous Waste Facility: Ideas for Communities and Local Assessment Committees. Citizens for Citizens, Inc., Fall River, MA, 1982.

Hendrickson, M. L. and S. A. Romano. "Citizen Involvement in Waste Facility Siting." Public Works, 113, 5 (1982): 76-79.

Hickman, H. L. "EPA Reports on Implementation of the Resource Conservation and Recovery Act of 1976." Solid Wastes Management, 20, 7 (1977): 52-56.

"How Massachusetts 'Markets' Hazardous Waste Siting." Environmental Forum, 1, 4 (1982): 34-.

Howell, J. A Citizen's Guide to the Major Hazardous Waste Facilities Siting Act. 3rd edition. Trenton, NJ: New Jersey Hazardous Waste Facilities Siting Commission, 1983.

Hudson, J. F. et al. "Disposal Technology: Site Selection Issues." In Evaluation of Policy-Related Research in the Field of Municipal Solid Waste Management. Cambridge, MA: Civil Engineering Systems Laboratory, Massachusetts Institute of Technology, 1974, pp. 199-203.

Hutt, P. B. "Public Participation in Toxicology Decisions." Food Drug Cosmetic Law Journal, 32, 6 (1977): 275-285.

Institute for Environmental Negotiation. Not-In-My-Backyard: Community Reaction to Locally Unwanted Land Use. University of Virginia, Charlottesville,VA, 1985. 68 p.

Institute of Environmental Research, Inc. Consulting with the Public When Operating Hazardous Waste Management Facilities: A Handbook for Developers and Public Agencies. U. S. Environmental Protection Agency, Washington, DC, 1981.

Institute of Environmental Research, Inc. The Design of a Public Consultation Program for a Hazardous Waste Management Facility. Waste Management Branch, Fisheries and Environment, Ottawa, Canada, June 1979.

Institute of German Studies. German and American Toxic Substances Legislation and Citizen Participation in Environmental Affairs. University of Indiana, Bloomington, IN, 1977. 23 p.

"Involving Public Aids Landfill Siting Process." Management of World Wastes, 26,12 (1983): 19-22+.

Isaak Walton League of America. Waste Alert Spotlight: Guide to State Hazardous Waste Management Program. Arlington, VA, 1982.

Jakubs, J. F. "Port Sivad: A Locational Decision Game for a Noxious Public Facility." Journal of Geography, 76, 4 (1977): 124-135.

Janis, J. R. "The Public and Superfund." EPA Journal, 7 (June 1981): 14-16.

Johnson, C. A. "Waste Facility Siting Process Requires State Backing, Candor, Credibility." Solid Wastes Management, 23 (May 1980): 84-85+.

Jubak, J. "The Struggle Over Siting." Environmental Action, 13, 7 (1982): 14-17.

Keystone Center. The Keystone Siting Process Handbook: A New Approach to Siting Hazardous Waste Management Facilities. Report LP-194. Texas Department of Water Resources, January 1984. 52 p.

Keystone Center. Siting Non-Radioactive Hazardous Waste Facilities: An Overview. Final Report of the First Keystone Workshop on Managing Non-Radioactive Hazardous Wastes. Keystone Center, CO, 1980.

Keystone Center. Siting Waste Management Facilities in the Galveston Bay Area: A New Approach. Keystone, CO, November 1982. 50 p.

Kovalick, W. W. Jr. (ed.). State Decision-Makers' Guide for Hazardous Waste Management. U. S. Environmental Protection Agency, Washington, DC, 1977.

Kraft, M. E. and R. Kraut. "The Impact of Citizen Participation on Hazardous Waste Policy Implementation: The Case of Clermont County, Ohio." Policy Studies Journal, 14, 1 (1985): 52-61.

Krawetz, N. M. Hazardous Waste Management: A Review of Social Concerns and Aspects of Public Involvement. Department of the Environment of Alberta, Canada, 1979.

Krivit, D. "Public Education and Relations in Waste Management." Paper presented at Evaluating Waste Management Options Conference, Brooklyn Park, MN, February 1984. 4 p.

Laden, G. M. "FDA Rule-Making Hearings: A Way Out of the Peanut Butter Quagmire." George Washington Law Review, 40, 4 (1972): 726-748.

League of Women Voters. A Hazardous Waste Primer. Report No. LWV 545. Education Fund, Washington, DC, 1980. 8 p.

League of Women Voters. Siting Hazardous Waste Facilities: A Dialogue. Report No. LWV 516. Education Fund, Washington, DC, October 1980. 4 p.

League of Women Voters. SOCs in Drinking Water: A Community Guide. Report No. LWV 532. Education Fund, Washington, DC, 1980. 4 p.

League of Women Voters. Solid Waste: It Won't Go Away Unless . . . A Sampling of What Citizen Leaders Can Do. LWV Education Fund, Washington, DC, 1974.

League of Women Voters of Massachusetts. Hazardous Waste Management (Massachusetts). Boston, MA, 1981.

Leffler, M. L. "Citizen Involvement Can Provide Valuable Insights." Solid Wastes Management, 23, 5 (1980): 74+.

Lennett, D. "State Regulation of Hazardous Waste." Ecology Law Quarterly, 12, 2 (1984): 183-270.

Lester, J. P. "Hazardous Waste, Politics, and Public Policy: A Comparative State Analysis." Western Political Quarterly, 36, 2 (1983): 257-285.

Levine, A. G. Love Canal: Science, Politics and People. Lexington, MA: Lexington Books, 1982.

Magorian, C. Public Participation and Hazardous Waste Facility Siting. Philadelphia, PA: Pennsylvania Environmental Research Foundation, 1982.

Maine Association of Conservation Commissions. Watching Our Wastes: A Citizen's Guide to Hazardous Waste in Northern New England. Bridgton, MA, n. d.

Mayo, D. G. "Increasing Public Participation in Controversies Involving Hazards: The Value of Metastatistical Rules." Science, Technology, and Human Values, 53 (1985): 55-68.

McAvoy, J. F. "Hazardous Waste Management in Ohio: The Problem of Siting." Capital University Law Review, 9 (Spring 1980): 435-450.

McMahon, R. et al. Using Compensation and Incentives When Siting Hazardous Waste Management Facilities: A Handbook. Report No. SW-942. Washington, DC: U. S. Government Printing Office, 1982.

McNulty, H. "Citizens' Role in Sludge Utilization Policy." In 5th National Acceptable Sludge Disposal Techniques Conference, Orlando, FL, January-February 1978: Proceedings, pp. 142-125.

Miletich, J. J. Hazardous Substances in Canada: A Selected Annotated Bibliography. Chicago, IL: Council of Planning Librarians, October 1982.

Morell, D. Siting Hazardous Waste Facilities: Local Opposition and the Myth of Preemption. Cambridge, MA: Ballinger Pub. Co., 1982.

Morell, D. and C. Magorian. "Siting Hazardous Waste Facilities: Local Opposition and the Myth of Preemption." Environment, 25 (April 1983): 45.

National Conference of State Legislatures. Hazardous Waste Management: A Survey of State Legislation 1982. Denver, CO, November 1982.

National Conference of State Legislatures. A Survey and Analysis of the Policy Options to Encourage Alternatives to Land Disposal of Hazardous Waste. Denver, CO, 1981.

Neumann, C. and B. Drake. "Citizen Participation in the Superfund Program." In Management of Uncontrolled Hazardous Waste Sites National Symposium, Washington, DC, November-December 1982: Proceedings. U. S. Environmental Protection Agency, pp. 350-353.

New Jersey. Legislature. Senate. Committee on Energy and Environment. Public Hearing before the Senate Energy and Environment Committee on the Senate Committee Substitute for S-1300 (Major Hazardous Waste Facilities Siting Act). Trenton, NJ, 1980.

O'Hare, M. "Not on My Block You Don't: Facility Siting and the Strategic Importance of Compensation." Public Policy, 25 (Fall 1977): 407-458.

O'Hare, M., Bacow, L., and J. Rose. Facility Siting and Public Opposition. New York: Van Nostrand-Reinhold, 1982.

"On a Two-Way Street: The Superfund Community Relations Program." EPA Journal, 9 (July-August 1982): 8-9.

Paigen, B. "Controversy at Love Canal." Hastings Center Report, 12, 3 (June 1982): 29-37.

Pennsylvania Department of Environmental Resources. Citizens Handbook on Hazardous Waste Management: A Guide to Citizen Action on Hazardous Waste Issues in Pennsylvania. Harrisburg, PA, 1982.

Pollock, E. L. "Residents Against Landfill." Solid Wastes Management, 16 (July 1974): 80+.

Popper, F. J. "Siting LULU's." Planning, 47 (April 1981): 12-15.

Quarles, J. Federal Regulation of Hazardous Wastes: A Guide to RCRA. Environmental Law Institute, Washington, DC, 1982.

Regens, J. L. "Siting Hazardous Waste Management Facilities." Paper presented at the Research Conference on Public Involvement and Social Impact Assessment, University of Arizona, Tucson, AZ, February 1981.

Ristoratae, M. "Siting Toxic Waste Disposal Facilities in Canada and the United States: Problems and Prospects." Policy Studies Journal, 14, 1 (1985): 140-148.

Romano, S. A. "Citizen and Local Official Involvement in Waste Management Facility Siting." In 4th Applied Research and Practice on Municipal and Industrial Waste Conference, Madison, WI, September 1981: Proceedings, pp. 1-15.

Rosenbaum, W. A. "The Politics of Public Participation in Hazardous Waste Management." In J. P. Lester and A. O. Bowman (eds.), The Politics of Hazardous Waste Management. Durham, NC: Duke University Press, 1983, pp. 177-195.

Schweitzer, G. E. "The Toxic Substances Control Act: Where Are We Going?" In 1st Toxic Substances Law Seminar, Washington, DC, December 1976: Proceedings, pp. 117-130.

Scott, M. "South Cayuga I and II: Lessons in the Need for Public Participation and the Role of the Ontario Waste Management Corporation." Alternatives, 10, 2-3 (1982): 5-11.

Segel, E. The Toxic Substances Dilemma: A Plan for Citizen Action. Washington, DC: National Wildlife Federation, 1980.

Seley, J. E. The Politics of Public-Facility Planning. Lexington, MA: Lexington Books, 1983. 236 p.

Sierra Club. Training Materials on Toxic Substances: Tools for Effective Action. 2nd ed. San Francisco, 1981. 2 vols. 604 p.

Smiley, C. "Landfill Siting Requires Public Education Effort." Management of World Wastes, 26 (September 1983): 52-54.

Sobetzer, J. G. and L. A. Corson. Hazardous Waste Management in Michigan: A Guide for Local Government and Citizens. Continuing Education Service, Institute for Community Development, Michigan State University, East Lansing, MI, 1982.

Sproul, C. A. "Public Participation in the Point Conception LNG Controversy: Energy Wasted or Energy Well-Spent." Ecology Law Quarterly, 13, 1 (1986): 73-153.

Sullivan, M. "Watching Our Wastes: A Citizen's Guide to Hazardous Waste in Northern New England. Maine Association of Conservation Commissions, n. d. 69 p.

Susskind, L. E. and S. R. Casell. "The Dangers of Pre-emptive Legislation: The Case of LNG Facility Siting in California." Environmental Impact Assessment Review, 1, 1 (1980): 8-26.

Tomboulian, A. and P. Tomboulian. Hazardous Waste Siting Response: A Handbook for Michigan Citizens and Local Government. Michigan Environmental Policy Institute, East Michigan Environmental Action Council, Troy, MI, 1983.

Tourbier, J. "Public Acceptance of Sludge Land Application is Vital." Water and Sewage Works, 125, 9 (1978): 126-128.

U. S. Congress. House. Committee on Government Operations. Environment, Energy, and Natural Resources Subcommittee. Hazardous Waste Facility Siting Problems. Washington, DC: U. S. Government Printing Office, 1982.

U. S. Congress. Office of Technology Assessment. "Public Participation and Public Confidence in the Superfund Program." In Superfund Strategy. OTA Report ITE-252. Washington, DC, pp. 257-274.

U. S. Environmental Protection Agency. Everybody's Problem: Hazardous Wastes. SW-826. Office of Water and Waste Management, Washington, DC, 1980.

U. S. Environmental Protection Agency. Hazardous Waste Regulations under RCRA: A Summary. SW-939. Washington, DC, 1981.

U. S. Environmental Protection Agency. Siting Hazardous Waste Management Facilities: Dilemma and Challenge. Report No. SW-951. Washington, DC, 1981.

U. S. Environmental Protection Agency. Waste Alert: A Citizen's Introduction to Public Participation in Waste Management.   SW-800. Office of Water and Waste Management, Washington, DC, 1979.

Urban Systems Research and Engineering, Inc. A Handbook for the States on the Use of Compensation and Incentives in the Siting of Hazardous Waste Management Facilities. U. S. Environmental Protection Agency, Washington, DC, 1980.

Vlachos, E. "Social Aspects of Solid Waste Development and Management: Refuse, Recovery, and Reuse." Water, Air, and Soil Pollution, 4, 2 (1975): 293-301.

Warnock, J. W. and J. Lewis. "The Political Ecology of 2,4-D." Alternatives, 10, 2-3 (1982): 33-39.

Washington Suburban Sanitary Commission. Guidelines for Citizen Participation in the WSSC Facilities Planning Process. Washington, DC, 1980.

Wetmore, R. D. "Massachusetts' Innovative Process for Siting Hazardous Waste Facilities." Environmental Impact Assessment Review, 1 (June 1980): 182-184.

Winsor, E. W. "Hazardous Wastes: Facility Siting." Solid Wastes Management, 23, 12 (1980): 48-50.

Winsor, E. W. "Public Should Have a Role in Siting Hazwaste Facility." Sanitation Industry Yearbook, (1982): 18-22.

Wolf, S. M. "Public Opposition to Hazardous Waste Sites." Boston College Environmental Affairs Law Review, 8, 3 (1980): 463-540.

Wynne, B. "A Case Study: Hazardous Waste in the European Community." In H. Otway and M. Peltu (eds.), Regulating Industrial Risks: Science, Hazards and Public Protection. Boston: Butterworths, 1985, pp. 149-176.

Water Pollution

Bruvold, W. H. "Public Participation in Environmental Decisions: Water Reuse. "Public Affairs Report, 22 (February 1981): 1-6.

Carlson, K. T. "The People's Lake." Environment, 17, 2 (1975): 16-20.

Crisp, H. W. "Successful Citizen Participation Methods for Wastewater Collection and Treatment Programs." Water Science and Technology, 13, 6 (1981):1-9.

Crusberg, C. C. et al. "The Water Quality Resource Study Group: An Interdisciplinary Community Effort in Worcester, Massachusetts." Environmental Professional, 5, 2 (1983): 162-167.

Davis, A. C. Public Participation in Water Pollution Control Policy and Decision Making. Report No. 88. Water Resources Research Institute, University of North Carolina, Raleigh, NC, December 1973. 66 p.

Greater Egypt Regional Planning and Development Commission. Areawide Waste Treatment and Water Quality Management Planning: Public Participation Activities. Carbondale, IL, 1980.

Harris, E. S. "To Clean a Harbor." In Citizens Advisory Committee on Environmental Quality, Citizens Make the Difference: Case Studies of Environmental Action. Washington, DC, January 1973, pp. 27-34.

Kamieniecki, S. Public Representation in Environmental Policymaking: The Case of Water Quality Management. Boulder, CO: Westview Press, 1980.

National Association of Counties Research Foundation. Community Action Program for Water Pollution Control. Washington, DC: U. S. Government Printing Office, 1961.

Paluszek, J. L. "Water Quality and the Public Policy Process." Paper presented at the Water Pollution Control Federation 14th Annual Government Affairs Seminar, Washington, DC, March 1980. 17 p.

Ragan Associates. The Water Pollution Control Act of 1972: Institutional Assessment -- Public Participation. Report PB 245 410. National Technical Information Service, Springfield, VA, October 1975. 278 p.

Reid, B. and G. Speth. Water Pollution Control Handbook: Citizens' Guide to the Federal Water Pollution Control Amendments of 1972. Project Clean Water, Natural Resources Defense Council, March 1973. 19 p.

Robadue, D. D. Jr., and V. K. Tippie. "Public Involvement in Offshore Oil Development: Lessons from New England." Coastal Zone Management Journal, 7, 2-4 (1980): 237-270.

Segree, C. R. "Public Participation: Boon or Boondoggle?" Journal of the Water Pollution Control Federation, 51, 5 (1979): 880-883.

Vogt, S. F. Public Participation Handbook for Water Quality Management. Water Planning Division, U. S. Environmental Protection Agency, Washington, DC, June 1976. 81 p.

U. S. General Accounting Office. Federal, State, Local, and Public Roles in Constructing Waste Water Treatment Facilities. Report No. RED-76-45. Washington, DC, December 1975. 51 p.

Zinn, J. A. (ed.) "Theme Issue: Energy and the Coastal Zone: A Question of Risk." Coastal Zone Management Journal, 7, 2-4 (1980): 123-337.

Part II

Energy-Related Decision Making

General

Barbour, I. G. et al. Energy and Human Values. New York: Praeger, 1982. 239 p.

Commoner, B. The Poverty of Power: Energy and the Economic Crisis. New York: Alfred Knopf, 1976.

Elder, P. S. "Project Approval, Environmental Assessment and Public Participation." Environmentalist, 2, 1 (1982): 55-61.

"Energy and the Environment." Energy Consumer, 3 (January 1981): entire issue (43 p.).

Grossman, R. and G. Daneker. Energy, Jobs, and Economy. Boston: Alyson Publications, 1979.

Johnson, W. A. Muddling Through Frugality. Boulder, CO: Shambhala Publications, 1979.

Kelsey, J. and D. Wiener. "The Citizen-Labor Energy Coalition." Social Policy, 13, 4 (1983): 15-18.

Kloman, E. H. Public Participation in Energy-Related Decision-Making. National Academy of Public Administration, Washington, DC. 1976.

Lake, L. M. "Participatory Evaluations of Energy Options for California: A Case Study in Conflict Avoidance." In L. M. Lake (ed.), Environmental Mediation: The Search for Consensus. Boulder, CO: Westview Press, 1980, pp. 147-172.

Mitre Corporation. Public Participation in Energy-Related Decision Making: Workshop Proceedings. MTR-7367. Metrek Division, McLean, VA, 1977.

"Transportation and Energy ." Energy Consumer, 2 (September 1980): entire issue.

Alternative Energy Development

Antunes, G. E. and G. Halter. "The Politics of Resource Recovery, Energy Conservation, and Solid Waste Management." Administration and Society, 8, 1 (1976): 55-77.

Bender, T. "Sharing Smaller Pies." In G. J. Coates (ed.), Resettling America: Energy, Ecology, and Community. Andover, MA: Brick House Publishing, 1981.

Bossong, K. Solar Organizing Ideas. Report Series No. 53. Citizens' Energy Project, Washington, DC, 1978. 5 p.

Center for Renewable Resources. Shining Examples: Model Projects Using Renewable Resources. Washington, DC, 1980. 210 p.

Center for Renewable Resources. Solar Action: 27 Communities Boost Renewable Energy Use. Washington, DC, May 1981. 83 p.

Citizens' Advisory Committee on Environmental Quality. Citizen Action Guide to Energy Conservation. Washington, DC, September 1973. 61 p.

Citizens' Energy Project. Citizens' Energy Directory: A Guide to Alternative Energy Resources. Washington, DC, March 1982. 185 p.

Frankena, F. "Defeat of the Hersey Wood-Fired Power Plant: The Ideology and Politics of Technology in a Nonmetropolitan Community." Paper presented at the 1st National Symposium on Social Science in Resource Management, Corvallis, OR, May 1986. 22 p.

Frankena, F. "Facts, Values, and Technical Expertise in a Renewable Energy Siting Dispute." Journal of Economic Psychology, 4 (1983): 131-147.

Frankena, F. "Facts, Values, and Technical Expertise in a Renewable Energy Siting Dispute." In P. Ester et al. (eds.), Consumer Behavior and Energy Policy: Selected/Edited Proceedings of the 1st International Conference, Noordwijkerhout, September 1982. New York: North-Holland, 1984, pp. 417-433.

Frankena, F. The Impact of Technical Expertise in a Nonmetropolitan Siting Dispute: A Case Study of the Hersey Wood-Fired Power Plant Controversy. Ph. D. Dissertation. Michigan State University, East Lansing, MI, 1983. Avail. University Microfilms International, Ann Arbor, MI.

Henderson, H. The Politics of the Solar Age: Alternatives to Economics. Garden City, NY: Anchor Press, 1981.

"A National Solar Strategy and Solar Resource Guide." Energy Consumer, 1 (August-September 1979): entire issue (35 p.).

Reece, R. The Sun Betrayed. Boston: South End Press, 1979.

Ridgeway, J. and B. Connor. New Energy: Understanding the Crisis and a Guide to an Alternative Energy System. Boston: Beacon Press, 1975.

Shama, A. and K. Jacobs. Social Values and Solar Energy Policy: The Policymaker and the Advocate. Solar Energy Research Institute, Golden, CO, 1980(?). v. p.

Snyder, R. (ed.). Reaching Up, Reaching Out: A Guide to Organizing Local Solar Events. SERI SP-62-326. Washington, DC: U. S. Government Printing Office, 1979. 204 p.

Snyder, R. (ed.). Saving Home Energy: A Handbook for Organizing a Hands-On Energy Conservation and Passive Solar Energy Workshop. Estes Park, CO: Colorado Solar Energy Association, 1978.

Solar Action. Sun Day Press Handbook Or, I Like Your Song and Dance, But Is It News? Washington, DC: Solar Action, n. d.

Stern, P. C., Black, J. S., and J. T. Elworth. Home Energy Conservation: Programs and Strategies for the 1980s. Institute for Consumer Policy Research, Consumers Union Foundation, Mount Vernon, NY, 1981. 152 p.

Stokes, B. "Small Is Bountiful." In Helping Ourselves: Local Solution to Global Problems. New York: Norton, 1981.

U. S. General Accounting Office. How Solar Energy Was Treated in the AEC Chairman's Report, "The Nation's Energy Future." GAO Report B-178205, Washington, DC, October 1974. 36 p.

Young, E. "Energy Conservation: Nashville Metro's Response." Tennessee Town and City, 28, 1 (1977): 14-17.

Community Energy Management

Alschuler, J. H. Community Energy Strategies. Hartford Policy Center, Hartford, CT,1980.

Antigone, S. People Power: What Communities Are Doing to Counter Inflation. U. S. Office of Consumer Affairs, Washington, DC, 1980. 411 p.

Bronfman, B. H., Carnes, S. A., and R. Ahmad. "Community Based Technology Assessment: Four Communities Plan Their Energy Future." In F. Porter, F. A. Rossini, and C. P. Wolf (eds.), Integrated Impact Assessment. Boulder, CO: Westview Press, 1983, pp. 202-218.

Coates, G. J. (ed.). Resettling America: Energy, Ecology, and Community. Andover, MA: Brick House Publishing, 1981. 560 p.

Cobb, T. B. "Community Energy Policy Project." Paper presented at the International Conference on Energy Education, Providence, RI, August 1981.

"Communities and Energy." Energy Consumer, 2 (February-March 1980): entire issue (47 p.).

"Community Self-Help." Energy Consumer, 1 (October 1979): 20-29.

Conference on Alternative State and Local Policies. Citizen Involvement in Community Energy Planning. Washington, DC, 1981. 51 p.

Cose, E. Decentralizing Energy Decisions: The Rebirth of Community Power. Boulder, CO: Westview Press, 1983. 140 p.

Critical Mass Energy Project. Town Energy Planning: A Framework for Action. Public Citizen, Washington, DC, 1983. 102 p.

Hughes, K. and B. Pape. Citizen Involvement in Community Energy Planning. Community Skills and Resource Report No. 5. Energy Project, Conference on Alternative State and Local Policies, Washington, DC, 1981. 48 p.

Illinois Department of Energy and Natural Resources. Project Evanston Completion Report: A Community Energy Management Planning Assistance (CEMPA) Program. Springfield, IL, 1983.

Johnson, L. "Neighborhood Energy: Designing for Democracy in the 1980s." In L. deMoll and G. Coe (eds.), Stepping Stones: Appropriate Technology and Beyond. New York: Schocken Books, 1978.

Morris, D. Planning for Energy Self-Reliance. Institute for Local Self-Reliance, Washington, DC, 1979.

Morris, D. Self-Reliant Cities: Energy and the Transformation of Urban America. San Francisco: Sierra Club, 1980.

Okagaki, A. and J. Benson. County Energy Plan Guidebook: Creating a Renewable Energy Future. Fairfax, VA: Institute for Ecological Policies, 1979. 164 p.

Schaefer, E. and J. Benson. Energy and Power in Your Community: How to Analyze Where It Comes From, How Much It Costs, and Who Controls It. Fairfax, VA: Institute for Ecological Policies, 1980. 129 p.

Solar Energy Research Institute. What Your Community Can Do About Energy. Community and Consumer Branch, Golden, CO, 1980. 28 p.

Conventional Energy Development

Aldrich, B. C. Communities of Opposition: Energy Facility Siting in Minnesota. Urban and Community Studies, Department of Sociology and Social Work, Winona State University, Winona, MN, 1980. 81 p.

Anagnoson, J. T. "Can an Industrialized Society Accelerate the Processing of Important Energy Projects? New Zealand's National Development Act." Energy Systems and Policy, 9, 3 (1985): 249-270.

Bailey, J., Bacigalupi, L. and M. Warner. Local Citizens Participation in Coal Development. Foundation for Urban and Neighborhood Development, Denver, CO, 1975.

Briggs, M. J. and M. L. Moss. Community Decisionmaking and Energy Exploration: The Pacific Palisades Conflict. Sea Grant Program, University of Southern California, Los Angeles, 1973.

Buchan, G. "Institutional Design for Energy Systems/Environmental Decision Making." In MIT Symposium, Cambridge, MA, February 12-14, 1973: Proceedings, pp. 261-271.

Cannon, J. "Public Coal and Private Profits." Business and Society Review, 31 (Fall 1979): 28-32; Reply by W. N. Warhol, 34 (Summer 1980): 64-65.

Clemente, F. et al. Public Participation in Energy-Related Decisionmaking: Six Case Studies. Report No. M76-53. Mitre Corporation and National Academy of Public Administration, McLean, VA, December 1977.

Comstock, R. W. "Open Planning and Power Plant Siting: How to Satisfy the Environmentalists and Still Stay in Business." Remarks before the Westinghouse International School for Environmental Management Course, Colorado State University, Fort Collins, CO, July 1975. 25 p.

Creighton, J. L. Public Involvement Manual: Involving the Public in Water and Power Resources Decisions. U. S. Department of the Interior, Water and Power Resources Service, Washington, DC, January 1980. 333 p.

Curry, M. G. and M. E. Olsen. Citizen Involvement in Energy Decision Making. BNWL-2084 (RAP-14). Battelle Pacific Northwest Labs, Richland, WA, 1977. 24 p.

Deal, D. "Durham Controversy: Energy Facility Siting and Land Use Planning and Control Process." Natural Resources Lawyer, 8, 3 (1975): 437-453.

Ducsik, D. W. "Citizen Participation in Power Plant Siting: Aladdin's Lamp or Pandora's Box?" Journal of the American Planning Association, 47, 2 (1981): 154-166.

Edmunds, C. M. W. "The Politics of Public Participation and the Siting of Power Plants in Japan." Environmental Professional, 6, 3-4 (1984): 293-302.

Gerlach, L. P. "Citizen Resistance to Energy Development in the Upper Midwest and Northern Tier States." Paper presented at the Annual Manager's Conference of the Rural Electric Cooperative Association, Louisville, KY, August 1976. 15 p.

Gerlach, L. P. "The Great Energy Standoff." Natural History, 87, 1 (1978): 22-32.

Holtz, S. "Public Concerns over the Combustion of Coal." In APCA 6th Annual Symposium, New Brunswick, Canada, September 1982: Proceedings, pp. 105-107.

Jackson, J. and P. Weller. "South Cayuga I: Lessons in the Need for Public Participation." Alternatives, 10, 2-3 (1982): 5-12.

Mack, E. and B. C. Aldrich. "Local Opposition to Power Plant Siting: Resource Mobilization Networks." In R. P. Wolensky and E. J. Miller (eds.), The Small City and Regional Community: Proceedings of the Conference on the Small City and Regional Community. Vol. 2. Stevens Point, WI: Foundation Press, Inc., 1979, pp. 150-157.

Mitnick, B. M. and C. Weiss, Jr. "The Siting Impasse and a Rational Choice Model of Regulatory Behavior: An Agency for Power Plant Siting." Journal of Environment, Economics, and Management, 1, 2 (1974): 150-171.

Nassikas, J. N. "Public Participation in Locating Facilities." Public Utilities Fortightly, 88 (September 16, 1971): 108-114.

Nelkin, D. "Experts and Citizens: Problems of Participation in Power Plant Siting Decisions." Paper presented at the Annual Meeting of the American Association for the Advancement of Science, San Francisco, CA, February 1974.

Parfit, M. Last Stand at Rosebud Creek: Coal, Power, and People. New York: Dutton, 1980. 304 p.

Robadue, D. D. Jr., and V. K. Tippie. "Public Involvement in Offshore Oil Development: Lessons from New England." Coastal Zone Management Journal, 7, 2-4 (1980): 237-270.

Sanderson, D. R. Compensation in Facility Siting Conflicts. Energy Impacts Project, Massachusetts Institute of Technology, Cambridge, MA, 1979.

Sanderson, D. R. Facility Siting, Social Costs, and Public Conflict. Energy Impacts Project, Massachusetts Institute of Technology, Cambridge, MA, 1979.

Seiple, W. R. "New Approach to Site Selection Studies." Journal of the Power Division, Proceedings of the American Society of Civil Engineers, 100 (July 1974): 63-69.

Sive, D. "The Role of Litigation in Environmental Policy: The Power Plant Siting Problem." Natural Resources Journal, 11 (July 1971): 467-476.

Sproul, C. A. "Public Participation in the Point Conception LNG Controversy: Energy Wasted or Energy Well-Spent." Ecology Law Quarterly, 13, 1 (1986): 73-153.

Starr, R. "Power and the People: The Case of Con Edison." Public Interest, 26 (Winter 1972): 75-99.

Susskind, L. E. and S. R. Casell. "The Dangers of Pre-emptive Legislation: The Case of LNG Facility Siting in California." Environmental Impact Assessment Review, 1, 1 (1980): 8-26.

Talbot, A. R. Power Along the Hudson: The Storm King Case and the Birth of Environmentalism. New York: Dutton, 1972.

Tobin, R. J. and R. A. Carpenter. "Public Participation in the Environmental Review Process, with Special Reference to Coal-Fired Power Plant Siting." Environmental Conservation, 10, 4 (1983): 315-321.

U. S. Department of Housing and Urban Development. Rapid Growth from Energy Projects: Ideas for State and Local Action. Washington, DC, 1976.

Wengert, N. and M. S. Hamilton. "Citizen Participation in State and Local Government Control of Power Plant Siting." In G. A. Daneke et al. (eds.), Public Involvement and Social Impact Assessment. Boulder, CO: Westview Press, 1983, pp. 129-142.

West, S. Opportunites for Company-Community Cooperation in Mitigating Energy Facility Impacts. Working Paper No. 9. Laboratory of Architecture and Planning, Massachusetts Institute of Technology, Cambridge, MA, April 1977.

Zinn, J. A. (ed.) "Theme Issue: Energy and the Coastal Zone: A Question of Risk." Coastal Zone Management Journal, 7, 2-4 (1980): 123-337.

Electric Power / Utilities

Alexander, G. R. "Consumer Advocates Before Public Utility Commissions." State Government, 48 (Summer 1975): 194-197.

Alpert, G. "Consumer Advisory Boards and Investor-Owned Utilities: Rhetoric and Reality." Public Utilities Fortnightly, 108 (August 27, 1981): 19-22.

"Angry Users, Unhappy Utilities -- Battle Over Runaway Rates." U. S. News and World Report, 77 (September 30, 1974): 83-84+.

Blair, J. P. "Policies of Government Pricing: Political Influences on Rate Structures of Public-ly-Owned Electric Utilities." American Journal of Economics and Sociology, 35 (June 1976): 31-36.

Brom, T. and E. Kirshner. "Buying Power: Community-Owned Electric Systems." Working Papers, 2 (Summer 1974): 46-55.

Bryan, W. W. State Offices for Utility Consumer Intervention. U. S. Office of Consumers' Education, Washington, DC, 1978.

Casper, B. M. and P. D. Wellstone. "Rural Energy War -- Report from the Front Lines." Nation, 233 (December 26, 1981): 699-700.

Casper, B. M. and P. D. Wellstone. Powerline: The First Battle of America's Energy War. Amherst, MA: University of Massachusett Press, 1981. 328 p.

"Citizen Participation in Utility Cases." Consumer News, 9 (April 1,1979): 2.

Coalition for Consumer Justice. Dictionary of Utility Loopholes and Language. Central Falls, RI, 1977. 18 p.

"Community Participation: A Case Study." Electrical World, 180 (October 15, 1973): 32-34.

Comstock, R. W. "Critical Precedent." Water Spectrum, 4 (Winter 1972): 1-6.

Comstock, R. W. "Participatory Decision-Making: Putting the Public in Public Utilities." Paper presented at the New York State Environment Advisor Conference, Tarrytown, NY, November 19, 1971. 6 p.

"Consumers Challenge Utilities on Fuel Costs." Business Week, (April 3, 1978): 27-28.

Cose, E. Decentralizing Energy Decisions: The Rebirth of Community Power. Boulder, CO: Westview Press, 1983. 140 p.

Council on Economic Priorities. The Price of Power -- Update: Electric Utilities and the Environment. New York, NY, 1977. 429 p.

Creighton, J. L. Public Involvement Manual: Involving the Public in Water and Power Resources Decisions. U. S. Department of the Interior, Water and Power Resources Service, Washington, DC, January 1980. 333 p.

Critical Mass Energy Project. Electric Utilities: Alternatives to Traditional Planning. Public Citizen, Washington, DC, 1985. 2 p.

Critical Mass Energy Project. Petitioning for Least-Cost Planning: A Model Proposal for Texas. Public Citizen, Washington, DC, 1986. 30 p.

Critical Mass Energy Project. Pushing the Power of Alternative Energy Resources: Making Better Use of PURPA. Public Citizen, Washington, DC, 1987. 14 p.

Ducsik, D. W. "Power Plants and People: A Profile of Electric Utility Initiatives in Cooperative Planning." Journal of the American Planning Association, 50, 2 (1984): 162-174.

Environmental Action Foundation. A Citizen's Guide to the Fuel Adjustment Clause. Washington, DC, 1975. 52 p.

Environmental Action Foundation. Phantom Taxes in Your Electric Bill: A Report on Federal Income Tax Avoidance by Electric Utilities. EAF Utility Project, Washington, DC, 1976.

"Funding Siting Evaluation Is a Thorny Risk." Electrical World, 173 (May 18, 1970): 21.

Gerlach, L. P. "The Great Energy Standoff." Natural History, 87, 1 (1978): 22-32.

Gormley, W. T. Jr. "Participation in Public Utility Regulation." Citizen Participation, 1 (July-August 1980): 3+.

Gormley, W. T. Jr. "Policy, Politics, and Public Utility Regulation." American Journal of Political Science, 27 (February 1983): 86-105.

Gormley, W. T. Jr. "Public Advocacy in Public Utility Commission Proceedings." Journal of Applied Behavioral Science, 17, 4 (1981): 446-463.

Gormley, W. T. Jr. "Statewide Remedies for Public Underrepresentation in Regulatory Proceedings." Public Administration Review, 41, 4 (1981): 454-462.

Grant, F. P. "Community Groups Study Alternative Rate Structures." Public Power, 35, 2 (1977): 27-29.

Guitar, M. A. Property Power: How to Keep the Bulldozer, the Power Line, and Highwaymen Away from Your Door. Garden City, NY: Doubleday and Co., 1972.

Henderson, L. J. Jr. "Public Utility Regulations: The Socioeconomic Dimensions of Reform." Review of Black Political Economy, 9 (Spring 1979): 260-275.

Lake, L. M. "Mediating Electric Power Plant Options for California: A Case Study in Conflict Avoidance." Paper presented at the Symposium on Environmental Mediation Case Studies held at the Annual Meetng of the American Association for the Advancement of Science, Denver, CO, 1977.

Leflar, R. and M. Rogol. "Consumer Participation in the Regulation of Public Utilities: A Model Act." Harvard Journal of Legislation, 13 (February 1976): 235-297.

Levy, P. F. "Politics of Rate Reform." Technology Review, 80 (February 1978): 36-43.

Mann, P. C. "User Power and Electricity Rates." Journal of Law and Economics, 17 (October 1974): 433-443.

Morgan, R. and S. Jerabek. How to Challenge Your Local Electric Utility: A Citizen's Guide to the Power Industry. Washington, DC: Environmental Action Foundation, 1974. 112 p.

Morgan, R., Riesenberg, T. and M. Troutman. Taking Charge: A New Look at Public Power. Washington, DC: Environmental Action Foundation, 1977.

Morris, D. "A Power Struggle: For the First Time in American History, Citizens Are Planning Their Region's Energy Future." Solar Age, 8 (February 1983): 43.

Myers, E. A. Jr. "Consumerists and Consumer Affairs." Public Utilities Fortnightly, 103 (May 24, 1979): 25-27.

Ridgeway, J. and B. Connor. New Energy: Understanding the Crisis and a Guide to an Alternative Energy System. Boston: Beacon Press, 1975.

Rubin, S. "An Agenda for a Public Service Commission." Public Utilities Fortnightly, 103 (June 7, 1979): 13-18.

Samprone, J. C. Jr. and N. Riddell-Dudra. "State Regulatory Climate: Can It Be Predicted?" Public Utilities Fortnightly, 108 (October 8, 1981): 41-43.

"San Diego Gas and Electric Brings Community into Plant Siting." Power, 118 (December 1974): 20-22.

Selznick, P. T.V.A. and the Grass Roots. New York: Harper and Row, 1966.

Smith, L. G. "Electric Power Planning in Ontario: Public Participation at a Normative Level." Canadian Public Administration, 26, 3 (1983): 360-377.

Sullivan, J. P. "Measuring Utilities' Consumer Affairs." Public Utilities Fortnightly, 100 (November 24, 1977): 43-45.

Wasserman, H. "People Against Power." Progressive, 42 (April 1978): 16-19.

Young, L. B. Power Over People. Fairlawn, NJ: Oxford University Press, 1975.

Energy Action

Alexander, G. R. "Consumer Advocates Before Public Utility Commissions." State Government, 48 (Summer 1975): 194-197.

Bossong, K. "Organizing for Effective Citizen Action." In Conservation Foundation, Energy Conservation Training Institute. Washington, DC, n. d., pp. V37-V72.

Bossong, K. Solar Organizing Ideas. Report Series No. 53. Citizens' Energy Project, Washington, DC, 1978. 5 p.

Cameron, J. and G. Wood. "Energy Organizing in the 1980s." Socialist Review, 10 (July-August 1980): 120-132.

Center for Renewable Resources. Solar Action: 27 Communities Boost Renewable Energy Use. Washington, DC, May 1981. 83 p.

Citizens' Advisory Committee on Environmental Quality. Citizen Action Guide to Energy Conservation. Washington, DC, September 1973. 61 p.

Citizens' Energy Project. Citizens' Energy Directory: A Guide to Alternative Energy Resources. Washington, DC, March 1982. 185 p.

Conference on Alternative State and Local Policies. Community Energy Cooperatives: How to Organize, Manage, and Finance Them. Washington, DC, 1982.

Cose, E. Decentralizing Energy Decisions: The Rebirth of Community Power. Boulder, CO: Westview Press, 1983. 140 p.

Dunlap, R. E. "Hard-Path Versus Soft-Path Advocates: A Study of Energy Activists." Policy Studies Journal, 13, 2 (1984): 319-330.

"Energy Saving at the Grass Roots: American Ingenuity Scores Again." Commerce America, 1, 19 (1976): 7-9.

Freeman, J. "Energy Cooperatives: A New Self-Help Tradition." Citizen Participation, 3 (July-August 1982): 20.

Gerlach, L. P. "The Great Energy Standoff." Natural History, 87, 1 (1978): 22-32.

Guitar, M. A. Property Power: How to Keep the Bulldozer, the Power Line, and Highwaymen Away from Your Door. Garden City, NY: Doubleday and Co., 1972.

Haines, P. and W. Moyer. People's Energy Movement: A Strategy for the 1980s. Philadelphia: New Society Press, 1980.

Hardt, J. and A. Fritsch. Citizens' Resource Handbook. Citizens Energy Project, Appalachia-Science in the Public Interest, Livingston, KY, 1979. 86 p.

Morgan, R. and S. Jerabek. How to Challenge Your Local Electric Utility: A Citizen's Guide to the Power Industry. Washington, DC: Environmental Action Foundation, 1974. 112 p.

Morgan, R., Riesenberg, T. and M. Troutman. Taking Charge: A New Look at Public Power. Washington, DC: Environmental Action Foundation, 1977.

"Plan an Energy Fair." Energy Consumer, 2 (October-November 1980): entire issue (51 p.).

Snyder, R. (ed.). Reaching Up, Reaching Out: A Guide to Organizing Local Solar Events. SERI SP-62-326. Washington, DC: U. S. Government Printing Office, 1979. 204 p.

Snyder, R. (ed.). Saving Home Energy: A Handbook for Organizing a Hands-On Energy Conservation and Passive Solar Energy Workshop. Estes Park, CO: Colorado Solar Energy Association, 1978.

Solar Action. Sun Day Press Handbook Or, I Like Your Song and Dance, But Is It News? Washington, DC: Solar Action, n. d.

U. S. Department of Energy. Act/One, Activitate Communities Today/Organize Now for Energy. Office of Consumer Affairs, Washington, DC, January 1981. 66 p.

Willens, H. "Crusade: Work for Citizens for Energy Action." New Yorker, 52 (June 14, 1976): 24-26.

Woolf, D. Energy Teach-Ins: Organizing for a Brighter Future. Massachusetts Public Interest Research Group, Amherst, MA, n. d. 95 p.

Government

Foster, C. R. (ed.). "Energy Policy." Part II in Comparative Public Policy and Citizen Participation: Energy, Education, Health, and Local Governance in the U.S.A. and Germany. Elmsford, NY: Pergamon, 1980.

Gershinowitz, H. Citizen's Policy Guide to Environmental Priorities for New York City, 1974-1984: Part I -- Energy and the New York City Environment. Council of the Environment of New York City, NY, February 1974. 59 p.

Hendricks, J. W. "Public Participation and Democratic Decision Making on Energy Issues." Social Science Energy Review, 1, 2 (1978): 1-25.

Hughes, S. "Greater Public Involvement -- Excerpts from Testimony before the House Subcommittee on Advanced Energy Technologies and Energy Conservation, Research, and Development and Demonstration, Committee on Science and Technology." DOE Energy Insider, (March 6, 1978): 7.

League of Women Voters. Citizens: The Untapped Energy Source. Publication No. 436. League of Women Voters Education Fund, Washington, DC, 1980. 8 p.

McFarland, A. Public-Interest Lobbies: Decision Making on Energy. American Enterprise Institute for Public Policy Research, Washington, DC, 1976.

National Academy of Sciences. Energy Choices for a Democratic Society. Supporting Paper 7. Committee on Nuclear and Alternative Energy Systems (CONAES), Consumption, Location, and Occupational Patterns Resources Group Synthesis Panel, Washington, DC, 1980. 136 p.

Orr, D. W. "U. S. Energy Policy and the Political Economy of Participation." Journal of Politics, 41 (November 1979): 1027-1056.

U. S. Executive Office of the President. Energy Policy and Planning. The National Energy Plan Summary of Public Participation. Washington, DC: U. S. Government Printing Office, 1977.

Nuclear Power

Alba, E. "Citizen Participation in Nuclear Energy Policy." Journal of Voluntary Action Research, 9, 1-4 (1980): 232-236.

"Anti-Nuclear Explosion." Economist, 274 (March 15, 1980): 44.

Bachman, L. "Public Decision Making on a Nuclear Power Plant." Transactions of the American Nuclear Society, 17 (1973): 409.

Barkan, S. E. "Strategic, Tactical, and Organizational Dilemmas of the Protest Movement Against Nuclear Power." Social Problems, 27 (October 1979): 19-37.

Boyle, M. J. and M. E. Robinson. "Plogoff Says No to Nuclear Power." Geographical Magazine, 53 (August 1981): 681-683.

Bright, G. O. "Some Effects of Public Intervention on the Reactor Licensing Process." Nuclear Safety, (January-February 1972): 13-21.

Bronfman, L. M. and T. J. Mattingly, Jr. "Critical Mass: Politics, Technology and the Public Interest." Nuclear Safety, 17, 5 (1976): 539-549.

Brown, O. "Anti-Nuclear Activists." Far Eastern Economic Review, 108 (June 13,1980): 54.

Burt, R. S. Resolving Community Conflict in the Nuclear Power Issue. U. S. Department of Energy, Washington, DC, 1978.

Butz, T. "Surveillance of the Anti-Nuke Movement." Public Eye, 1, 2 (1978): 40-47.

Caldicott, H. Nuclear Madness. New York: Bantam Books, 1979.

Cherry, M. M. "Use of Discovery Procedures by Intervenors in Nuclear Power Licensing Cases." Atomic Energy Law Journal, 13 (Fall 1971): 260-281.

Cohen, E. "The Clamshell Alliance." Citizen Participation, 1 (January-February1980): 14.

Cotter, B. P. "Nuclear Licensing: Innovation Through Evolution in Administrative Hearings." Administrative Law Review, 34, 4 (1982): 497-532.

"Creative Socioeconomics: Developing the Role of Impact Assessment in Nuclear Siting and Licensing." Groundswell, (1979): 4-6.

Critical Mass Energy Project. Double Jeopardy: Short-Run Tax Savings Threaten Nuclear Safety. Public Citizen, Washington, DC, 1987. 16 p.

Critical Mass Energy Project. The Economic Benefits of a Nuclear Phase-Out. Public Citizen, Washington, DC, 1986. 14 p.

Critical Mass Energy Project. Lost in the Dark: TVA Stumbling Blindly Over Its Nuclear Program. Public Citizen, Washington, DC, 1987. 35 p.

Critical Mass Energy Project. National Directory of Safe Energy Organizations. Public Citizen, Washington, DC, 1987. 17 p.

Critical Mass Energy Project. Nuclear Power Safety Report: 1979-1986. Public Citizen, Washington, DC, 1986. 6 p.

Critical Mass Energy Project. Shutdown Strategies: Citizen Efforts to Close Nuclear Power Plants. Public Citizen, Washington, DC, 1987. 60 p.

Curry, M. et al. State and Local Planning Procedures Dealing with Social and Economic Impacts from Nuclear Power Plants. Battelle Memorial Institute, Seattle, WA, 1977.

Daleus, L. "A Moratorium in Name Only." Bulletin of the Atomic Scientists, 31, 8 (1975): 27-33.

Davies, R. "The Sizewell-B Nuclear Inquiry: An Analysis of Public Participation in Decision-Making About Nuclear Power." Science, Technology, and Human Values, 48 (1984): 21-32.

Davis, T. P. "Citizen's Guide to Intervention in Nuclear Power Plant Siting: A Blueprint for Alice in Nuclear Wonderland." Environmental Law, 6, 3 (1976): 621-674.

De Volpi, A. "Energy Policy Decision-Making: The Need for Balanced Input." Bulletin of the Atomic Scientists, 30, 10 (1974): 29-33.

Doub, W. O. "'Right to be Heard' -- Laying It on the Line." Atomic Energy Law Journal, 13 (Fall 1971): 211-224.

Ebbin, S. and R. Kasper. Citizen Groups and the Nuclear Power Controversy: Uses of Scientific and Technological Information. Cambridge, MA: MIT Press, 1974.

Environmental Action Foundation. Nuclear Power: The Bargain We Can't Afford. Washington, DC. 96 p.

"Environmental -- Three Mile Island in Your Neighborhood? -- People Against Nuclear Energy v. United States Nuclear Regulatory Commission." Arizona State Law Journal, (1982): 1009-1029.

Evans, B. "Sierra Club Involvement in Nuclear Power: An Evolution of Awareness." Oregon Law Review, 54 (1975): 607-621.

Ford, D. F. and H. W. Kendall. "Time for Public Review." Trial, 9 (July-August1973): 51-52.

Gardner, G. T. et al. "Risk and Benefit Perceptions, Acceptability Judgments, and Self-Reported Actions Toward Nuclear Power." Journal of Social Psychology, 116 (1982): 179-197.

Gendlin, F. "Palisades Protest: A Pattern of Citizen Intervention." Bulletin of Atomic Scientists, 27, 9 (1971): 53-56.

Glasser, I. "Nuclear Power, Rapid Technological Advancement, and Democratic Values." New York University Review of Law and Social Change, 10, 2 (1980-81): 347-355.

Green, H. P. "Nuclear Power Licensing and Regulation." Annals of the American Academy of Political and Social Sciences, 400 (March 1972): 116-126.

Green, H. P. "Public Participation in Nuclear Power Plant Licensing: The Great Delusion." William and Mary Law Review, 15 (Spring 1974): 503-525.

Gricar, B. G. and A. J. Baratta. "Bridging the Information Gap at Three Mile Island: Radiation Monitoring by Citizens." Journal of Applied Behavioral Science, 19, 1 (1983): 35-49.

Gyorgy, A. No Nukes: Everyone's Guide to Nuclear Power. Boston: South End Press, 1980.

Hedgpeth, J. W. "Bodega: A Case History of Intense Controversy. " In C. R. Goldman et al. (eds.), Environmental Quality and Water Development. San Francisco: W. H. Freeman, 1973, pp. 438-454.

Hedgepeth, J. W. "Bodega Head: A Partisan View." Bulletin of the Atomic Scientists, 21 (March 1965): 2-7.

Hensler, D. R. and C. P. Hensler. "Science Policy by Referendum: Voter Choice on the California Nuclear Energy Initiative." Paper presented at the Annual Meeting of the American Association for the Advancement of Science, January 1981. 41 p.

Hines, W. "Anti-Nuclear Ferment in Europe." Progressive, (September 1977): 14.

Hirsch, H. and H. Nowotny. "Information and Opposition in Austrian Nuclear Energy Policy." Minerva, 15, 3-4 (1977): 316-334.

Hogan, J. F. "Public Information : Whose Responsibility?" Nuclear Engineering International, 24 (July 1979): 27-28.

Hunt, J. P. and N. H. Katz. "Nonviolent Protest and Third-Party Public Opinion: A Study of the June 1978, Seabrook, New Hampshire, Antinuclear Power Protest." In J. C. Petersen (ed.), Citizen Participation in Science Policy. Amherst, MA: University of Massachusetts Press, 1984, pp. 215-228.

Ignatius, N. and J. Claybrook (eds.). A Citizen's Manual on Nuclear Energy. Washington, DC: Center for Responsive Law, 1974.

Institute for Environmental Studies. Citizen Concern with Power Plant Siting: A Report on Four Public Workshops. Portage Project, Environmental Monitoring and Data Acquisition Group, Madison, WI, August 1977.

Irwin, B. and G. Faison. "Why Nonviolence?: Nonviolence Theory and Strategy for the Anti-Nuclear Movement." Dandelion, Special Issue (April 1979): 1-4.

Jacks, W. T. "Public and the Peaceful Atom: Participation in AEC Regulatory Proceedings." Texas Law Review, 52 (March 1974): 466-525.

Jezer, M. "From the Movement: The Socialist Potential of the No-Nuke Movement." Radical America, 11 (September-October 1977): 63-71.

Kasperson, R. et al. Nuclear Energy, Local Conflict, and Public Opposition. Project RARE (Risk Assessment of Rare Events), Clark University, Worchester, MA, n. d.

Katz, N. H. and D. List. "Seabrook: A Profile of Anti-Nuclear Activists, June 1978." Peace and Change: A Journal of Peace Research, 7 (1981): 59-70.

Kemeny, J. G. "Saving American Democracy: The Lessons of Three Mile Island." Technology Review, 82 (June-July 1980): 65-75.

Key, W. "Bridging the Information Gap at Three Mile Island: Radiation Monitoring by Citizens-- Comments." Journal of Applied Behavioral Science, 19, 1 (1983): 49-51.

Klema, E. D. and R. L. West. Public Regulation of Site Selection for Nuclear Power Plants: Present Procedures and Reform Proposals -- An Annotated Bibliography. Baltimore, MD: Johns Hopkins University Press, 1977. 160 p.

Kovler, P. "Nuclear Dissidents: What They Can Tell Congress." Nation, 223 (December 18, 1976): 655-659.

Krannich, R. S. Siting Implications of Public Attitudes Toward Nuclear Generating Facilities. Center for the Study of Environmental Policy, Pennsylvania State University, University Park, PA, 1977.

Kronick, J. C. "Public Interest Group Participation in Congressional Hearings on Nuclear Power Development." In J. C. Petersen (ed.), Citizen Participation in Science Policy. Amherst, MA: University of Massachusetts Press, 1984, pp. 196-214.

Kuklinski, J. H., Metlay, D., and W. D. Kay. "Citizen Knowledge and Choices on the Complex Issue of Nuclear Energy." American Journal of Political Science, 26, 4 (1982): 615-642.

Laitner, S. Citizen's Guide to Nuclear Power. Washington, DC: Center for Study of Responsive Law, 1975. 93 p.

Lanoue, R. Nuclear Plants, the More They Build the More You Pay. Washington, DC: Center for Study of Responsive Law, 1976. 92 p.

League of Women Voters. Taking Nuclear Issues to the Village Square: A Guide for Community Leaders. Publication No. 155. League of Women Voters Education Fund, Washington, DC, 1981. 8 p.

Lewis R. S. "Citizens versus Atomic Power." New Scientist, 56 (November 23, 1972): 450-452.

Lewis, R. S. The Nuclear Power Rebellion: Citizens vs. the Atomic Power Establishment. New York: Viking Press, 1972. 313 p.

Lieberman, J. "Generic Hearings: Preparation for the Future." Atomic Energy Law Journal, 16 (Summer 1974): 141-174.

Milkovich, J. "Consumers' Challenges to the Construction of Nuclear Power Plants -- Closing the Door on Armageddon." New England Law Review, 19 (1983-1984): 19-126.

Mitchell, J. K. "Participation of Private Interest Representatives in Nuclear Power Plant Licensing Proceedings." Idaho Law Review, 13 (Summer 1977): 309-324.

Morgan, R. Nuclear Power: The Bargain We Can't Afford. Washington, DC: Environmental Action Foundation, 1977. 98 p.

Murphy, P. P. "Harnessing the Atomic Juggernaut: The Need for Multi-Lateral Input in Nuclear Energy Decision Making." Natural Resource Journal, 14, 3 (1974): 411-422.

Nelkin, D. "Nuclear Power and Its Critics: A Siting Dispute." In D. Nelkin (ed.), Controversy: The Politics of Technical Decisions. Beverly Hills, CA: Sage, 1979, pp. 49-68.

Nelkin, D. Nuclear Power and Its Critics: The Cayuga Lake Controversy. Science, Technology and Society Series No. 1. Ithaca, NY: Cornell University Press, 1971. 128 p.

Nelkin, D. "The Role of Experts in a Nuclear Siting Controversy." Bulletin of the Atomic Scientists, 30 (November 1974): 29-36.

Nelkin, D. and S. Fallows. "The Evolution of the Nuclear Debate: The Role of Public Participation." Annual Review of Energy, 3 (1978): 275-312.

Nelkin, D. and M. Pollak. The Atom Besieged: Extra Parliamentary Dissent in France and Germany. Cambridge, MA: MIT Press, 1980. 235 p.

Nelkin, D. and M. Pollak. "Ideology as Strategy: The Discourse of the Anti-Nuclear Movement in France and Germany." Science, Technology and Human Values, 15 (1980): 3-13.

Nelkin, D. and M. Pollak. "The Politics of Participation and the Nuclear Debate in Sweden, the Netherlands, and Austria." Public Policy, 25, 3 (1977): 333-357.

Nowotny, H. "Experts in a Participatory Experiment: The Austrian Debate on Nuclear Energy." Bulletin of Science, Technology, and Society, 2, 2 (1982): 109-124.

Nowotny, H. "Experts in a Participatory Experiment: The Austrian Debate on Nuclear Energy." In H. Skoie (ed.), Scientific Expertise and the Public: Conference Proceedings. Oslo: Institute for Studies in Research and Higher Education, Norwegian Research Council for Science and the Humanities, 1979, pp. 79-97.

"Nuclear Blows; West Germany." Economist, 278 (March 7, 1981): 48-49.

"Nuclear Power Plant Siting: A Comparative Analysis of Public Interaction in the Siting Process in France and the United States." Denver Journal of International Law and Policy, 8 (Winter 1979): 343-366.

Olson, M. C. Unacceptable Risk: The Nuclear Power Controversy. New York: Bantam, 1976. 285 p.

Organization for Economic Cooperation and Development. Siting of Major Energy Facilities. Report, 1977. 87 p.

"People vs. Nuclear Power: Public Participation in the Energy Debate." Perception, 2 (March-April 1979): 31-33.

"Proper Role of the Public in Nuclear Power Plant Licensing Decisions." Atomic Energy Law Journal, 15 (Spring 1973): 34-59.

Ramey, J. T. "Role of the Public in the Development and Regulation of Nuclear Power." Atomic Energy Law Journal, 12 (Spring 1970): 3-35.

Reinsdorf, W. "Public Participation: Nuclear Plant Licensing." Environment, 22, 5 (1980): 3-4.

Robinson, G. "Clam's Consensus." Environmental Action, 10, 6 (1978): 9-11.

Roizman, A., Sheldon, K., and E. Weiss. Nuclear Intervenor's Training Manual. Washington, DC: Nuclear Information and Resource Service, 1978.

Rolnick, P. "Increasing Citizen Participation in AEC Proceedings by Expanding Social Impact Considerations: The Maine Yankee Decision." George Washington Law Review, 42 (August 1974): 1062-1088.

Rose, J., Weinstein, A., and J. Wondolleck. Nuclear Energy Facilities and Public Conflict: Three Case Studies. Energy Impacts Project, Massachusetts Institute of Technology, Cambridge, MA, 1979.

Rothman, S. and S. R. Lichter. "The Nuclear Energy Debate: Scientists, the Media and the Public." Public Opinion, 5 (August-September 1982): 47-52.

Rubin, D. M. and D. P. Sachs. "Access to Environmental Information: Orchestrated Confusion in Atomic Energy." In Mass Media and the Environment: Water Resources, Land Uses and Atomic Energy in California. New York: Praeger, 1973.

Rydell, R. J. "Solving Political Problems of Nuclear Technology: The Role of Public Participation." In J. C. Petersen (ed.), Citizen Participation in Science Policy. Amherst, MA: University of Massachusetts Press, 1984, pp. 182-195.

Sailor, V. L. and A. Carl. "Scientist vs. Citizen: The Shoreham Controversy." Bulletin of the Atomic Scientists, 28 (June 1972): 24-26.

Sax, J. L. "Public Participation." Paper presented at the Atomic Industry Forum Conference, Miami, FL, October 1971.

Starr, R. "Power and the People: The Case of Con Edison." Public Interest, 26 (Winter 1972): 75-99.

Stott, M. "Nuclear Confrontation." Town and Country Planning, 49 (March 1980): 91-93.

Stroube, H. "Operation Fishbowl." Public Utilities Fortnightly, 93 (June 20, 1974): 31-33.

Swann, M. "Citizen Opposition Shelves Energy Parks in Pennsylvania." Environmental Action Bulletin, 7, 11 (1976): 4-5.

Swann, M. "Citizens Talk Tough at Energy Park Hearings." Environmental Action Bulletin, 6, 14 (1975): 4-7.

Turnage, J. J. and A. A. Husseiny. "Public Participation in Siting Decisions." Transactions of the American Nuclear Society, 34 (June 1980): 689-691.

U. S. Congress. House. Committee on Science and Technology. Nuclear Public Information and Rational Public Policy Decisions: Hearings, December 15, 1981. 97th Congress, 1st Session. Washington, DC: U. S. Government Printing Office, 1982. 270 p.

Union of Concerned Scientists. Safety Second: A Critical Evaluation of the NRC's First Decade. Cambridge, MA, February 1985. 239 p.

Unsoeld, K. "Should Public Power Be Nuclear Power: Ratepayers Refuse to Finance Failure." Dollars and Sense, 83 (January 1983): 15-17.

Vlek, C. A. J. "Rise, Decline and Aftermath of the Dutch 'Societal Discussion on (Nuclear) Energy Policy' (1981-1983)." In H. A. Becker and A. G. Porter (eds.), Impact Assessment Today. Utrecht: Van Arkel, 1986.

Vogel, S. "The Limits of Protest: A Critique of the Anti-Nuclear Movement." Socialist Review, 10 (November-December 1980): 125-134.

Wade, N. "Nuclear Power and People's Power: Law-Making by Initiative." Science, (January 9, 1976): 48-50.

Walsh, E. J. "Resource Mobilization and Citizen Protest in Communities Around Three Mile Island." Social Problems, 29, 1 (1981): 1-21.

Wasserman, H. "The Clamshell Alliance: Getting It Together." Progressive, (September 1977): 14.

Weingast, B. R. "Congress, Regulation, and the Decline of Nuclear Power." Public Policy, 28 (Spring 1980): 231-255.

Wenner, L. M. and M. W. Wenner. "Nuclear Policy and Public Participation." American Behavioral Scientist, 22, 2 (1978): 277-310.

Whitney, S. C. "Enhancing Public Acceptance of Nuclear Decision-Making." William and Mary Law Review, 15 (Spring 1974): 557-566.

Wilcox, F. Grass Roots: An Anti-Nuke Source Book. Trumansburg, NY: Crossing Press, 1980. 192 p.

Williams, R. M. "Massing at the Grass Roots." Saturday Review, (January 22, 1977): 14+.

Wolfe, R. R. "Individual Participation in Governmental Decisions." Bulletin of the Atomic Scientists, 24, 10 (1968): 32.

Wondolleck, J. M. The Montague Nuclear Power Plant: Negotiation, Information and Intervention. Energy Impacts Project, Massachusetts Institute of Technology, Cambridge, MA, 1979.

Wynne, B. "The Rationality and Ritual of Nuclear Decision Making." In H. Skoie (ed.), Scientific Expertise and the Public: Conference Proceedings. Oslo: Institute for Studies in Research and Higher Education, Norwegian Research Council for Science and the Humanities, 1979, pp. 115-138.

Radioactive Waste

Abbotts, J. "Radioactive Waste: A Technical Solution." Bulletin of the Atomic Scientists, 35, 8 (1979): 12-18.

Abrahamson, D. "Social, Ethical, and Moral Issues in the Implementation of Radioactive Waste Management Objectives." In Proceedings of the Symposium on Waste Management, Tucson, AZ, 1976.

Abrams, N. E. and J. R. Primack. "Helping the Public Decide: The Case of Radioactive Waste Management." Environment, 22 (April 1980): 14-20+.

Abrams, N. E. and J. R. Primack. "The Public and Technological Decisions." Bulletin of the Atomic Scientists, 36 (June 1980): 44-48.

Albrecht, S. L. "Community Response to Large-Scale Federal Projects: The Case of the MX." In S. H. Murdock et al. (eds.), Nuclear Waste: Socioeconomic Dimensions of Long-Term Storage. Boulder, CO: Westview Press, 1983, pp. 233-250.

Allen, J. "One Woman's Crusade Against Nuclear Crud: Kay Drey Knows the Cleanser Won't Work." Progressive, 43 (August 1979): 41-42.

Amonette, E. L. et al. "Prepared Statements from the Public." In EPA Workshop on Policy and Technical Issues Pertinent to Development of Environmental Protection Criteria for Radioactive Wastes, Albuquerque, NM, April 12-14, 1977: Proceedings, pp. 280-326.

Anderson, M. Fallout on the Freeway; the Hazards of Transporting Radioactive Wastes in Michigan. Public Interest Research Group in Michigan, Lansing, MI, 1974. 60 p.

Anderson, R. Y. Report to Sandia Laboratories on Deep Dissolution of Salt, Northern Delaware Basin, New Mexico. Southwest Research and Information Center, Albuquerque, NM, January 1978.

Bishop, A. B., McKee, M., and R. D. Hansen. Public Consultation in Public Policy Information: A State-of-the-Art Report. Intermountain Consultants and Office of Waste Isolation, Energy Research and Development Administration, Washington, DC, 1977.

Bodde, D. L "Radioactive Wastes: Pragmatic Strategies and Ethical Perspectives." In D. MacLean and P. G. Brown (eds.), Energy and the Future. Totowa, NJ: Rowman and Littlefield, 1983, pp. 120-128.

Bord, R. "Problems in Siting Low-Level Radioactive Waste: A Focus on Public Participation." In S. K. Majumdar and E. W. Miller (eds.), Management of Radioactive Materials and Wastes: Issues and Progress. Easton, PA: Pennsylvania Academy of Science, 1985, pp. 189-202.

Bord, R. J. "The Low-Level Radioactive Waste Crisis: Is More Citizen Participation the Answer?" Abstracts of Papers of the American Chemical Society, 191 (April 1986): 3.

Bord, R. J. "Problems in Siting Low-Level Radioactive Wastes: A Focus on Public Participation." Transactions of the American Nuclear Society, 45 (1983): 516-517.

Boulton, J. and E. R. Frech. Nuclear Waste Management Program: An Approach to Community Relations. Technical Record TR-30. Atomic Energy of Canada Limited, Pinawa, Manitoba, Canada, March 1979.

Braine, B., Hohenemser, C., Kasperson, R., and R. Kates. "West Valley Nuclear Wastes: Who Gains; Who Loses?" Unpublished manuscript. Center for Technology, Environment, and Development, Clark University, Worcester, MA, n. d.

Bronfman, L. M. "Public Information on Radioactive Waste, 1973-1978: A Study of an Emerging Issue in the United States." International Journal of Environmental Studies, 19, 3-4 (1982): 245-258.

Bronfman, L. M. et al. Public Information on Radioactive Waste: A Study of Emerging Issues. Oak Ridge National Laboratory, Oak Ridge, TN, 1978.

Brooks, J. "The Public Concern in Radioactive Waste Management." In Proceedings of the International Symposium on the Management of Wastes from the LWR Fuel Cycle. CONF-76-0701. National Technical Information Service, Springfield, VA, 1979, pp. 52-57.

Brown, P. G. and W. L. Rankin. "Proxy for the Unborn: Future Generations." Bulletin of the Atomic Scientists, 35 (November 1979): 64-65.

Brunn, S. D., Johnson, J. H. Jr, and B. J. McGirr. "Locational Conflict and Attitudes Regarding the Burial of Nuclear Wastes." East Lakes Geographer, 15 (August 1980): 24-40.

Burt, R. S. et al. Resolving Community Conflict in the Nuclear Power Issue. U. S. Department of Energy, Office of Waste Isolation, Oak Ridge, TN, 1978. 193 p.

Carnes, S. A. et al. "Incentives and Nuclear Waste Siting: Prospects and Constraints." Energy Systems and Policy, 7, 4 (1983): 323-351.

Carnes, S. A. et al. Incentives and the Siting of Radioactive Waste Facilities. ORNL-5880. Oak Ridge National Laboratory, Oak Ridge, TN, August 1982. Avail. National Technical Information Service, Springfield, VA.

Clugston, M. "Deadly Corpse of Nuclear Power." MacLeans, 93 (September 1, 1980): 46+.

Cochran, T. B. "A Criterion for Radioactive Waste Management: A Case Study of Intergenerational Justice." In D. MacLean and P. G. Brown (eds.), Energy and the Future. Totowa, NJ: Rowman and Littlefield, 1983, pp. 113-120.

Conservation Foundation. Managing the Nation's High-Level Radioactive Waste: Key Issues and Recommendations. Washington, DC, 1981.

Craig, R. "The Keystone Process in Radioactive Waste Management." Environmental Consensus, (Winter 1980):

"DOE Weighs Paying States Off to Calm Opposition to Nuclear Waste Disposal." Inside DOE, (July 6, 1979): 5.

Duberg, J. A., Frankel, M. L. and C. M. Niemczewski. "Siting Hazardous Waste Management Facilities and Public Opposition." Environmental Impact Assessment Review, 1 (March 1980): 84-88.

Enbar, M.   "Equity in the Social Sciences." In R. E. Kasperson (ed.), Equity Issues in Radioactive Waste Management. Cambridge, MA: Oelgeschlager, Gunn and Hain, 1983, pp. 3-23.

Environmental Policy Institute. "How Safe is Radioactive Low-Level Waste Transportation?
A Case Study of a Major Shipping Company's Casks and NRC Cask Regulation." Washington,
DC, December 1981. 28 p.

Environmental Policy Institute. Summary and Excerpts from "Social and Economic Aspects of
Radioactive Waste Disposal: Considerations for Institutional Management". Washington,
DC, October 1981. 8 p.

Fallows, S. "The Nuclear Waste Disposal Controversy." In D. Nelkin (ed.), Controversy: The
Politics of Technical Decisions. Beverly Hills, CA: Sage, 1979, pp. 87-110.

Gobel, R. L. "Time Scales and the Problem of Radioactive Waste." In R. E. Kasperson (ed.),
Equity Issues in Radioactive Waste Management, Cambridge, MA: Oelgeschlager, Gunn and
Hain, 1983, pp. 139-174.

Goodin, R. E. "No Moral Nukes." Ethics, 90, 3 (1980): 417-449.

Graff, T. J. "Legal Constraints on Consultation and Concurrence." In R. Reiser et al. (eds.),
Consultation and Concurrence. ONWI-87. National Technical Information Service,
Springfield, VA, 1980.

Green, H. P. "Legal Aspects of Intergenerational Equity Issues." In R. E. Kasperson (ed.), Equity
Issues in Radioactive Waste Management. Cambridge, MA: Oelgeschlager, Gunn and Hain,
1983, pp. 189-202.

Gyorgy, A. et al. No Nukes: Everyone's Guide to Nuclear Power. Boston: South End Press, 1979.

Hadden, S. et al. High Level Nuclear Waste Disposal: Information Exchange and Conflict Resolution. Austin, TX: Texas Energy and Natural Resources Advisory Council and U. S. Department of Energy, 1981.

Hammond, R. P. "Nuclear Wastes and Public Acceptance." American Scientist, 67 (March
1979): 146-150; Discussion, 67 (September 1979): 516+.

Hancock, D. "The Nuclear Legacy--How Safe Is It?" Workbook (Southwest Research and
Information Center), 8, 4-5 (1983): 149-172.

Harwood, S. et al. Activation Products in a Nuclear Reactor. New York Public Interest Research
Group, Buffalo, NY, 1976.

Hebert, J. A. et al. Nontechnical Issues in Waste Management: Ethical, Institutional, and Political Concerns. PNL-2400. Battelle Human Affairs Research Centers, Seattle, WA, May
1978. 106 p.

Hilberry, N. "Remarks on Managerial Errors and Public Participation." In W. P. Bishop et al.,
Essays on Issues Relevant to the Regulation of Radioactive Waste Management. NUREG-
0412. U. S. Nuclear Regulatory Commission, Washington, DC, May 1978, pp. 47-50.

Hill, D. "Management of High-Level Waste Repository Siting." Science, 218 (November 26,
1982): 859-854.

Hoos, I. "The Credibility Issue." In W. P. Bishop et al., Essays on Issues Relevant to the Regulation of Radioactive Waste Management. NUREG-0412. U.S. Nuclear Regulatory Commission, Washington, DC, May 1978, pp. 21-30.

Howell, R. E. and D. Olsen. Citizen Participation in Nuclear Waste Repository Siting: Technical Report (microform). Office of Nuclear Waste Isolation, Battelle Project Management Division, Columbus, OH, 1982. Avail. National Technical Information Service, Springfield, VA.

Howell, R. E. and D. Olsen. Citizen Participation in the Socio-Economic Analysis of Nuclear Waste Repository Siting. Department of Rural Sociology, Washington State University, Pullman, WA, 1981.

Howell, R. E. et al. "Citizen Participation in Nuclear Waste Repository Siting." In S. H. Murdock et al. (eds.), Nuclear Waste: Socioeconomic Dimensions of Long-Term Storage. Boulder, CO: Westview Press, 1983, pp. 267-288.

Hyde, M. O. Everyone's Trash Problem: Nuclear Wastes.   New York: McGraw-Hill, 1979.

Jakimo, A. and I. C. Bupp. "Nuclear Waste Disposal: Not in My Backyard." Technology Review, 80 (March 1978): 64-72.

Jarrett, C. et al. ONWI Initiating Actions: Strategy Leading to a Comprehensive Community Development Program. Battelle Human Resource Center, Seattle, WA, n. d.

Johansen, A. "Environmentalists Stopper Germany's Nuclear Energy." New Scientist, (March 22, 1979): 934.

Johansen, A. "Expert Confusion at Nuclear Hearings." New Scientist, (April 26, 1979): 247.

Kasperson, R. E. Nuclear Waste Management and the Public: Considerations for Public Policy. Clark University Graduate School of Geography, Worcester, MA, 1977.

Kasperson, R. E. "Social Issues in Radioactive Waste Management: The National Experience." In R. E. Kasperson (ed.), Equity Issues in Radioactive Waste Management. Cambridge, MA: Oelgeschlager, Gunn and Hain, 1983, pp. 24-65.

Kasperson, R. E. and R. W. Kates. "Confronting Equity in Radioactive Waste Management." Paper presented at the Meetings of the American Association for the Advancement of Science, Toronto, Canada, January 1980.

Kasperson, R. E. and B. L. Rubin. "Siting a Radioactive Waste Repository: What Role for Equity?" In R. E. Kasperson (ed.), Equity Issues in Radioactive Waste Management, Cambridge, MA: Oelgeschlager, Gunn and Hain, 1983, pp. 118-136.

Kasperson, R. E., Derr, P., and R. W. Kates. "Confronting Equity in Radioactive Waste Management: Modest Proposals for a Socially Just and Acceptable Program." In R. E. Kasperson (ed.), Equity Issues in Radioactive Waste Management, Cambridge, MA: Oelgeschlager, Gunn and Hain, 1983, pp. 331-368.

Kelly, J. E. and C. E. Shea. "The Subseabed Disposal Program for High-Level Radioactive Waste--Public Response." Oceanus, 25, 2 (1982): 42-53.

Kemp, L. Radioactive Waste: A Handbook for Minnesotans. The Minnesota Project, Minneapolis, MN, February 1983.

Kemp, R., O'Rioridan, T. and M. Purdue. "Environmental Politics in the 1980s: The Public Examination of Radioactive Waste Disposal." Policy and Politics, 14,1 (1986): 8-26.

Keystone Center. An Overview of the Keystone Radioactive Waste Management Process: An Exercise in Problem Solving. Keystone, CO, 1980.

Keystone Center. Public Participation in Developing National Plans for Radioactive Waste Management. Keystone, CO, October 1980.

Krawetz, N. M. Hazardous Waste Management: A Review of Social Concerns and Aspects of Public Involvement. Research Secretariat, Department of the Environment of Alberta, Edmonton, Alberta, Canada, November 1979.

Kress, H. W. Workshops for State Review of Site Suitability Criteria for High-Level Radioactive Waste Repositories: Analysis and Recommendation. Vol. 1. Report No. NUREG-0354-VOL-1. U. S. Nuclear Regulatory Commission, Washington, DC, 1978. 74p.

Lash, T. R. Radioactive Waste, Nuclear Energy's Dilemma. Natural Resources Defense Council, NY, Fall 1979.

Lash, T. R., Bryson, J. E., and R. Cotton. Citizens' Guide: The National Debate on the Handling of Radioactive Wastes from Nuclear Power Plants. Palo Alto, CA: Natural Resources Defense Council, 1975. 50 p.

League of Women Voters Education Fund. A Nuclear Waste Primer: A Handbook for Citizens. New York: Nick Lyons Books, 1985. 90 p.

League of Women Voters Southern California Regional Task Force. Disposing of Low-Level Radioactive Waste in California. Sacramento, CA, 1984. 28 p.

Lindell, M. K. et al. Radioactive Wastes: Public Attitudes Toward Disposal Facilities. Battelle Human Affairs Research Centers, Seattle, WA, 1978.

Lindell, K. K., Earle, T. C., and R. W. Perry. Social Issues and Energy Alternatives: The Context of Conflict Over Nuclear Waste. B/HARX-411/80/033. Battelle Human Affairs Research Centers, Seattle, WA, June 1980. 64 p.

Lipschutz, R. D. Radioactive Waste: Politics, Technology and Risk. Cambridge, MA: Ballinger Pub. Co., 1980. 247 p.

Lotts, A. L. et al. "Low-Level Radioactive Waste Disposal: Panel Discussion Tuesday Afternoon." In NRC/ORNL Low-Level Waste Disposal Site Suitability Requirements Symposium, Crystal City, VA, December 8-9, 1981: Proceedings, Vol. 1, pp. 107-133.

Lucas, A. R. "Legal Foundations for Public Participation in Environmental Decision-Making." Natural Resources Journal, 16, 1 (1976): 73-102.

MHB Technical Associates. Spent Fuel Disposal Costs. Natural Resources Defense Council, New York, NY, August 1978.

MacKerron, C. "Haste May Waste A Repository: Disposing of Nuclear Garbage." Critical Mass Energy Journal, 8, 7 (January 1983): 5-7.

MacLean, D. "Radioactive Wastes: A Problem of Morality Between Generations." In R. E. Kasperson (ed.), Equity Issues in Radioactive Waste Management. Cambridge, MA: Oelgeschlager, Gunn and Hain, 1983, pp. 175-188.

MacLean, D. and P. G. Brown. E. (eds.) "Conflicting Views on a Neutrality Criterion for Radioactive Waste Management." In Energy and the Future. Totowa, NJ: Rowman and Littlefield, 1983, pp. 110-113.

Marcus, A. A. et al. "Analysis of Participation at Nuclear Waste Meetings: The Representation of Divergent Concerns." Radioactive Waste Management, 2, 4 (1982): 363-380.

Marcus, S. J. "Democracy, Nuclear Waste, and a Modest Proposal." Technology Review, 81, 8 (1979): 82-83.

Maynard, W. S. et al. Public Values Associated with Nuclear Waste Disposal. BNWL-1997. Battelle Human Affairs Research Centers, Seattle, WA, June 1976. 181 p.

Mazur, A. and B. Conant. "Controversy Over a Local Nuclear Waste Repository." Social Studies of Science, 8 (1978): 235-243.

Metlay, D. S. "History and Interpretation of Radioactive Waste Management in the United States." In W. P. Bishop et al., Essays on Issues Relevant to the Regulation of Radioactive Waste Management. NUREG-0412. Office of Nuclear Material Safety and Safeguards, U. S. Nuclear Regulatory Commission, May 1978, pp. 1-19.

Metlay, D. and G. I. Rochlin. "Radioactive Waste Management in the United States: An Interpretive History of Efforts to Gain Wider Social Consensus." Paper prepared for RESOLVE Nuclear Waste Management Process Review Workshop, Palo Alto, CA, December 1979.

Michigan Governor's Nuclear Waste Disposal Task Force. Public Concerns and Attitudes Regarding Nuclear Waste Disposal in Michigan. Lansing, MI, 1977. 134 p.

Millerd, W. "Public Acceptability of Risk Associated with Nuclear Waste." In Proceedings: A Workshop on Policy and Technical Issues Pertinent to the Development of Environmental Protection Criteria for Radioactive Wastes, Albuquerque, NM, April 1977. ORP/CSD-77-2. Office of Radiation Programs, U. S. Environmental Protection Agency, Washington, DC,1977.

Minnesota Public Interest Research Group. Nuclear Waste in Minnesota. Minneapolis, MN, 1977.

Monroe, A. "Radioactive Wastes: How to Evaluate Solutions." Workbook (Southwest Research and Information Center), 6 (March/April 1981): 45-54.

Montague, K. and P. Montague. "Proposal for Broader Participation in Radioactive Waste Management." Underground Space, 6 (January/April 1982): 280-288.

Montague, P. "Representing the Unrepresented in Radioactive Waste Management Decisions." Paper presented at the American Association for the Advancement of Science Symposium on Radioactive Waste Management, Houston, TX, January 5, 1979.

National Conference of State Legislatures. Public Participation and Siting of LLW. Issue Brief Series. Denver, CO, 1981. 4 p.

National Research Council. Social and Economic Aspects of Radioactive Waste Disposal. Washington, DC: National Academy Press, 1984. 175 p.

National Science Foundation. Proceedings of the Conference on Public Policy Issues in Nuclear Waste Management, October 27-29, 1976. Report No. NSF C-1044. Mitre Corporation, McLean, VA, October 1976.

Natural Resources Defense Council, Inc. Memoradum of Points and Authorities in Support of NRC Licensing of the ERDA High-Level Waste Storage Facilities Under the Energy Reorganization Act of 1974. New York, NY, July 1975.

Natural Resources Defense Council, Inc. Memorandum of Points and Authorities in Support of the Natural Resources Defense Council's Petition for Rulemaking and Request for a Programmatic Environmental Impact Statement Regarding NRC Licensing of Disposal of Low-Level Radioactive Wastes. New York, NY, August 1976.

Nealey, S. M. and J. Hebert. "Public Attitudes Toward Radioactive Wastes." In C. A. Walker et al. (eds.), Too Hot to Handle? Social and Policy Issues in the Management of Radioactive Wastes. New Haven, CT: Yale University Press, 1983, pp. 94-111.

Nealey, S. M. and L. M. Redford. Public Policy Issues in Nuclear Waste Management. Battelle Human Affairs Research Centers, Seattle, WA, 1978.

Nelkin, D. and S. Fallows. "The Evolution of the Nuclear Debate: The Role of Public Participation." Annual Review of Energy, 3 (1978): 275-312.

Nienaber, J. et al. "The Public and the Nuclear Management Question: Assessing Information Dissemination." In Waste Management and Fuel Cycles Symposium, Tucson, AZ, March 6-8, 1978: Proceedings, pp. 74-91.

Nuclear Information and Resource Service. NIRS Resource Guide on Nuclear Waste. RW-2. Washington, DC, n.d. 6 p.

"Nuclear Waste Disposal." People and Energy Newsletter, 2, 7 (July 1976): 4.

"Nuclear Wastes Report to Include Public Comment." Commerce America, (January 19, 1976): 14.

Olsen, M. E. Results of Research on the Social Impacts of Nuclear Waste Isolation Being Conducted by the Battelle Human Affairs Research Centers. Battelle Human Affairs Research Centers, Seattle, WA, 1977.

Paige, H., Lipman, D. S., and J. E. Owens. Assessment of National Systems for Obtaining Local Acceptance of Waste Management Siting and Routing Activities. International Energy Associates Limited, Washington, DC, 1980.

Perkins, B. "Radioactive Waste and Public Acceptance." In Proceedings: A Workshop on Policy and Technical Issues Pertinent to the Development of Environmental Protection Criteria for Radioactive Wastes, Albuquerque, NM, April 1977. OAP/CSD-77-2. Office of Radiation Programs, U. S. Environmental Protection Agency, Washington, DC, 1977.

"The Public and the AEC." Nation, 189 (October 24, 1959): 242.

Rankin, W. L. and S. M. Nealey. Public Concerns and Choices Regarding Nuclear Waste Repositories. Battelle Human Affairs Research Centers, Seattle, WA, June 1981.

Reiser, R. et al. (eds.) Consultation and Concurrence: Workshop Proceedings [September 1979]. OWNI-87. Battelle Office of Nuclear Waste Isolation, Columbus, OH, January 1980. Avail. National Technical Information Service, Springfield, VA.

Resnikoff, M. "When Does Consultation Become Co-optation? When Does Information Become Propaganda? An Environmental Perspective." In E. W. Colglazier, Jr. (ed.), The Politics of Nuclear Waste. Elmsford, NY: Pergamon, 1982, pp. 188-201.

Resolve. Nuclear Waste Management Process Review Forum -- Executive Summary. Resolve-Center for Environmental Conflict Resolution, Palo Alto, CA, July 1980.

Resolve. Nuclear Waste Management Process Review Forum -- Final Report. Resolve-Center for Environmental Conflict Resolution, Palo Alto, CA, 1980.

Rochlin, G. I. The Role of Participatory Impact Assessment in Radioactive Waste Management Program Activities. Office of Nuclear Waste Isolation, Battelle Memorial Institute, Columbus, OH, 1981.

Rosenthal, B. et al. "Prepared Statements from the Public." In EPA Workshop on Issues Pertinent to Development of Environmental Protection Criteria for Radioactive Wastes, VA, February 3-5, 1977: Proceedings, pp. 4-1 to 17.

Rowe, W. D. et al. "Approaches to Radioactive Waste Management Criteria Development." In EPA Workshop on Issues Pertinent to Development of Environmental Protection Criteria for Radioactive Wastes, VA, February 3-5, 1977: Proceedings,pp. 1-3 to 55.

Schilling, H. and S. M. Nealey. Public Participation in Nuclear Waste Management. Battelle Human Affairs Research Centers, Seattle, WA, 1978.

Sierra Club Radioactive Waste Campaign. Low-Level Waste Primer. Buffalo, NY, n. d.

Sierra Club Radioactive Waste Campaign. Shipping Casks: Are They Safe? Buffalo,NY, 1980.

Skolnikoff, E. "Interactions Between Scientific Experts and Lay Public in Implementation of Nuclear Waste Management Goals." In Proceedings of Conference on Public Policy Issues in Nuclear Waste Management. NSF-C-1044. National Science Foundation, Washington, DC, October 1976.

Southwest Research and Information Center. Relate to Nuclear Waste Disposal Issues. Albuquerque, NM, n.d.

Stensvaag, J. M. "Regulating Radioactive Air Emissions from Nuclear Generating Plants: A Primer for Attorneys, Decisionmakers, and Intervenors." Northwestern University Law Review, 78 (March 1983): 1-197.

U. S. Congress. House. Committee on Interior and Insular Affairs. Subcommittee on Energy and the Environment. Nuclear Waste Management: Oversight Hearings, January 25 and 26, 1979. 96th Congress, 1st session. Washington, DC: U. S. Government Printing Office, 1979. 602 p.

U. S. Department of Energy. Consumer Briefing #8 [Public Meetings on Nuclear Waste Management--San Francisco, Denver, Boston]. Office of Consumer Affairs, Washington, DC, 1979 (?)

U. S. Department of Energy. Proceedings of the 1983 Civilian Radioactive Waste Management Information Meeting, December 12-15, 1983. Washington, DC, February 1984.

U. S. Department of Energy. Summary Report of Public and Small Group Meetings Sponsored by the Interagency Review Group on Nuclear Waste Management, July 14-August 5, 1978. DOE Chicago Operations Office, Chicago, IL, 1978.

U. S. Department of Energy. Transcripts of Proceedings: Public Meetings on Nuclear Waste Disposal Held April-August in New Mexico and Texas. Washington, DC, 1978.

U. S. Department of Energy. Western New York Nuclear Service Center Study: Final Report for Public Comment. TID-28905-1. Washington, DC, November 1978.

U. S. Environmental Protection Agency. Proceedings: A Workshop of Policy and Technical Issues Pertinent to the Development of Environmental Protection Criteria for Radioactive Wastes, Albuquerque, NM, April 12-14, 1977. ORP/CSD-77/2. Office of Radiation Programs, Washington, DC, 1977. 323 p.

U. S. Environmental Protection Agency. Proceedings: A Workshop on Issues Pertinent to the Development of Environmental Protection Criteria for Radioactive Wastes, Reston, VA, February 3-5, 1977. ORP/CDS-77/1. Office of Radiation Programs, Washington, DC, 1978. 226 p.

U. S. Environmental Protection Agency. Proceedings of a Public Forum on Environmental Protection Criteria for Radiation Wastes, Denver, CO, March 30-April 1, 1978. Office of Radiation Programs, Washington, DC, 1978. 152 p.

U. S. Interagency Review Group on Nuclear Waste Management. Report to the President. TID-29442. Washington, DC, March 1979. 149 p. Avail. National Technical Information Service, Springfield, VA.

U. S. Nuclear Regulatory Commission. Task Force Report on Review of the Federal/State Program for Regulation of Commercial Low-Level Radioactive Waste Burial Grounds: Analysis of Public Comments. NUREG-0217-SUPPL-1. Washington, DC, 1977. 22 p.

U. S. Nuclear Regulatory Commission. Workshops for State Review of Site Suitability Criteria for High-Level Radioactive Waste Repositories. NUREG-0353. Washington, DC, 1977.

Union of Concerned Scientists. The Nuclear Fuel Cycle: A Survey of the Public Health, Environmental and National Security Effects of Nuclear Power. Cambridge, MA: MIT Press, 1975. 275 p.

Unruh, C. M. et al. "Public Comments on the Draft Generic Environmental Impact Statement for Management of Commercially Generated Radioactive Waste." In Waste Management 80 Symposium, Tucson, AZ, March 10-14, 1980: Proceedings, Vol. 2, pp. 331-338.

Varanini, E. E., III. "Consultation and Concurrence: Process or Substance." In E. W. Colglazier, Jr. (ed.), The Politics of Nuclear Waste. Elmsford, NY: Pergamon, 1982, pp. 138-159.

Vermont Public Interest Research Group. Radwaste on the Roadways: Transportation of Radioactive Materials in Vermont. Montpelier, VT, n. d. 17 p.

Voth, D. E. The Implications of Community Development for Nuclear Waste Isolation. Department of Agricultural Economics and Rural Sociology, University of Arkansas, Fayetteville, AR, 1980.

Voth, D. E. and B. E. Herrington. "Community Development in Nuclear Waste Isolation." In S. H. Murdock et al. (eds.), Nuclear Waste: Socioeconomic Dimensions of Long-Term Storage. Boulder, CO: Westview Press, 1983, pp. 251-265.

Walsh, E. J. "Resource Mobilization, Three Mile Island Protest, and Nuclear Waste Repository Siting." Paper prepared for the Office of Nuclear Waste Isolation, Battelle-Columbus. Pennsylvania State University, University Park, PA, January 1982.

Wiltshire, S. and M. Pendleton. "Public Involvement in Nuclear Waste Management Decisions: The Information Office Concept." In DOE National Waste Terminal Storage Symposium, Washington, DC, December 1982: Proceedings, pp. 214-217.

Woodhouse, E. J. "If We Really Wanted Public Participation in Nuclear Waste Management." Paper presented at the New York State Political Science Association Annual Conference, Albany, April 1982. 25 p.

Woodhouse, E. J. "Managing Nuclear Wastes: Let the Public Speak." Technology Review, 85 (October 1982): 12-13.

Woodhouse, E. J. "The Politics of Nuclear Waste Management." In C. A. Walker et al. (eds.), Too Hot to Handle? Social and Policy Issues in the Management of Radioactive Wastes. New Haven, CT: Yale University Press, 1983, pp. 151-183.

Worby, L. The Citizen's Nuclear Waste Manual. Nuclear Information and Resource Services, Washington, DC, May 1984, 150 p.

Yuan, G. "Public Participation in Licensing Decisions -- A Necessary Partner for Technical Site Suitability." In NRC/ORNL Low-Level Waste Disposal Site Suitability Requirements Symposium, Crystal City, VA, December 8-9, 1981: Proceedings, Vol. 1, pp. 55-77.

Zinberg, D. "The Public and Nuclear Waste Management." Bulletin of the Atomic Scientists, (January 1979): 34-39.

Zinberg, D. S. "Public Participation: U.S. and European Perspectives." In E. W. Colglazier, Jr. (ed.), The Politics of Nuclear Waste. New York: Pergamon Press, 1982, pp. 160-167.

Transportation

Adkins, W. G. and D. Burke. Social, Economic, and Environmental Factors in Highway Decision Making. Texas Transportation Institute, College Station, TX, November 1974.

Amir, G. Conservation Kills a Highway: The Hudson River Expressway Controversy. Discussion Paper IV. Research on Conflict in Locational Decisions, Regional Science Department, University of Pennsylvania, Philadelphia, PA, 1970.

Anderson, G. "Citizen Participation and the Minority Viewpoint." In Highway Research Board, Citizen Participation in Transportation Planning. Special Report No. 142. National Academy of Sciences, Washington, DC, 1973.

Ayer, G. A. Guidelines for Public Participation in the Transportation Planning Process. Planning Division, Ministry of Transportation and Communication, Ontario Government, Canada, 1972.

Bain, H. The Reston Express Bus: A Case History of Citizen Action to Improve Urban Transportation. Washington Center for Metropolitan Studies, Washington, DC, 1969.

Baumbach, R. O. and W. E. Borah. The Second Battle of New Orleans: A History of the Vieux Carre Riverfront Expressway Controversy. University, AL: University of Alabama Press, 1981.

Bishop, A. B., Oglesby, C. H. and G. E. Willeke. Socio-Economic and Community Factors in Planning Urban Freeways. Stanford, CA: Stanford University Press, 1969. 216 p.

Bleiker, H. et al. "Community Interaction as an Integral Part of the Highway Decision-Making Process." Highway Research Record, 356 (1971): 12-25.

Bowman, W. E. "Hearing Procedures in Illinois." In Papers and Proceedings of the 56th Annual Meeting of the American Association of State Highway Officials. Houston, TX, 1970.

Bradley, P. "Citizen Participation and the Citizen's Viewpoint." In Highway Research Board, Citizen Participation in Transportation Planning. Special Report No. 142. National Academy of Sciences, Washington, DC, 1973, pp. 96-102.

Brown, B. A. "Citizen Opposition to a Suburban Freeway, a Semi-Hypothetical Scenario: The Seattle Experience." Urban Law Annual, (1972): 105-130.

Buchanan, C. and A. Macewen. "Alternatives for Edinburgh: Public Participation in Transport Policy." Traffic Engineering and Control, 13, 11 (1972): 503-505.

Burwell, D. G. A Citizen's Guide to Clean Air and Transportation: Implications for Urban Revitalization. Washington, DC: U. S. Environmental Protection Agency, 1980.

Campbell, B. and M. T. Gruenbaum. "Community Participation in the Development of an Area-wide Topics Plan in Massachusetts." Traffic Engineering, 42, 7 (1972): 46-47.

Clary, B. B. and R. F. Goodman. "Community Attitudes and Actions in Response to Airport Noise." Environment and Behavior, 8 (September 1976): 441-470.

Connors, W. J. et al. "Validation of Citizen Participation in Aviation Decisions." Town Planning Review, 48, 2 (1977): 173-186.

Conservation Society. "How to Fight a Road." Ecologist, 2, 11 (1972): 30-31.

Cornelio, P. S. and L. G. Grimm. "A Case Study of Citizen Participation in the Planning of New Transportation Facilities for the Sunbelt States." In Institute of Transportation Engineers 52nd Annual Symposium, Chicago, August 22-26, 1982: Proceedings, pp. 266-272.

Cotham, J. C. and F. L. Hendrix. "Mobilizing Community Leadership in Urban Transit Planning: An Overview." High Speed Ground Transport Journal, 5, 1 (1971): 25-32.

Crawford, G. L. and C. E. Sweet. "Citizen Participation in Planning Transportation." Traffic Engineering, 43, 8 (1973): 14-16.

Creighton, J. L. Community Involvement Manual. Washington, DC: Federal Aviation Administration, 1979.

Devine, E. Multi-Discipline Design Teams for Transportation Facilities: A Study of Administrative Planning and Community Participation. State Planning and Community Affairs Agency, Olympia, WA, 1971.

Fellman, G. "Neighborhood Protest of an Urban Highway." Journal of the American Institute of Planners, 35, 2 (1969): 118-122.

Fellman, G. and G. Brandt. "Working-Class Protests Against an Urban Highway: Some Meanings, Limits and Problems." Environment and Behavior, 3, 1 (1971): 61-80.

Ferreri, M. G. "Public Participation in Urban Transit." Journal of Transportation Engineering Division-ASCE, 99, 4 (1973): 701-710.

Fielding, G. J. "Citizen Participation: An Administrative Strategy for Transportation Improvements." In P. Stringer and H. Wenzel (eds.), Transportation Planning for a Better Environment. New York: Plenum Press, 1976, pp. 417-428.

Fielding, G. J. Group Dynamics in the Urban Freeway Decision Process. School of Social Sciences, University of California, Irvine, CA, 1972. 103 p.

Fielding, G. J. "Locating Urban Freeways: A Method for Resolving Community Conflict." In F. Horton (ed.), Geographic Studies of Urban Transportation and Network Analysis. Studies in Geography No. 16. Evanston, IL: Northwestern University, 1968, pp. 76-101.

Fielding, G. J. Locating Urban Freeways: Methods for Resolving Community Conflict. Irvine, CA: University of California, 1968-69.

Finley, J. R. and J. K. Baker. "Social Elements in Environmental Planning." Battelle Research Outlook, 4, 2 (1972): 8-11.

France, E. A. "Effects of Citizen Participation in Governmental Decision-Making." Highway Research Record, 356 (1971): 1-5.

Gakenheimer, R. Transportation Planning as a Response to Controversy: The Boston Case. Cambridge, MA: MIT Press, 1976. 377 p.

Glickman, N. J. Conflict Over Public Facility Location in Japan. Discussion Paper XVI. Research on Conflict in Locational Decisions, Regional Science Department, University of Pennsylvania, Philadelphia, PA, 1972.

Gonen, A. The Spadina Expressway in Toronto: Decision and Opposition. Discussion Paper V. Research on Conflict in Locational Decisions, Regional Science Department, University of Pennsylvania, Philadelphia, PA, 1970.

Graven, D. L. "Citizen Participation in Regional Planning." In Highway Research Board, Citizen Participation in Transportation Planning. Special Report No. 142. National Academy of Sciences, Washington, DC, 1973, pp. 52-61.

Grisby, J. E. and B. Campbell. "A New Rule for Planners: Working with Community Residents in Formulating Alternative Plans for Street Patterns -- Before Decision Making." Transportation, 1, 2 (1972): 125-150.

Guitar, M. A. Property Power: How to Keep the Bulldozer, the Power Line, and Highwaymen Away from Your Door. Garden City, NY: Doubleday and Co., 1972.

Gurchin, M. H. et al. "Proposals for Improving Transportation and Environmental Planning at the State and Local Level." Harvard Environmental Law Review, 2 (1978): 542-561.

Hall, D. and D. Lock. "Participation in Road Planning: A Consultation Paper. TCPA Comments on the Department of the Environment Publication of March 1973." Town and Country Planning, 41, 7-8 (1973): 354-356.

Hamilton, G. D. "Citizen Participation in the Transportation Planning Process: A Review." Transportation Engineer, 47, 9 (1977): 32-36.

Hardy, M. F. et al. "The Construction of Highways: The Environment and Public Participation." Highway Engineer, 22, 2 (1975): 4-27.

Healey, P. "The Sociology of Urban Transportation Planning: A Socio-Political Perspective." In D. A. Hensher (ed.), Urban Transport Economics. London: Cambridge University Press, 1977, pp. 199-227.

Highway Research Board. "Boston Transportation Planning Review Papers." In Highway Research Board, Citizen Participation in Transportation Planning. Special Report No. 142. National Academy of Sciences, Washington, DC, 1973.

Highway Research Board. Citizen Participation in Transportation Planning. Special Report No. 142. National Academy of Sciences, Washington, DC, 1973.

Highway Research Board. "Social, Economic, and Environmental Factors of Transportation." Highway Research Record, 356 (1971): entire issue.

Highway Research Board. Transportation and Community Values. Special Report 105. National Academy of Sciences, Washington, DC, 1969.

Hill, S. L. "Watts-Century Freeway." In Highway Research Board, Transportation and Community Values. Special Report 105. National Academy of Sciences, Washington, DC, 1969, pp. 117-121.

Holland, A. J. "Citizen Participation and an Elected Official's Viewpoint." In Highway Research Board, Citizen Participation in Transportation Planning. Special Report No. 142. National Academy of Sciences, Washington, DC, 1973.

Hoover, J. H. and A. A. Alshuler. Involving Citizens in Metropolitan Region Transportation Planning. PB-279 847. National Technical Information Service, Springfield, VA, June 1977. 167 p.

Howe, M. "The Transport Act, 1962 and the Consumers' Consultative Committees." Public Administration, 42 (Spring 1964): 45-56.

Hunt, R. "Improving Snelling Avenue: A Chronicle of Citizen Participation." Nations Cities, 16 (February 1978): 27-29.

Hunt, R. "St. Paul Citizens Influence Street Improvement." Minnesota Cities, 62, 13 (1977): 4-5.

Jordan, D. et al. Effective Citizen Participation in Transportation Planning. Volume I. Community Involvement Processes; Volume II. A Catalog of Techniques. Socioeconomic Studies Division, Federal Highway Administration, U. S. Department of Transportation, Washington, DC, 1976. Vol. I-129 p.; Vol. II-298 p.

Joyner, H. R. "Regional-Local Conflicts in Transportation Planning." Journal of Transportation Engineering, 98, 3 (1972): 515-519.

Kelly, B. The Pavers and the Paved. New York: Charles Scribner's Sons, 1971.

Kihl, M. R. "Alternative Reuses of Abandoned Highway Right-of-Way." Transportation Research Record, 812 (1981): 75-80.

Kinstingler, J. and L. E. Keefer. "Citizen Participation in the Urban State." In Highway Research Board, Citizen Participation in Transportation Planning. Special Report No. 142. National Academy of Sciences, Washington, DC, 1973, pp. 71-89.

Legarra, J. A. and T. R. Lammers. "The Highway Administrator Looks at Values." In Highway Research Board, Transportation and Community Values. Special Report 105. National Academy of Sciences, Washington, DC, 1969, pp. 109-116.

Lockwood, S. C. "The Boston Transportation Planning Review: A Case Study in Community/ Technical Inter-Action." Planners Notebook (AIP), 2, 4 (1972): entire issue.

Lockwood, S. C. "Participation: Its Influence on Planning Methodology." In Highway Research Board, Citizen Participation in Transportation Planning. Special Report No. 142. National Academy of Sciences, Washington, DC, 1973, pp. 116-120.

Lupo, A., Colcord, F. C., and E. P. Fowler. Rites of Way: Politics of Transportation and the U. S. City. Boston: Little and Brown, 1971.

Maller, R. L. "The Fallacy of the Design Public Hearing as a General Concept." In Papers and Proceedings of the 56th Annual Meeting of the American Association of State Highway Officials. Houston, TX, 1970.

Manheim, M. L. "Reaching Decisions about Technological Projects with Social Consequences: A Normative Model." Transportation, 2, 1 (1973): 1-24.

Manheim, M. L. and J. H. Suhrbier. The Automobile and the Environment: Implications for the Planning Process. Environmental Report No. 6. Organization for Economic Cooperation and Development, Paris, 1974. 107 p.

Manheim, M. L. et al. Community Values in Highway Location and Design: A Procedural Guide. Report 71-4. Urban Systems Laboratory, Massachusetts Institute of Technology, Cambridge, MA, 1971.

Manheim, M. L. et al. Transportation Decision-Making: A Guide to Social and Environmental Considerations. NCHRP Report No. 156. Transportation Research Board, Washington, DC, 1975.

Massachusetts Institute of Technology. The Impacts of Highways Upon Environmental Values. Report No. USL-69-1. Urban Systems Laboratory, Cambridge, MA, March 1969.

McCarty, B. "Participation in Transportation-Air Quality Plans." In Transportation and the 1977 Clean Air Act Amendments Conference, San Francisco, November 12-14, 1979: Proceedings, pp. 375-381.

McGrath, D. C. Jr. "Multidisciplinary Environmental Analysis: Jamaica Bay and Kennedy Airport." Journal of the American Institute of Planners, 37, 4 (1971): 243-252.

McKie, D. A Sadly Mismanaged Affair: A Political History of the Third London Airport. London: Croom Helm, 1973. 256 p.

Metropolitan Toronto Transportation Plan Review. Public Participation Program. Toronto, Canada,1972.

Metzger, J. F. and D. C. Colony. "Citizens and Project Design: Management Team." Journal of the Urban Planning and Development Division-ASCE, 106, 1 (1980): 56-66.

Michaels, L. P. "More Public Consultation on Airport Plans." Airport Forum, 8,1 (1978): 25-36.

Milch, J. E. "Feasible and Prudent Alternatives: Airport Development in the Age of Protest." Public Policy, 24, 1 (1976): 82-109.

Milch, J. E. "The Toronto Airport Controversy." In D. Nelkin (ed.), Controversy: The Politics of Technical Decisions. Beverly Hills, CA: Sage, 1979, pp. 25-47.

Miller, J. H. "Citizen Participation in Transport System Planning: A Case Study." Transportation Research Record, 618 (1976): 47-52.

Mitchell, H. R. "Citizen Participation in Transportation Decision Making." Traffic Engineering, 45 , 8 (1975): 7-11.

Mumphrey, A. J. The New Orleans Riverfront Expressway Controversy: An Analytical Account. Discussion Paper I. Research on Conflict in Locational Decisions, Regional Science Department, University of Pennsylvania, Philadelphia, PA, 1970.

Mumphrey, A. J. Jr. and C. B. Fromherz. "Citizens, Politicians, and Decisionmakers: A Helix Game for Transportation Planning." Geoforum, 9, 4-5 (1978): 279-291.

Mumphrey, A. J. and J. Wolpert. "Equity Considerations and Concessions in the Siting of Public Facilities." Economic Geography, 49, 2 (1973): 109-121.

Mumphrey, A. J., Seley, J. E., and J. Wolpert. "A Decision Model for Locating Controversial Facilities." Journal of the American Institute of Planners,(November 1971): 397-402.

Murphy, R. H. "The Boston Transportation Planning Review: A Reevaluation of Expressways' Value in an Urban Area." Traffic Engineering, (June 1971): 18-22.

National Wildlife Federation/Environmental Action Foundation. The End of the Road: A Citizen's Guide to Transportation Problemsolving. Report NWF79409. Washington, DC, 1977. 159 p.

Nowlan, D. and N. Nowlan. The Bad Trip: The Untold Story of the Spadina Expressway. Toronto: New Press, 1970.

Odell, R. "To Stop Highways Some Citizens Take to the Streets." Smithsonian, 3,1 (1972): 24-29.

Onibokun, A. G. and M. Curry. "An Ideology of Citizen Participation: The Metropolitan Seattle Transit Case Study." Public Administration Review, 36, 3 (1976): 269-277.

Park, K. S. "Achieving Positive Community Participation in the Freeway Planning Process." Highway Research Record, 380 (1972): 14-22.

Partridge, T. J. Transportation Advocacy Planning in Winnipeg: The Case of COST." Institute of Urban Studies, University of Winnipeg, Winnipeg, Canada, 1973.

Patterson, T. W. "Public Participation in Railroad Relocation." Journal of the Urban Planning and Development Division-ASCE, 110, 1 (1984): 9-21.

Patton, L. K. and G. W. Cormick. "Mediation and the NEPA Process: The Interstate 90 Experience." Paper presented at the Environmental Impact Analysis Conference, University of Illinois, Champaign-Urbana, IL, May 1977.

Perfater, M. A. Citizen Participation and the Role of the Public Hearings. VHTRC No. 75-R36. Virginia Highway and Transportation Research Council, Charlottesville, VA, September 1975.

Peters, J. L. and K. R. White. "New Directions and Techniques in Highway Location Planning." Journal of the Transportation Engineering Division-ASCE, 100, 2 (1974): 305-312.

Pilarsky, M. "Chicago's Crosstown Expressway: Mod-Highway for Urban America." In Highway Research Board, Transportation and Community Values. Special Report 105. National Academy of Sciences, Washington, DC, 1969, pp. 123-137.

Praeger, P. "Extinction by Thruway: The Fight to Save a Town." Harpers, (December 1958): 61-71.

Primack, J. and F. von Hippel. "Scientists, Politics and SST: A Critical Review." Bulletin of the Atomic Scientists, 28, 4 (1972): 24-30.

Reiner, T. et al. The Crosstown Controversy: A Case Study. Discussion Paper XXII. Research on Conflict in Locational Decisions, Regional Science Department, University of Pennsylvania, Philadelphia, PA, 1971.

Rice, H. "The Overton Park-Interstate 40 Conflict." In Citizens Advisory Committee on Environmental Quality, Citizens Make the Difference: Case Studies of Environmental Action. Washington, DC, January 1973, pp. 43-53.

Robinson, J. "Citizen Participation and Environmental Considerations in Transportation Planning." In Highway Research Board, Environmental Considerations in Planning, Design and Construction. Special Report No. 138. National Academy of Sciences, Washington, DC, 1973.

Rock, M. A. "How to Fight a Freeway -- and Win!" National Parks and Conservation Magazine, 52, 8 (1978): 12-16.

Roden, D. Community Involvement in Transportation Planning. NCTCOG Technical Report Series 37. North Central Texas Council of Governments, Arlington, TX, May 1984. v. p.

Ross, H. S. and G. M. Smerk. "Institutionalization of Mass Transportation in the Community." Traffic Quarterly, 33, 4 (1979): 511-524.

Sager, T. "Citizen Participation and Cost-Benefit Analysis." Transportation Planning and Technology, 5, 3 (1979): 161-168.

Saltzman, A. "Transportation Research for Community Objectives." Journal of Transportation Engineering, 98, TE4 (1972): 855-862.

Schary, P. B. "Consumers as Participants in Transportation Planning." Transportation, 6, 2 (1977): 135-148.

Schimpeler, C. C. and W. L. Grecco. "The Community-Systems Evaluation: An Approach Based on Community Structures and Values." Highway Research Record, 238 (1968): 123-152.

Seley, J. Development of a Sophisticated Opposition: The Lower Manhattan Expressway Issue. Discussion Paper VII. Research on Conflict in Locational Decisions, Regional Science Department, University of Pennsylvania, Philadelphia, PA, 1970.

Sloan, A. K. Citizen Participation in Transportation Planning: The Boston Experience. Cambridge, MA: Ballinger Publishing Co., 1974.

Sloan A. K. "Technical Assistance and Community Liason." In Highway Research Board, Citizen Participation in Transportation Planning. Special Report No. 142. National Academy of Sciences, Washington, DC, 1973, pp. 128-131.

Stanley, J. K. and C. A. Nash. "The Evaluation of Urban Transport Improvements." In D. A. Hensher (ed.), Urban Transport Economics. London: Cambridge University Press, 1977, pp. 55-71.

Steger, W. A. "Reflections on Citizen Involvement in Urban Transport Planning: Towards a Positive Approach." Transportation, 3, 2 (1974): 127-144.

Stevens, D. H. "Citizen Participation in a Rural State." In Highway Research Board, Citizen Participation in Transportation Planning. Special Report No. 142. National Academy of Sciences, Washington, DC, 1973.

Symposium on Citizen Participation: 50th Annual Meeting of the Highway Research Board. National Research Council, Washington, DC, 1971.

Taebel, D. A. "Citizen Groups, Public Policy and Urban Transportation." Traffic Quarterly, 27, 4 (1973): 503-515.

Thomas, E. N. and J. L. Schofer. Strategies for the Evaluation of Alternative Transport Plans. National Cooperative Highway Research Program Report No. 96. Highway Research Board, National Academy of Sciences, Washington, DC, 1970. 111 p.

Thorsen, J. H. "How to Conduct Controversial Public Hearings." Airport Management Journal, 1, 3 (1976): 5-7.

Torrey, W. R. and F. W. Mills. Selecting Effective Citizen Participation Techniques. Office of Program and Policy Planning, Federal Highway Administration, U. S. Department of Transportation, Washington, DC, 1977. 27 p.

"Transportation and Energy ." Energy Consumer, 2 (September 1980): entire issue.

U. S. Department of Transportation, Citizens' Advisory Committee on Transportation Quality. Community Participation in Highway Planning. Office of Consumer Affairs, Washington, DC, October 1972.

U. S. Department of Transportation. Community Involvement in Highway Project Planning. Federal Highway Administration, Washington, DC, March 1971.

U. S. Department of Transportation. Identification of Community Values through Analysis of Public Hearings. Washington, DC, March 1972.

U. S. Department of Transportation. A Manual of Community Involvement Techniques for Designing and Implementing Community Involvement in Highway Planning and Design. Washington, DC: Office of Environmental Policy, Federal Highway Administration, 1977. 360 p.

Urban Systems Laboratory, MIT (ed.). Proceedings of a Panel Discussion on Community Involvement in Highway Planning and Design. Federal Highway Administration, U. S. Department of Transportation, 1973.

Vodrazka, W. C. et al. "Citizen Participation in Louisville Airport Site Selection." Transportation Research Record, 555 (1975): 37-49.

Vogel, H. H. "Interstate Expressway Versus Parkway." Environmental Policy and Law, 5, 4 (1979): 186-189.

Voorhees, A. M. "Techniques for Determining Community Values." Highway Research Record, 102 (1965): 11-18.

Wachs, M. "A Survey of Citizens' Opinions of the Effectiveness, Needs and Techniques of Urban Transportation Planning." Highway Research Record, 229 (1968): 65-76.

Wachs, M., Barclay, M. H., and J. L. Schofer. Integrating Localized and Systemwide Objectives in Transportation Planning. School of Architecture and Urban Planning, University of California, Los Angeles, CA,1973. 43 p.

Walton, L. E. Jr. and J. R. Saroff. "Proposed Strategy for Public Hearings." Highway Research Record, 356 (1971): 26-31.

Watkins, L. H. et al. "Evaluation of Environmental Factors of Road and Road Traffic." Highway Engineer, 22, 2 (1975): 27-41.

Webber, M. M. "Alternative Styles for Citizen Participation in Transport Planning" Highway Research Record, 356 (1971): 6-11.

Webber, M. M. "On the Techniques and the Politics of Transport Planning." In Highway Research Board, Citizen Participation in Transportation Planning. Special Report No. 142. National Academy of Sciences, Washington, DC, 1973.

Weiner, P. and E. J. Deak. Environmental Factors in Transportation Planning. Lexington, MA: Lexington Books, 1972. 283 p.

Weiner, P. and E. J. Deak. "Nonuser Effects in Highway Planning." Highway Research Record, 356 (1971): 55-68.

Wellman, B. "Public Participation in Transportation Planning." Traffic Quarterly, 31, 4 (1977): 639-656.

Wofford, J. G. "Participatory Planning in Boston Metro-Area Transport." Civil Engineering-ASCE, 43, 4 (1973): 78-81.

Wofford, J. G. "Public Participation in Balanced Transportation Planning." In Highway Research Board, Citizen Participation in Transportation Planning. Special Report No. 142. National Academy of Sciences, Washington, DC, 1973, pp.107-115.

Wulkan, A. "Dade County Experience: Model for Citizen Participation." Transit Journal, 2, 1 (1976): 20-30.

Yukubousky, R. Community Interaction in Transportation Systems and Project Development: A Framework for Application. New York State Department of Transportation, Albany, NY, September 1973.

Zimmerman, J. F. "Citizen Involvement in Urban Transportation Planning and Development." Planning and Administration, 3, 2 (1976): 65-71.

Part III

Natural Resources Decisionmaking

General

Bolle, A. W. "Public Participation and Environmental Quality." Natural Resources Journal, 11, 3 (1971): 497-505.

Bultena, G. L. and D. L. Rogers. "Considerations in Determining the Public Interest." Journal of Soil and Water Conservation, 29, 4 (1974): 168-173.

Burch, W. R. Jr. "Who Participates: A Sociological Interpretation of Natural Resource Decisions." Natural Resources Journal, 16 (January 1976): 41-54.

Cutler, M. R. "New Role for Government Information and Education Personnel." Transactions of the North American Wildlife and Natural Resources Conference, 39 (1974): 397-405.

Fairfax, S. and L. Burton. "A Decade of NEPA: Milestone or Millstone?" Fisheries, 8, 6 (1983): 5-8.

Gammell, A. "Public Involvement." Naturopa, 39 (1981): 26-.

Heberlein, T. A. "Some Observations on Alternative Mechanisms for Public Involvement: The Hearing, Public Opinion Poll, the Workshop, and the Quasi-Experiment." Natural Resources Journal, 16, 1 (1976): 197-212.

Hendee, J. C., Gale, R. P., and J. Harry. "Conservation, Politics and Democracy." Journal of Soil and Water Conservation, 24, 6 (1969): 212-215.

Kacmar, S. A. and A. R. Brecher. "The Public as an Ally." In Western Water and Energy Conference, Fort Collins, CO, June 1982: Proceedings. American Society of Civil Engineers, pp. 610-615.

Kelly, H. W. "Communicating Conservation." Journal of Soil and Water Conservation, 39, 1 (1984): 23-25.

Lindaman, E. B. Alternatives for Washington, Vol. I; Pathways to Washington 1985, A Beginning; Citizens' Recommendations for the Future. Report No. 1. Alternatives for Washington, Statewide Citizen Task Force, May 1975.

O'Riordan, T. "Towards a Strategy of Public Involvement." In W. R. D. Sewell and I. Burton (eds.), Perceptions and Attitudes in Resources Management. Ottawa, Canada: Department of Energy Mines and Resources, 1971, pp. 99-110.

Portney, P., Sonstelie, J., and A. Kneese. "Environmental Quality, Household Migration, and Collective Choice." In E. T. Haefele (ed.), The Governance of Common Property Resources. Baltimore, MD: Johns Hopkins University Press, 1974, pp. 65-93.

Potter, H. R. Citizen Participation in Natural Resources Decision-Making: Conceptual Issues and Approaches. Department of Sociology, Purdue University, West Lafayette, IN, 1978.

Reidel, C. H. "Importance of Legal Constraints in Maintaining Public Resource Values." In Proceedings of North American Wildlife and Natural Resources Conference, 40 (1975): 19-26.

Sewell, W. R. D. "Integrating Public Views in Planning and Policymaking." In W.R. D. Sewell and I. Burton (eds.), Perceptions and Attitudes in Resources Management. Ottawa, Canada: Department of Energy Mines and Resources, 1971, pp. 125-131+.

Sewell, W. R. D. and S. D. Phillips. "Models for the Evaluation of Public Participation Programmes." Natural Resources Journal, 19, 2 (1979): 337-358.

Thompson, D. L. Politics, Policy, and Natural Resources. New York: The Free Press, 1972.

U. S. Department of the Interior. Private Sector Involvement Workbook. Washington, DC: Heritage Conservation and Recreation Service, 1979. 84 p.

Waddell, K. B. A Survey of Public Review Hearings in Northern Canada. Department of Indian Affairs and Northern Development, Ottawa, Ontario, Canada, 1981.

Wengert, N. Natural Resources and the Political Struggle. New York: Doubleday, 1955. 71 p.

Coastal Zone Management

Ashbaugh, J. "Identifying the 'Public' for Participation in Coastal Zone Management." Coastal Zone Management Journal, 2, 4 (1976): 383-408.

Bennett, D. W. 202 Questions for the Endangered Coastal Zone. Highlands, NJ: American Littoral Society, 1970. 28 p.

Conservation Foundation. The Sanibel Report: Formulation of a Comprehensive Plan Based on Natural Systems. Washington, DC, 1976. 405 p.

"Drive to Save America's Shorelines." U. S. News and World Report, 73 (July 31, 1972): 38-40.

Duddleson, W. J. "How the Citizens of California Secured Their Coastal Management Program." In Conservation Foundation, Protecting the Golden Shore. Washington, DC, 1978, pp. 3-65.

Farrell, B. H. "Cooperative Tourism and the Coastal Zone." Coastal Zone Management Journal, 14, 1-2 (1986): 113-130.

Healy, R. G. and J. A. Zinn. "Environment and Development Conflicts in Coastal Zone Management." American Planning Association Journal, 51, 3 (1985): 299-311.

Kinsey, D. N. "Organizing a Public Participation Program: Lessons Learned from the Development of New Jersey's Coastal Zone Management Program." Coastal Zone Management Journal, 8, 1 (1980): 85-101.

Kreutzwiser, R. D. "Ontario Cottager Associations and Shoreline Management." Coastal Zone Management Journal, 14, 1-2 (1986): 93-111.

Lakshminarayana, J. S. S. "Integration of Interfaces of Coastal Systems and Technology in Coastal Zone Management." Water Science and Technology, 16, 3-4 (1984): 591-598.

Lassey, W. R. and C. P. Ditwiler. "Land Use Planning and Coastal Zone Management: The Oregon Story." Environmental Law, 5, 3 (1975): 661-673.

Robadue, D. D. Jr., and V. K. Tippie. "Public Involvement in Offshore Oil Development: Lessons from New England." Coastal Zone Management Journal, 7, 2-4 (1980): 237-270.

Rosener, J. B. "Can Citizen Involvement Make Bureaucrats Responsive? A Test of the Effectiveness of Citizen Involvement in Public Hearing Held by California Coastal Commissions." Paper presented at the Research Conference on Public Involvement and Social Impact Assessment, University of Arizona, Tucson, February 1981.

Rudenberg, F. "Coastal Management: What Is Managed and by Whom? Is the Public Being Given a Fair Shake?" In Coastal Society 7th Conference, Galveston, TX, October 1981: Proceedings, pp. 109-115.

Shabman, L. A. "Effective Public Participation in Coastal Zone Management: Toward Effective Coastal Zone Management." Coastal Zone Management Journal, 1, 2 (1974): 197-207.

Simon, A. W. "Who Speaks for the Coast -- and Who Listens?" Coastal Zone Management Journal, 6, 4 (1979): 311-316.

Spencer, J. Evaluation of Public Participation in the Wisconsin Coastal Management Program. Office of Coastal Management, Madison, WI, 1976.

Stoffle, R. W. et al. "Perceptions of Resource Regulation: A Comparison of North Carolina Fisherman and Managers." Coastal Zone Management Journal, 10, 4 (1983): 407-427.

Willeke, G. E. A Program for Involving the Public in Coastal Zone Planning in South Carolina. Environmental Resources Center and Department of City Planning, Georgia Institute of Technology, Atlanta, GA, 1973.

Zinn, J. A. (ed.) "Theme Issue: Energy and the Coastal Zone: A Question of Risk." Coastal Zone Management Journal, 7, 2-4 (1980): 123-337.

Forest Resources

Allen, G. M. and E. M. Gould Jr. "Complexity, Wickedness and Public Forests." Journal of Forestry, 84 (April 1986): 20-23.

Alston, R. M. Forest Goals and Decision Making in the Forest Service. Research Paper IN T-128. Intermediate Forest and Range Experiment Station, U. S. Forest Service, Ogden, UT, 1972. 84 p.

Arnold, R. "Loggers vs. Environmentalists: Friends? or Foes?" Logging Management, (February 1978): 16-19.

Arvola, T. F. "State vs. Local Forest Practice Regulation in California." Journal of Forestry, 68, 11 (1970): 688-691.

Behan, R. W. "Citizen vs. Bureaucrat: The Need for Para-Politics on Professionalized Bureaucracy." Paper presented at the Forest Service Supervisors' Staff Meeting, Missoula, MT, December 1970.

Behan, R. W. "Forestry and the End of Innocence." American Forests, 81 (May 1975): 16-19+.

Behan, R. W. "The Myth of the Omnipotent Forester." Journal of Forestry, 64, 6 (1966): 398-400+.

Behan, R. W. Wilderness Decisions in Region I, U. S. Forest Service: A Case Study of Professional Bureau Policy Making. Unpublished Ph. D. dissertation. University of California, Berkeley, CA, 1971.

Benfield, F. K. "The Forest Service: Can It Learn to Listen?" Environment, 27, 7 (1985): 4-5+.

Blahna, D. J. "Social Bases for Forest Resource Conflicts in Areas of Reverse Migration." Paper presented at the First National Symposium on Social Science in Resource Management, Corvallis, OR, May 1986.

Blahna, D. J. and S. Yonts-Shepard. "Preservation or Use: Identifying and Using Public Issues in National Forest Planning." Policy Studies Review, (forthcoming).

Blonski, K. S. Moving Towards Excellence: Social Design for Future U. S. Forest Service Land Management Planning. California State University, Hayward, CA, 1985. 34 p.

Bolle, A. W. "Public Participation and Environmental Quality." Natural Resources Journal, 11, 3 (1971): 497-505.

Bultena, G. L. and J. C. Hendee. "Forester's Views of Interest Group Positions on Forest Policy." Journal of Forestry, 70, 6 (1972): 337-342.

Burch, W. R. Jr. "Social Aspects of Forest Policy Research." In M. Clawson (ed.), Research in Forest Economics and Forest Policy. Research Paper R-3. Resources for the Future, Washington, DC, 1977 pp. 329-382.

Bush, M. "The Last Big Battle?" American Forests, 77, 1 (1971): 46-47.

Butcher, R. D. "Conservationists Go to Court." American Forests, 77, 6 (1971): 32-35+ (Part I); 77, 7 (1971): 32-35 (Part II).

Campion, T. B. Jr. (ed.). Public Involvement in Decision-Making in the Shoshone National Forest. Ford Foundation Environmental Law Intern Program, University of Colorado Law School, May 1972. 106 p.

Carroll, M. Polarization and Forest Service Public Involvement: The Case of the Indian Peaks. Unpublished M. S. thesis. West Virginia University, Morgantown, WV, 1979. 137 p.

Carter, D. R. and C. H. Oglesby. Unified Planning and Decision-Making: A Conceptual Framework for Forest Service Management. Report EEP-49. Stanford University Program in Engineering-Economic Planning, Stanford, CA, October 1973. 252 p.

Case, P. J., Edgmon, T. D., and D. A. Renton. Public -- A Procedure for Public Involvement. Range Science Department, College of Forestry and Natural Resources, Colorado State University, Fort Collins, CO, 1976.

Claeyssens, P. "Rethinking Significance: Is There Room for Public Input in Cultural Resource Allocation Strategies?" Paper presented at the First National Symposium on Social Science in Resource Management, Corvallis, OR, May 1986.

Clark, R. N., Stankey, G. H., and J. C. Hendee. An Introduction to Codinvolve: A System for Analyzing, Storing, and Retrieving Public Input to Resource Decisions. Research Note PNW-223. Pacific Northwest Forest and Range Experiment Station, U. S. Forest Service, Portland, OR, 1974. 16 p.

Copeland, C. J. Communication During a Forest Service Public Involvement Process. Unpublished M. S. thesis. West Virginia University, Morgantown, WV, 1976. 88 p.

Cortner, H. J. and M. T. Richards. "The Political Component of National Forest Planning." Journal of Soil and Water Conservation, 38, 2 (1983): 79-81.

Cortner, H. J. et al. "Uses of Public Opinion Surveys in Resource Planning." Environmental Professional, 6 (1984): 265-275.

Crafts, E. C. "Foresters on Trial." Living Wilderness, 36, 120 (1972-73): 38+; reprinted in Journal of Forestry, 71, 1 (1973): 14+.

Culhane, P. Public Lands Politics: Interest Group Influence on the Forest Service and the Bureau of Land Management. Baltimore, MD: Johns Hopkins University Press, 1981.

Dana, S. T. and S. K. Fairfax. Forest and Range Policy. New York: McGraw-Hill Book Co., 1980. 458 p.

Davis, L. S. "Opening Question: What Is the Purpose of Public Involvement in Public Land Management." In Proceedings of the Society of American Foresters National Convention, New York, 1974, pp. 136-139.

Davis, L. S. et al. Citizens and Natural Resources: A Perspective on Public Involvement. Department of Forestry and Outdoor Recreation, College of Natural Resources, Utah State University, Logan, UT, 1975. 20 p.

Devall, W. B. "The Forest Service and Its Clients: Input to Forest Service Decision-Making." Environmental Affairs, 2 (Spring 1973): 732-757.

Devall, W. B. and S. Metcalf. "The Forest Service and Its Clients: A Study in Conflict Resolution." Paper presented at the American Sociological Convention, New Orleans, LA, 1972.

Dravniecks, D. and D. C. Pitcher. Public Participation in Resource Planning: Selected Literature Abstracts. Management Science Staff, U. S. Forest Service, Berkeley, CA, April 1981. 77 p.

Elison, R. "The What and Why of Land Use Planning and Design: The Planning Process in Action: Techniques and Tools." Society of American Foresters National Conference, Albuquerque, NM, 1977, pp. 295-322.

Ellefson, D. V. "Roles and Responsibilities of Forestry Professionals." Journal of Forestry, 72, 7 (1974): 408-410.

Fairfax, S. K. Public Involvement: An Evaluation of the Southern Region, Forest Service. U. S. Forest Service, Atlanta, GA, 1974. 43 p.

Fairfax, S. K. "Public Involvement and the Forest Service." Journal of Forestry, 71 (October 1975): 657-659.

Fairfax, S. K. and G. L. Achterman. "The Monogahela Controversy and the Political Process." Journal of Forestry, 75 (August 1977): 485-487.

Finison, B. F. "National Forests in Florida." Forest Farmer, 33, 6 (1974): 12-14.

Folkman, W. S. and A. J. Wagar. "The Case for Small Groups: Public Participation in Forest Management Decisions." Journal of Forestry, 72, 7 (1974): 405-407.

Forest, L. B. Attitudes Toward Scenic Corridor Development - Shawnee National Forest: A Study of Involvement Input Using Content Analysis Procedures. Department of Agriculture and Extension Education, University of Wisconsin, Madison, WI, 1974. 65 p.

Fox, B. Public Involvement and the Forest Service: Conceptual Framework, Legal Requirements, Organizational Analysis and Recommendations. School of Natural Resources, University of Michigan, Ann Arbor, Michigan, 1978. 99 p.

Frankena, F. "Defeat of the Hersey Wood-Fired Power Plant: The Ideology and Politics of Technology in a Nonmetropolitan Community." Paper presented at the 1st National Symposium on Social Science in Resource Management, Corvallis, OR, May 1986. 22 p.

Frankena, F. "Facts, Values, and Technical Expertise in a Renewable Energy Siting Dispute." Journal of Economic Psychology, 4 (1983): 131-147.

Frankena, F. "Facts, Values, and Technical Expertise in a Renewable Energy Siting Dispute." In P. Ester et al. (eds.), Consumer Behavior and Energy Policy: Selected/Edited Proceedings of the 1st International Conference, Noordwijkerhout, September 1982. New York: North-Holland, 1984, pp. 417-433.

Frankena, F. The Impact of Technical Expertise in a Nonmetropolitan Siting Dispute: A Case Study of the Hersey Wood-Fired Power Plant Controversy. Ph. D. dissertation. Michigan State University, East Lansing, MI, 1983. Avail. University Microfilms International, Ann Arbor, MI.

Frear, S. T. "Confrontation vs. Communication: Confessions of a Government PR Man." Journal of Forestry, 71, 10 (1973): 650-652.

Freeman, D. M. "Politics of Planning and the Problem of Public Confidence: A Sociology of Conflict Approach." In Proceedings of the Society of American Foresters, Hot Springs, AK, October 1972, pp. 184-199.

Gale, R. P. "Communicating with Environmentalists: A Look at Life on the Receiving End." Journal of Forestry, 71, 10 (1973): 653-655.

Garcia, M. W. "Public Involvement and Social Impact Assessment: A Case History of the Coronado National Forest." In G. A. Daneke et al. (eds.), Public Involvement and Social Impact Assessment. Boulder, CO: Westview Press, 1983, pp. 195-206.

Garcia, M. Y. W. Citizen Participation in Forest Service Planning in Arizona. Unpublished Ph. D. dissertation. University of Arizona, Tucson, AZ, 1980. 172 p.

Gould, E. M. Jr. "Whatever Became of the Invisible Hand?" Forest History, 12 (1969): 7-9.

Graves, P. F. and W. F. LaPage. "Participant Satisfaction with Public Involvement in U. S. Forest Service Recreation Policy." In B. Sadler (ed.), Involvement and Environment: Proceedings of the Canadian Conference on Public Participation. Vol. 2: Working Papers and Case Studies. Edmonton, Alberta: Environment Council of Alberta, 1979, pp. 297-311.

Hagan, M. and E. Valfer. Analysis of the RARE II Public Involvement Process. Management Sciences Staff, U. S. Forest Service, University of California, Berkeley, CA, May 1978. 35 p.

Hahn, B. W. and C. B. White. National Forest Management: A Handbook for Public Input and Review. Stanford Environmental Law Society, Stanford, CA, September 1978. 267 p.

Haigh, J. A. and J. V. Krutilla. "Clarifying Policy Directives: The Case of National Forest Management." Policy Analysis, 16 (Fall 1980): 409-439.

Hendee, J. C. "Public Involvement in the United States Forest Service Roadless-Area Review: Lessons from a Case Study." In W. R. Sewell and J. T. Coppock (eds.), Public Participation in Planning. New York: John Wiley and Sons, 1977.

Hendee, J. C. "Public Opinion and What Foresters Should Do About It." Journal of Forestry, 82 (June 1984): 340-344.

Hendee, J. C. and R. N. Clark. "Concepts, Assumptions, and Philosophy Underlying the Analysis of Written Inputs from Public Involvement." Paper presented at the R-6 Forest Service I & E Conference, May 9, 1972.

Hendee, J. C. and R. Harris. "Foresters' Perception of Wilderness -- User Attitudes and Preferences." Journal of Forestry, 68 (1970): 759-762.

Hendee, J. C. and R. M. Lake. "Public Involvement in Resource Decisions: RARE I and II and Their Implications for the Future." In Published Proceedings of the Multiple-Use Management Symposium, Clemson University, 1979, pp. 217-232.

Hendee, J. C. and G. H. Stankey. "Commentary: Applied Social Research Can Improve Public Participation in Resource Decision Making." Rural Sociology, 40,1 (1975): 67-74.

Hendee, J. C., Clark, R. N., and G. H. Stankey. "A Framework for Agency Use of Public Input in Resource Decision-Making." Journal of Soil and Water Conservation, 29, 2 (1974): 60-66.

Hendee, J. C., Clark, R. N., and G. H. Stankey. A Rational Approach for Using Public Inputs in Decision Making. U. S. Forest Service, n. d.

Hendee, J. C. et al. Public Involvement and the Forest Service: Experience, Effectiveness and Suggested Direction. Administrative Study of Public Involvement, U. S. Forest Service, Washington, DC, 1973. 162 p.

Huser, V. "Mediating Forestry Issues: This Three-Pronged Process Holds Great Promise in Resolving Resource Disputes, Including Turf Battles Over Forest Plans." American Forests, 92 (October 1986): 29-34.

Johnson, H. "The Flaws of RARE II." Sierra Club Bulletin, (May-June 1979): 8-10.

Kaplan, R. "Visual Resources and the Public: An Empirical Approach." In Our National Landscape Conference, Nevada, April 1979: Proceedings. U. S. Forest Service, pp. 209-216.

Keaton, G. D. and R. W. Stickel. "Ad Hoc Committee Is Used in Land Planning Study." Journal of Forestry, 73, 11 (1975): 705-708.

Keeny, K. et al. Forest Service -- Public Understanding, A Candid Evaluation: Report of Forest Public Understandings Committee. Northern Region, U. S. Forest Service, 1968. 27 p.

Kelly, G. "Helping to Hold the Soil." American Forests, 89, 1 (1983): 12-15.

Kelly, G. "Helping to Save Endangered Species." American Forests, 88, 11 (1982): 12-15.

Kelly, G. "Quorum in the Woodlot." American Forests, 88, 8 (1982): 12-15.

Kelly, G. "Promise and Compromise on the National Forests." American Forests, 88, 9 (1982): 12-15.

Kelly, G. "Tightrope Act in the National Parks." American Forests, 88, 10 (1982): 12-15.

Kelly, G. "Water: Searching for a Solution in Arizona." American Forests, 89, 2 (1983): 12-15.

Knopp, T. B. and E. S. Caldbeck. "Portraying Choices for Meaningful Public Input to Decision Making." Paper presented at the First National Symposium on Social Science in Resource Management, Corvallis, OR, May 1986.

Koenigs, R. H. "Commitment to Purpose and Expectations of Public Involvement by the Bureau of Land Management." In Proceedings of the Society of American Foresters, National Convention, 1974.

Lake, R. M. Administrative Study of Public Involvement. U. S. Forest Service, 1973.

LaPage, W. F. and P. F. Graves. A Comparison of Participant Satisfaction Among Three Styles of Public Involvement in Forest Service Recreation Policy Making. Northeastern Forest and Range Experiment Station, U. S. Forest Service, 1977.

Lee, R. G. An Administrative Study of the Public Participation Program on the Tongass National Forest: Final Report. Pacific Northwest Forest and Range Experiment Station, Portland, OR, 1982.

Lee, R. G. "Pluralism and Public Participation in Natural Resource Decision Making." Paper presented at the Annual Meetings of the Pacific Sociological Association, San Jose, CA, April 1983. 32 p.

Martin, P. L. "Conflict Resolution Through the Multiple Use Concept in Forest Service Decision-Making." Natural Resources Journal, 9 (April 1969): 228-236.

Mater, J. Citizens Involved: Handle with Care, A Forest Industry Guide to Working with the Public. Forest Grove, OR: Timber Press, 1977. 156 p.

McCann, B. D. "Administrative Environment for Planning: The Case of Statewide Forest Resources Programs in the United States." Resource Management and Optimization, 2, 3 (1983): 205-224.

McCloskey, J. M. "Expectations from Public Involvement by the Sierra Club." In Proceedings of the Society of American Foresters Convention, New York, 1974, pp. 150-153.

Middaugh, G. B. Effectiveness of Selected Forest Service Public Meetings and Implications for Decision Making. Unpublished M.S. thesis. Department of Forest Science, Utah State University, Logan, UT, 1973.

Miller, M. L. and R. P. Gale. "The Sociology of Science in Natural Resource Management Systems: Observations on Forestry and Marine Fisheries." Paper presented at the First National Symposium on Social Science in Resource Management, Corvallis, OR, May 1986.

Miller, W. R. "Judicial Control of Forest Service Discretion under the Multiple-Use Act." Environmental Law, 5, 1 (1974): 127-146.

Mohai, P. "Influence of Public Participation on Forest Service Decisions: Evidence from RARE II." Paper presented at the First National Symposium on Social Science in Resource Management, Corvallis, OR, May 1986.

Nelson, A. W. Jr. "Public Involvement in Public Land Management: Expectations from Public Involvement by the Public." In Proceedings of the Society of American Foresters National Convention, New York, 1974, pp. 154-156.

Nelson, M. M. "The Forest Service in the Seventies." Journal of Soil and Water Conservation, 26 (January-February 1971): 11-14.

Nelson, T. C. "Public Involvement in Forest Service Decision-Making." In Proceedings of the Society of American Foresters National Convention, New York, 1974, pp. 140-143.

Nienaber, J. O. The Politics and Policy of Environmental Decision-Making: A Case Study of the U. S. Forest Service. Coop-Agreement 21-142. Administrative study between University of California, Berkeley and the Pacific Southwest Forest and Range Experiment Station, U. S. Forest Service, 1973.

O'Brien, R. K. Consensus or Conflict: Communication in the Indian Peaks Public Involvement Process. Unpublished M.S. thesis. West Virginia University, Morgantown, WV, 1979. 141 p.

Ogden, D. M. "Wildland Policy Decisions -- By Whom?" Journal of Forestry, 68, 4 (1970): 200-204.

Ostheimer, J. M. The Forest Service Meets the Public: Public Involvement Experiences of the Coconino National Forest. Eisenhower Consortium Bulletin No. 5. Rocky Mountain Forest and Range Experiment Station, U. S. Forest Service, Fort Collins, CO, 1977. 224 p.

Pimlott, D. H. "Editorial: Toward Public Participation in Northern Decisions." Nature Canada, 1, 3 (1972): 2+.

Popovich, L. "Environmentalism and the New Conservatives." American Forests, 89, 3 (1983): 18-22.

Press, M. A. Public Involvement in the USDA Forest Service. Unpublished Master's thesis. University of Calgary, Calgary, Alberta, Canada, 1979. 226 p.

Rahm, N. M. "Public Participation in National Forest Management Decisions." Journal of Forestry, 68, 4 (1970): 205-207.

Randall, C. E. "People Power and Pollution: What Can I Do?" American Forests,76, 10 (1970): 28-36.

Reich, C. A. "The Public and the Nation's Forests." California Law Review, 50, 3 (1962): 381-407.

Reinke, K. B. and B. Reinke. "Public Involvement in Resource Decisions: A National Forest Seeks Public Input for Recreation Development." Journal of Forestry, 71, 10 (1973): 656-658.

Renton, D. A. Preference Representation and Conflict in the U. S. Forest Service. Unpublished Ph. D. dissertation. Colorado State University, Fort Collins, CO,1975. 140 p.

Rich, S. U. (ed.). Public Relations in an Era of Public Involvement -- Challenge for the Timber Industry: Proceedings of a Current Issues Conference, March 1973. Eugene, OR: University of Oregon Press, 1973. 104 p.

Robinson, G. O. The Forest Service: A Study in Public Land Management. Baltimore: Johns Hopkins University Press, 1975. 327 p.

Royer, L. et al. Public Involvement in Public Land Management: An Evaluation of Concepts, Methods and Effectiveness. Department of Forestry and Outdoor Recreation, Utah State University, Logan, UT, October 1975. 47 p.

Salazar, D. J. "Counties, States, and Regulation of Forest Practices." Paper presented at the First National Symposium on Social Science in Resource Management, Corvallis, OR, May 1986.

Sandor, J. A. "Public Involvement in National Forest Management." In C. Rupp et al. The Problems of Park Management in Canada and the U.S.A. Weyerhaeuser Lecture Series. Forestry Association and School of Forestry, Lakehead University, Thunder Bay, Ontario, March 1971, pp. 21-33.

Schoenfeld, C. "Environmentalism: Fad or Fixture?" American Forests, 78, 3 (1972): 17-19.

Schweitzer, D. L. et al. "Ensuring Viable Public Land-Use Decisions: Some Problems and Suggestions." Journal of Forestry, 73, 11 (1975): 705-708.

Searle, R. and P. Dearden. "Preservation Versus Development Conflicts and Assessment of the Role of Values." Paper presented at the First National Symposium on Social Science in Resource Management, Corvallis, OR, May 1986.

Seed, A. H. Jr. "Spirit of the Seventies." American Forests, 76, 4 (1970): 12-15+.

Serino, R. R. A Public Opinion and Reaction Survey in Regard to Off-the-Road Motorized Vehicle Use in the Uwharrie National Forest. Unpublished Master's thesis. Department of Recreation Resources Administration, North Carolina State University, Raleigh, NC, 1973.

Shannon, M. A. Assessing Communication Effectiveness in Developing Forest Plans and EIS Documents. Land and Resource Management Planning, U. S. Forest Service, Washington, DC, 1986.

Shannon, M. A. "Public Participation in Land Management Planning: The Formation of a Social Contract." Paper presented at the First National Symposium on Social Science in Resource Management, Corvallis, OR, May 1986.

Shannon, M. A. "Rationalizing the Forest Service Policy Formation Process: The Integration of Management with Planning, Politics and Law." Paper presented at the First National Symposium on Social Science in Resource Management, Corvallis, OR, May 1986.

Stankey, G. H. "The Use of Content Analysis in Resource Decision Making." Journal of Forestry, 70, 3 (1972): 148-151.

Thulin, S. "Swedish Forestry and the General Public." American Forests, 78, 2 (1972): 8-11+.

Twight, B. W. "Confidence or More Controversy: Whither Public Involvement?" Journal of Forestry, 75, 2 (1977): 93-95.

Twight, B. W. The Tenacity of Value Commitment: The Forest Service and the Olympic National Park. Unpublished Ph. D. dissertation. University of Washington, Seattle, WA, 1971.

Twight, B. W. and M. S. Carroll. "Workshops in Public Involvement: Do They Help Find a Common Ground?" Journal of Forestry, 81, 11 (1983): 732-735.

Twight, B. W. and W. R. Catton Jr. "The Politics of Images: Forest Managers vs. Recreation Publics." Natural Resources Journal, 15, 2 (1975): 297-306.

Twight, B. W. and J. J. Paterson. "Conflict and Public Involvement: Measuring Consensus." Journal of Forestry, 77, 12 (1979): 771-773+.

U. S. Forest Service. Evaluation of the RARE II Public Input Analysis Process. Washington, DC, November 1980.

U. S. Forest Service. Guide to Public Involvement in Decision Making. Rev. Ed. Washington, DC: U. S. Government Printing Office, 1974. 22 p.

U. S. Forest Service. Inform and Involve Handbook. Washington, DC, August 1977. 310 p.

U. S. Forest Service. The Principal Laws Relating to Forest Service Activities. Agriculture Handbook No. 453. Washington, DC, 1978. 359 p.

U. S. Forest Service. Public Participation Handbook. Washington, DC, January 1981.

U. S. Forest Service. State and Private Forestry Learning System: A Quick Reference Guide. Washington, DC: U. S. Government Printing Office, 1983.

Vaux, H. J. "Forest Taxation: A Citizen's Problem." Citizens' Conference on Pacific Northwest Forest Resources, Reed College, 1959.

Wagar, J. A. "Recreational and Esthetic Considerations." In O. P. Cramer (ed.), Environmental Effects of Forest Residues Management in the Pacific Northwest: A State-of-Knowledge Compendium. General Technical Report PNW-24. Pacific Northwest Forest and Range Experiment Station, U. S. Forest Service, Portland, OR, 1974.

Wagar, J. A. and W. S. Folkman. "Public Participation in Forest Management Decisions." Journal of Forestry, 72, 7 (1974): 405-407.

Watkins, C. "The Public Control of Woodland Management." Town Planning Review, 54, 4 (1983): 437-459.

Webster, H. H. "Forest Resource Management and Education -- Pressure, Pain and Constructive Change." Journal of Forestry, 73, 2 (1975): 75-79.

Widman, G. "Expectations from Public Involvement by the Public." In Proceedings of the Society of American Foresters National Convention, New York, 1974, pp. 157-160.

Wilderness Society et al. National Forest Planning: A Conservationist's Guide. Report. Washington, DC, 1983. 121 p.

Willhite, R. G., Bowlus, D. R., and D. Tarbet. "An Approach for Resolution of Attitude Differences Over Forest Management." Environment and Behavior, 5, 3 (1973): 351-366.

Williams, K. L. and J. E. Force. "Public Participation in National Forest Planning." Paper presented at the First National Symposium on Social Science in Resource Management, Corvallis, OR, May 1986.

Williams, K. L. and J. E. Force. Results of a Survey on Public Participation in National Forest Planning Processes. Technical Report 18. Forest, Wildlife and Range Experiment Station, University of Idaho, Boise, ID, 1985. 7 p.

Wilson, D. M. "Trees, Earth, Water and Ecological Upheaval: Logging Practices and Watershed Protection in California." California Law Review, 54, 2 (1966): 1117-1132.

Yannacone, V. J. "People Need Advocates." American Forests, 76, 4 (1970): 21-23+.

Yonts-Shepard, S. and D. J. Blahna. Evaluation of the Collection of Public Input in Forest Service Planning. Public Affairs Office, U. S. Forest Service, Washington, DC, October 1986. 33 p.

Land-Use

Aitken, L. L. Jr. "Public Land Law Review Commission: Public Participation." Rocky Mountain Mineral Law Institute, 13 (1967): 41-64.

Balmer, D. G. "The Use of Advisory Bodies in the Administration of the Public Lands." Appendix B in Public Land Law Review Commission, Organization, Administration, and Budgeting Policy, Vol. II: Appendices. Washington, DC: U.S. Government Printing Office, November 1970, pp. 90-192.

"Beating Developers at Their Own Game." Science News, 109 (January 3, 1976): 5.

Block, W. J. and M. Thullen. Citizen Participation in Land-Use Planning. Agricultural Extension Service, University of North Carolina, Raleigh, NC, 1973.

Bultena, G. L. and D. L. Rogers. "Studies of Public Preferences and Group Interactions to Guide Land Use Planning and Control." In Papers of the Land Use Planning Seminar: Focus on Iowa. Center for Agriculture and Rural Development, Iowa State University, Ames, IA, 1973, pp. 351-375.

Citizen Participation in Growth Management, 2nd Conference on Planning for Growth Management, Honolulu, HI, November 1979: Proceedings. Office of Council Services, Honolulu City Council, 1980. 72 p.

Connor, D. M. "Design Options for Public Involvement in Land Management." Paper presented at the First National Symposium on Social Science in Resource Management, Corvallis, OR, May 1986.

Culhane, P. Public Lands Politics: Interest Group Influence on the Forest Service and the Bureau of Land Management. Baltimore, MD: Johns Hopkins University Press, 1981.

Erickson, D. L., Cordell, H. K., and A. C. Davis. "Public Land Policy: An Evaluation of Decision and Citizen Involvement Systems." Journal of Environmental Management, 5 (October 1977): 365-377.

Fisher, A. C. and J. V. Krutilla. "Managing the Public Lands: Assignment of Property Rights and Valuation of Resources." In E. T. Haefele (ed.), The Governance of Common Property Resources. Baltimore, MD: Johns Hopkins University Press, 1974, pp. 35-59.

Godschalk, D. Citizen Participation in Environment/Land Use Management. Washington, DC: Center for Responsive Governance, 1980.

Godschalk, D. R. Evaluating Public Participation in Environment/Land Use Management: Strategies and Lessons. Department of City and Regional Planning, University of North Carolina, Chapel Hill, NC, January 1980.

Harris, T. D. Guidelines for Public Participation in Federal Land Use Planning. Extension Service, Oregon State University, Corvallis, OR, 1981. 18 p.

Henning, D. H. "The Public Land Law Review Commission: A Political and Western Analysis." Idaho Law Review, 7 (Spring 1970): 77-85.

"Interest Representation and the Federal Land Policy and Management Act." Michigan Law Review, 80 (May 1982): 1303-1325.

Irland, L. C. "Citizen Participation: A Tool for Conflict Management on the Public Lands." Public Administration Review, 35, 3 (1975): 263-269.

Irland, L. C. and J. R. Vincent. "Citizen Participation in Decision Making: A Challenge for Public Land Managers." Journal of Range Management, 27, 3 (1974):182-185.

Kelly, G. "Championing Prime Farmlands." American Forests, 88, 7 (1982): 12-15.

Koenigs, R. H. "Commitment to Purpose and Expectations of Public Involvement by the Bureau of Land Management." In Proceedings of the Society of American Foresters, National Convention, 1974.

Lassey, W. R. and C. P. Ditwiler. "Public Involvement in Federal Land Use Planning." Environmental Law, 5, 3 (1975): 643-659.

Landstrom, K. S. "Citizen Participation in Public Land Decisions." St. Louis Law Review, 9 (Spring 1965): 372-389.

Logan, C. J. Winning the Land-Use Game: A Guide for Developers and Citizen Protesters. New York: Praeger, 1982. 199 p.

McCormick, J. R., Shaffer, R., and M. Gorham. Land Use Planning and Citizen Involvement: The Case of Maple Grove, Wisconsin. Extension Service, University of Wisconsin, Madison, WI, 1975.

Mock, B. H. "Public Land Policy and the Public Land Law Review Commission." In P. O. Foss (ed.), Public Land Policy. Boulder, CO: Colorado University Associated Press, 1970, pp. 57-70.

Montjor, R. S. Citizen Participation in Land-Use Governance. Cooperative Extension Service, Virginia Polytechnic Institute and State University, Blacksburg, VA, 1977.

Public Technology. Land Management: A Technical Report on Selected Participatory Techniques for State and Local Governments. PB 281 314. National Technical Information Service, Springfield, VA, 1977. 64 p.

Reimers, M. A. Involving the Public in the Land Planning of the Rock Creek Drainage. Unpublished Masters thesis. Department of Natural Resources, Cornell University, Ithaca, NY, 1973.

Royer, L. et al. Public Involvement in Public Land Management: An Evaluation of Concepts, Methods and Effectiveness. Department of Forestry and Outdoor Recreation, Utah State University, Logan, UT, October 1975. 47 p.

Sax, A. and B. Brundage. Holding Our Ground: A Directory of Citizens' Efforts to Preserve Farmland in Illinois. Herrin, IL: Illinois South Project, Inc., 1982.

Sewell, W. R. D. "Perceptions, Attitudes and Public Participation in Countryside Management in Scotland." Journal of Environmental Management, 2, 3 (1974): 235-257.

Shaffer, R. E. "Citizen Involvement in Land Use Planning: A Tool and an Example." Journal of Soil and Water Conservation, 30, 5 (1974): 211-214.

Stoddard, C. H. "Public Participation in Public Land Decisions." In P. O. Foss (ed.), Public Land Policy. Boulder, CO: Colorado University Associated Press, 1970, pp. 71-82.

Susskind, L. E. "Citizen Involvement in Growth Management and Local Land Use Planning." In Land Use/Growth Management National Conference, San Francisco, CA,March 1979: Proceedings. Golden Gate University, pp. 90-102.

Susskind, L. E. The Importance of Citizen Participation and Consensus-Building in the Land Use Planning Process. Laboratory of Architecture and Planning, Massachusetts Institute of Technology, Cambridge, MA, 1978.

Thelander, A. L. "Citizen Participation in Land and Water Use." Acta Sociologica, 24, 4 (1981): 321-329.

Thomsen, A. L. Public Participation in Water and Land Management. Technical Report 57. Cornell University, Ithaca, NY, January 1973. 194 p.

Tossett, O. Land, Water, and People. St. Paul, MN: Soil Conservation Districts Foundation, Inc., 1961.

Wald, J. et al. "Public Use and Abuse, and Input in Decision Making in the Grazing Issue." In Grazing and Riparian/Stream Ecosystems Symposium, Denver, CO, November 1978: Proceedings. Trout Unlimited, pp. 61-67.

White, L. G. "Approaches to Land Use Policy." American Planning Association Journal, 45, 1 (1979): 62-71.

Natural Resources Action

Allen, R. How to Save the World: Strategy for World Conservation. Totowa, NY: Barnes and Noble Books, 1980. 150 p.

Caldwell, L. K., Hayes, L. R., and I. M. MacWhirter. Citizens and the Environment: Case Studies in Popular Action. Bloomington, IN: Indiana University Press, 1976. 449 p.

Coan, G. (ed.). Sierra Club Political Handbook: Tools for Action. 5th ed. San Francisco: Sierra Club, 1979. 76 p.

League of Women Voters. Overview of Citizen Participation. WRIS Technical Bulletin No. 17. Washington State Department of Ecology, Olympia, WA, December 1975.

Logan, C. J. Winning the Land-Use Game: A Guide for Developers and Citizen Protesters. New York: Praeger, 1982. 199 p.

McConnell, G. "The Failures and Successes of Organized Conservation." In R. Nash (ed.), Environment and Americans: The Problem of Priorities. New York: Holt, Rinehart, and Winston, 1972, pp. 45-53.

McCluney, W. R. (ed.). The Environmental Destruction of South Florida: A Handbook for Citizens. Coral Gables, FL: University of Miami Press, 1969.

Mohai, P. "Public Concern and Elite Involvement in Environmental-Conservation Issues." Social Science Quarterly, 66, 4 (1985): 820-838.

Reeves, M. B. "The Politics of Making Conservation Happen: A Panel Discussion." Journal of Soil and Water Conservation, 37, 5 (1982): 259-268.

Robertson, J. and J. Lewallen. The Grass Roots Primer. San Francisco: Sierra Club, 1975.

Selznick, P. T.V.A. and the Grass Roots. New York: Harper and Row, 1966.

Stokes, B. "Helping Ourselves." Futurist, 15 (August 1981): 44-51.

Stokes, B. Helping Ourselves: Local Solutions to Global Problems. New York: Norton, 1981. 160 p.

U. S. Citizens' Advisory Committee on Environmental Quality. Citizens Make the Difference: Case Studies of Environmental Action. Washington, DC: U. S. Government Printing Office, 1973. 71 p.

U. S. Department of the Interior. It's Your World: The Grass Roots Conservation Story. Conservation Yearbook No. 5. Washington, DC: U. S. Government Printing Office, 1969.

Natural Resources Management

Allen, D. R. "The Problem of Standing to Sue and Public Involvement in Federal Resources Management." Natural Resources Lawyer, 74, 7 (1974): 87-95.

Alston, R. M. and D. M. Freeman. "The Natural Resources Decision Maker as Political and Economic Man: Toward a Synthesis." Journal of Environmental Management, 3, 3 (1975): 167-183.

Clark, R. N. and D. H. Stankey. "Analyzing Public Input to Resource Decisions: Criteria, Principles and Case Examples of the Codinvolve System." Natural Resources Journal, 16, 1 (1976): 213-236.

Clark, R. N., Stankey, G. H., and J. C. Hendee. An Introduction to Codinvolve: A System for Analyzing, Storing, and Retrieving Public Input to Resource Decisions. Research Note PNW-223. Pacific Northwest Forest and Range Experiment Station, U. S. Forest Service, Portland, OR, 1974. 16 p.

Erickson, D. L. "Public Involvement in Resource Agency Decision-Making." Journal of Soil and Water Conservation, 35, 5 (1980): 224-229.

Folkman, W. S. Public Involvement in the Decision-Making Process of Natural Resource Management Agencies with Special Reference to the Pacific Northwest. Public Affairs Paper No. 3. Institute of Government Research, Seattle, WA, June 1973. 29 p.

Freeman, A. M. III. "Advocacy and Resource Allocation Decisions in the Public Sector." Natural Resources Journal, 9, 2 (1969): 166-175.

Fulton, J. K. Development and Evaluation of Citizen Participation Techniques for Inland Lake and Shoreland Management. Huron River Watershed Council, Ann Arbor, MI, 1971.

Haefele, E. T. (ed.). The Governance of Common Property Resources. Baltimore, MD: Johns Hopkins University Press, 1974. 181 p.

Harrington, J. T. and B. A. Frick. "Opportunities for Public Participation in Administrative Rulemaking." Natural Resources Lawyer, 15, 3 (1983): 537-567.

Henning, D. H. "Natural Resources Administration and the Public Interest." Public Administration Review, 30, 2 (1970): 134-140.

Henning, D. H. "The Politics of Natural Resources Administration." Annals of Regional Science, (December 1968): 239-247.

Kiely-Brocato, K. A. et al. "An Attitude Matrix Scaling System with Relevance for Resource Management." Journal of Environmental Management, 10, 1 (1980): 71-81.

Leitch, J. A. and D. F. Scott. Public Participation in Natural Resource Decision Making. Department of Agricultural Economics, North Dakota State University , Fargo, ND, 1977. 13 p.

Lord, W. B. and M. L. Warner. "Aggregates and Externalities: Information Needs for Public Natural Resources Decision Making." Natural Resources Journal, 13, 1(1973): 106-117.

Potter, H. R. Citizen Participation in Natural Resources Decision-Making: Conceptual Issues and Approaches. Department of Sociology, Purdue University, West Lafayette, IN, 1978.

Ryan, M. P. "The Role of Citizen Advisory Boards in the Administration of Natural Resources." Oregon Law Review, 50 (Winter 1971): 153-177.

Tester, F. J. "Northern Renewable Resources Management: Socio-Psychological Dimensions of Participation." In Association of Canadian Universities for Northern Studies, Banff, Alberta, May 1981: Proceedings, pp. 190-197.

Wandesforde-Smith, G. "The Bureaucratic Response to Environmental Politics." In A. E. Utton and D. H. Henning (eds.), Environmental Policy. New York: Praeger, 1973, pp. 76-85.

Natural Resources Planning

Cortner, H. J. et al. "Uses of Public Opinion Surveys in Resource Planning." Environmental Professional, 6 (1984): 265-275.

Dravniecks, D. and D. C. Pitcher. Public Participation in Resource Planning: Selected Literature Abstracts. Management Science Staff, U. S. Forest Service, Berkeley, CA, April 1981. 77 p.

Greenhalgh, R. Improving Public Involvement in USDA Natural Resource Planning. Working Paper No. 15. NRE Economic Research Service, U. S. Department of Agriculture, Washington, DC, 1976. 12 p.

Institute for Environmental Studies. A Case Study of Citizen Participation in Resource Planning: The Crawford County Critical Resource Information Workshop. IES Report No. 44. University of Wisconsin, Madison, WI, 1975. 61 p.

Sewell, W. R. D. "Integrating Public Views in Planning and Policymaking." In W.R. D. Sewell and I. Burton (eds.), Perceptions and Attitudes in Resources Management. Ottawa, Canada: Department of Energy Mines and Resources, 1971, pp. 125-131+.

U. S. Army Corps of Engineers. Proceedings of the Social Scientists Conferences, Vol. 1: Social Aspects of Comprehensive Planning. Institute for Water Resources, Fort Belvoir, VA, December 1977. 287 p.

Wallace, L. T. et al. "Citizen Options for Resource Planning." Planning, 39, 7(1973): 23-24.

Parks, Recreation, and Wildlife

Alden, H. R. "Citizen Involvement in Gravel Pit Reclamation: A Case Study." In Wildlife Values of Gravel Pits Symposium, Crookston, MN, June 1982: Proceedings. University of Minnesota, Minneapolis, MN, 1982, pp. 95-101.

Allen, B. and M. H. Haefele (eds.). In Defense of Rivers: A Citizens Workbook on Impacts of Dam and Canal Projects. Delaware Valley Conservation Association, Stillwater, NJ, 1976. 190 p.

American Rivers Conservation Council. How to Save Your River: A Citizens Guide to Water Projects. Washington, DC, n. d. 8 p.

Balsamo, V. M. (ed.). Management of Small Lakes Programs Symposium: Local Self Reliance, Barrington, IL, 1982. Springfield, IL: Illinois Department of Energy and Natural Resources, 1982. 108 p.

Banes, R. E. "Maximizing Human Resources." Parks and Recreation, 10, 2 (1975):27-29.

Bromley, D. W. and V. L. Arnold. "Social Goals, Problem Perception and Public Intervention: The Fishery." San Diego Law Review, 7, 3 (1970): 469-487.

Citizens Committee for the Outdoor Recreation Resources Review Commission Report. Action for Outdoor Recreation for America. Washington, DC, 1964. 37 p.

Conservation Foundation. National Parks for the Future: An Appraisal of the National Parks as They Begin Their Second Century in a Changing America. Washington, DC, 1972. 254 p.

Cormick, G. W. and J. McCarthy. Environmental Mediation: Flood Control, Recreation and Development in the Snoqualmie River Valley. Social Science Institute, Washington University, St. Louis, MO, 1974.

Dearden, P. "Public Participation and Scenic Quality Analysis." Landscape Planning, 8, 1 (1981): 3-19.

Diamant, R. Citizen's Guide to River Conservation. Washington, DC: Conservation Foundation, 1984. 124 p.

Duttweiler, M. W. "Use of Questionnaire Surveys in Forming Fishery Management Policy." Transactions of the American Fisheries Society, 105 (1976): 232-239.

Fulton, J. K. Development and Evaluation of Citizen Participation Techniques for Inland Lake and Shoreland Management. Ann Arbor, MI: Huron River Watershed Council, 1971.

Gillette, E. "The Making of a Wild and Scenic River." Sierra Club Bulletin, 60, 8 (1975): 15-19.

Grima, A. P. "Public Participation in Great Lakes Management: An Overview." In R. McCalla (ed.), Coastal Studies in Geography. Occasional Papers in Geography No. 4. St. Mary's University, Halifax, Canada, 1980, pp. 62-80.

Hackman, A. "Shaping a Future for Ontario Parks: The Protagonists." Seasons, 22, 2 (1982): 26-34.

Hoole, A. F. "Public Participation in Park Planning: Riding Mountain Case." Canadian Geographer, 22, 1 (1978): 41-50.

"How to Help Plan Parks." National Parks and Conservation Magazine, 52, 3 (1978): 15-18.

"How to Save a River." Senior Scholastic, 105 (January 16, 1973): 4-7.

Kaplan, R. "Citizen Participation in the Design and Evaluation of a Park." Environment and Behavior, 12 (December 1980): 494-507.

Kasperson, R. E. "Political Behavior and the Decisionmaking Process in the Allocation of Water Resources Between Recreational and Municipal Use." Natural Resources Journal, 9, 2 (1969): 176-211.

Kelly, G. "Helping to Save Endangered Species." American Forests, 88, 11 (1982): 12-15.

Kelly, G. "Pioneer Park." American Forests, 88, 6 (1982): 12-15.

Klessig, L. L. "The Means and Ends of Public Participation." In Lake Restoration: Proceedings of a National Conference, August 1978, Minneapolis, MN. Office of Water Planning and Standards, U. S. Environmental Protection Agency, March 1979, pp. 27-31.

Langenau, E. E. "Organizational and Political Factors Affecting State Wildlife Management." Wildlife Society Bulletin, 12, 2 (1984): 107-116.

Lee, J. M. Jr. Citizen Participation in Wildlife Management Decision Making: The Squirrel Hunting Season as an Example. Unpublished Masters thesis. Virginia Polytechnic Institute and State University, Blacksburg, VA, 1972. 163 p.

Line, L. (ed.). What We Save Now: An Audubon Defense Primer. New York: Houghton Mifflin, 1973.

Lorenz, J. "Recreational Fishing." EPA Journal, 7 (May 1981): 30-32.

McCabe, R. "How to Save a Marsh." Journal of Environmental Education, 4, 1 (1972): 40-42.

National Association of Counties. County Action for Outdoor Recreation. Washington, DC, 1964. 48 p.

National Parks and Conservation Association. Citizen's Action Guide to the National Park System. Washington, DC, 1979. 23 p.

Ogden, D. M. "The Politics of Conservation: Establishing the Redwood National Park." In R. S. Ross (ed.), Public Choice and Public Policy: Seven Cases in American Government. Chicago, IL: Markham Pub. Co., 1971, pp. 81-109.

Paish, H. An Appraisal of the Contribution that National and Provincial Wildlife Organizations Could Make to "Man and the Land." H. Paish and Associates, Vancouver, B. C., Canada, October 1970.

Paish, H. Public Involvement in "Man and the Land": A Preliminary Appraisal for British Columbia. H. Paish and Associates, Vancouver, B. C., Canada, July 1970.

River Conservation Fund. Flowing Free: A Citizen's Guide for Protecting Wild and Scenic Rivers. Washington, DC, 1977. 76 p.

Rasch, D. L., Stoffle, R. W., and F. V. Jensen. "Urban Sports Anglers and Lake Michigan Fishery Policies." Coastal Zone Management Journal, 10, 4 (1983): 407-428.

Ross, J. E., Elfring, C. A., and W. R. Clingan. Community Attitudes and Political Environments in Relation to Lake Harvesting Programs: The Life and Times of Lake Wingra. IES Report 109. Center for Biotic Systems, Institute for Environmental Studies, University of Wisconsin, Madison, WI, 1980. 58 p.

Schectman, S. M. "The 'Bambi Syndrome': How NEPA's Public Participation in Wildlife Management Is Hurting the Environment." Environmental Law, 8, 2 (1978): 611-653.

Sefton, D. F. "Volunteer Lake Monitoring: Citizen Action to Improve Lakes." In 3rd Lake and Reservoir Management Conference, Knoxville, TN, October 1983: Proceedings, U. S. Environmental Protection Agency and North American Lake Management Society, pp. 473-477.

Shanklin, J. F. "Outdoor Recreation Planning: Behind Closed Doors?" American Forests, 78, 9 (1972): 6-7.

Simison, H. E. Oregonians Restore the Willamette: Joint Citizen, State, and Federal Efforts Clean River Waters. U. S. Environmental Protection Agency, Washington, DC. 2 p.

Sullivan, M. "The Little Town that Could." Conservation News Reprint. National Wildlife Federation, Washington, DC, January 1977.

Starbird, E. A. "A River Restored: Oregon's Willamette." National Geographic,1414 (June 1972): 816-836.

Resource Development

Aradeon, D. "Public Learning and Participation in the Development Process." Habitat International, 7, 5-6 (1983): 385-394.

Bailey, J., Bacigalupi, L. and M. Warner. Local Citizens Participation in Coal Development. Foundation for Urban and Neighborhood Development, Denver, CO, 1975.

Beckman, N. and L. Dworsky. "New Views on Public Responsibility for Resources Development: Jurisdictions, Consequences, and Remedies." In New Horizons for Resources Research: Issues and Methodology. Boulder, CO: University of Colorado Press, 1965, pp. 101-119.

Briggs, M. J. and M. L. Moss. Community Decisionmaking and Energy Exploration: The Pacific Palisades Conflict. Sea Grant Program, University of Southern California, Los Angeles, 1973.

Cann, B. R. Social Values Analysis for the Red Mountain Planning Unit. Resource Development Internship Program, Western Interstate Commission of Higher Education, Boulder, CO, 1976. 82 p.

Cohen, J. M. and N. T. Uphoff. Rural Development Participation: Concepts and Measures for Project Design, Implementation and Evaluation. Rural Development Committee, Cornell University, Ithaca, NY, 1977.

Environmental Policy Institute. The Strip Mine Handbook: A Citizens Guide to the New Federal Surface Mine Law: How to Use It to Protect Your Community and Yourself. Washington, DC, 1978. 107 p.

Erickson, E. E. and D. E. Moore. "Rural Development, Human Resources, and Leadership." Journal of Soil and Water Conservation, 29, 1 (1974): 20-22.

Galloway, L. T. and T. FitzGerald. "The Surface Mining Control and Reclamation Act of 1977: The Citizen's 'Ace in the Hole.'" Northern Kentucky Law Review, 8, 2 (1981): 259-276.

Gerlach, L. P. "Citizen Resistance to Energy Development in the Upper Midwest and Northern Tier States." Paper presented at the Annual Manager's Conference of the Rural Electric Cooperative Association, Louisville, KY, August 1976. 15 p.

Heberlein, T. A. Principles of Public Involvement. Staff Paper Series in Rural and Community Development. Extension Service, University of Wisconsin, Madison, WI, April 1976.

Murray, F. X. (ed.). Where We Agree: Summary and Synthesis. Report of the National Coal Policy Project. Boulder, CO: Westview Press, 1978.

Parfit, M. Last Stand at Rosebud Creek: Coal, Power, and People. New York: Dutton, 1980. 304 p.

Plesuk, B. The Only Game in Town: Public Involvement in Cold Lake. Alberta Environment, Canada, July 1981.

Robadue, D. D. Jr., and V. K. Tippie. "Public Involvement in Offshore Oil Development: Lessons from New England." Coastal Zone Management Journal, 7, 2-4 (1980): 237-270.

Talbot, A. R. Power Along the Hudson: The Storm King Case and the Birth of Environmentalism. New York: Dutton, 1972.

Templeton, C. H. "The Great Pipeline Debate of 1977: People Participation." In B. Sadler (ed.), Involvement and Environment: Proceedings of the Canadian Conference on Public Participation. Vol. 1: A Review of Issues and Approaches. Edmonton, Alberta, Canada: Environment Council of Alberta, 1978, pp. 165-173.

U. S. Department of Housing and Urban Development. Rapid Growth from Energy Projects: Ideas for State and Local Action. Washington, DC, 1976.

Western Interstate Nuclear Board. Plowshare Technology Assessment: Implications to State Governments. Lakewood, CO, 1973. 100 p.

Resource Recycling

Antunes, G. E. and G. Halter. "The Politics of Resource Recovery, Energy Conservation, and Solid Waste Management." Administration and Society, 8, 1 (1976): 55-77.

Copeland, V. S. "Recycling Success in Canada: 80% Participation!" Waste Age, 15, 11 (1984): 38-.

DeYoung, R. "Motivating People to Recycle: The Use of Incentives." Resource Recycling, 3, 2 (1984): 14-15+.

Eidson, B. Recycling in Your Community: A Guide to Make It Happen. Fresno County Economic Opportunities Commission, Fresno, CA, 1979. 81 p.

Engelhardt, A. L. How to Run a Community Recycling Center: A Resource Guide to Low-Technology Recycling in Illinois. Illinois Department of Energy and Natural Resources, Springfield, IL, 1982.

"Expanding Roles of State Recycling Associations." Resource Recycling, 1, 4 (1982): 16-19.

Friend, G. "Bronx Redevelopment Program Based on Value of Compost." Environmental Action Bulletin, 7, 23 (1976): 2-3.

Humphrey, C., Harris, G. R., and S. H. Mann. "Sociological Aspects of Waste Paper Recovery." Journal of Environmental Systems, 8, 2 (1978): 111-126.

League of Women Voters. Curbing Trash. Publication No. 147. LWV Education Fund, Washington, DC, 1977. 6 p.

Seldman, N. N. "Citizen and Institutional Participation in Resource Conservation and Recovery." In Appropriate Technology in Resource Conservation and Recovery Symposium, Atlanta, GA, October 1979: Proceedings. American Society of Civil Engineers, pp. 60-90.

Sullivan, M. "Good News in Garbage." Conservation News Reprint. National Wildlife Federation, Washington, DC, June 1976.

Water Resources

Ahmed, R. and L. E. Johnson. "Public Involvement in Water Resources Planning." In United River Basin Management Symposium: Proceedings, Atlanta, GA, October 1981. American Water Resources Association, 1981, pp. 183-199.

Albert, H. E. and D. N. Hall. Private Sector Reaction to Normal Political Institutional Procedures and Outcomes When Water Is an Issue. Report No. PB223 375. National Technical Information Service, Springfield, VA, June 1973. 290 p.

Allee, D. J. (ed.). The Role of Public Involvement in Water Resources Planning and Development. Report No. 79. Water Resources and Marine Sciences Center, Cornell University, Ithaca, NY, 1974. 160 p.

Allee, D. J. "Translating Theory into Action." In Proceedings of a Conference on Water Resources Planning and Public Opinion, University of Nebraska, Lincoln, NB, 1971, pp. 39-44.

Allen, B. and M. H. Haefele (eds.). In Defense of Rivers: A Citizens Workbook on Impacts of Dam and Canal Projects. Delaware Valley Conservation Association, Stillwater, NJ, 1976. 190 p.

Allen, C. M. and J. C. Killick. "Autocracy or Democracy? Public Involvement in Water Resources Planning." In Hydrology and Water Resources Symposium, Perth, Australia, September 1979: Proceedings. Australia Institute of Engineer, 1979, pp. 23-27.

American Rivers Conservation Council. How to Save Your River: A Citizens Guide to Water Projects. Washington, DC, n. d. 8 p.

Andrews, W. H. and D. C. Geertsen. Social Dimensions of Urban Flood Control Decisions. Institute for Social Science Research on Natural Resources, Utah State University, Logan, UT, 1974. 69 p.

Ashton, P. M. "Accountability of Public Water Agencies: Legal Institutions for Public Interaction." In J. M. Stewart (ed.), Proceedings: Conference on Public Participation in Water Resources Planning and Management. Raleigh, NC: North Carolina Water Resources Institute, North Carolina State University, 1974, pp. 51-75.

Axworthy, L. "Notes on Public Participation." In P. Bonner and R. Shimizu (eds.), Proceedings of a Workshop on Public Participation. Windsor, Ontario: International Joint Commission, Great Lakes Research Advisory Board, 1975, pp. 17-24.

Badyk, M., Roschlau, M., and A. Litterick. Public Involvement in Water Resource Management. Experience '78 Research Report. Library, Ontario Ministry of the Environment, Toronto, Canada, 1978.

Balsamo, V. M. (ed.). Management of Small Lakes Programs Symposium: Local Self Reliance, Barrington, IL, 1982. Springfield, IL: Illinois Department of Energy and Natural Resources, 1982. 108 p.

Bartal, K. A. and L. V. Gutierrez Jr. "Comprehensive Water Quality Management Planning." Journal of Hydraulics Division ASCE, 101, 4 (1975): 371-386.

Baumann, N., Ervin, O., and G. Reynolds. "The Policy Delphi and Public Involvement Programs." Water Resources Research, 18, 4 (1982): 721-728.

Beatty, K. M. and J. C. Pierce. "Representation and Public Involvement in Water Resource Politics: A Comparison of Six Participant Types." Water Resources Bulletin, 12, 5 (1976): 1005-1017.

Beatty, K. M. et al. "Water Resource Politics and Interest Group Tactics." Water Resources Bulletin, 14, 2 (1978): 394-403.

Behan, R. W. "Parapolitics and Resource Management in the Corps of Engineers, or What to Do While Waiting for the Sierra Club to Arrive." Paper presented to U. S. Army Corps of Engineers Park Managers Seminar, Fresno, CA, October 1974.

Berger, B. B. and C. O. Fisher. "Citizen Review Committee -- An Evaluation." In Report of the Citizen Review Committee on the Comprehensive Water-Related Land Resources Investigation. A Report to the New England River Basins Commission, Boston, MA, February 1971, Appendix I.

Bishop, A. B. Public Participation in Water Resources Planning. Report No. IWR 70-7. Institute for Water Resources, U. S. Army Corps of Engineers, Alexandria, VA, 1970. 109 p.

Bishop, A. B. Structuring Communications Programs for Public Participation in Water Resources Planning. Report 75-2. Institute for Water Resources, U. S. Army Corps of Engineers, Alexandria, VA, May 1975. 143 p.

Biswas, A. K. "Socio-Economic Considerations in Water Resources Planning." Water Resources Bulletin, 9, 4 (1973): 746-754.

Board of Engineers for Rivers and Harbors. Manual for Water Resource Planners. U. S. Army Corps of Engineers, Fort Belvoir, VA, 1980.

Borton, T. E. and K. P. Warner. "Involving Citizens in Water Resources Planning: The Communication-Participation Experiment in the Susquehanna River Basin." Environment and Behavior, 3, 3 (1971): 284-306.

Borton, T. E., Warner, K. P., and J. W. Wenrich. The Susquehanna Communication- Participation Study: Selected Approaches to Public Involvement in Water Resources Planning. Report No. IWR 70-6. Institute for Water Resources, U. S. Army Corps of Engineers, Alexandria, VA, December 1970. 128 p.

Botts, L. "Citizen Views on Water Recycling and Reuse." In 2nd National Conference on Complete Water Reuse: Water's Interface with Energy, Air and Solids, Chicago, 1975: Proceedings, pp. 104-128.

Bowen, G. T. and T. Gangaware. Institutional Barriers to Implementing 208 Water Quality Management Plans in the Southeast: Institutional Barriers. Vol. 1. Report No. PB 82-153537. National Technical Information Service, Springfield, VA, May 1981. 193 p.

Bowen, G. T. and T. Gangaware. Institutional Barriers to Implementing 208 Water Quality Management Plans in the Southeast: Issues, Problems, and Data. Vol. 2. Report No. PB 82-153545. National Technical Information Service, Springfield, VA, May 1981. 194 p.

Bracken, D. D. Trends in Environmental Law Related to Water Resources Planning. PB224 824/3WP. National Technical Information Service, Springfield, VA, September 1973. 123 p.

Bromley, D. W. et al. An Evaluation of Public Participation in the Upper Rock River Basin Survey. University of Michigan, Ann Arbor, MI, 1971.

Brown, C., Monks, J. G., and J. R. Park. Decision Making in Water Resource Allocation. Lexington, MA: Lexington Books, 1973.

Brown, C. A. "The Central Arizona Water Control Study: A Case for Multiobjective Planning and Public Involvement." Water Resources Bulletin, 20, 3 (1984): 331-337.

Bruvold, W. H. "Public Participation in Environmental Decisions: Water Reuse." Public Affairs Report, 22 (February 1981): 1-6.

Bruvold, W. H. and J. Crook. "Public Participation in the Adoption of Wastewater Reclamation Projects." In Water Reuse Symposium, Washington, DC, March 1979: Proceedings. American Water Works Association Research Foundation, 1979, pp. 1066-1074.

Bultena, G. L. Community Values and Collective Action in Reservoir Development. ISWRRI-69. Iowa State Water Resources Research Institute, Iowa State University, Ames, IA, 1975. 184 p.

Bultena, G. L. "Dynamics of Agency-Public Relations in Water Resource Planning." In D. R. Field et al. (eds.), Water and Community Development: Social and Economic Perspectives. Ann Arbor, MI: Ann Arbor Science Publishers,1974, pp. 125-149.

Bultena, G., Rogers, D., and V. Webb. Public Response to Planned Environmental Change: A Study of Citizens' Views and Actions on the Proposed Ames Reservoir. Sociology Report 106. Department of Sociology and Anthropology, Iowa State University, Ames, IA, January 1973. 108 p.

Burke, R. and J. P. Heaney. Collective Decisionmaking in Water Resource Planning. Lexington, MA: D. C. Health and Co., 1975.

Burke, R., Heaney, J. P., and E. E. Pyatt. "Water Resources and Social Choices." Water Resources Bulletin, 9, 3 (1973): 433-447.

Canada Inquiry on Federal Water Policy. Hearing about Water: A Synthesis of Public Hearings. Report. Ottawa, Canada, April 1985. 75 p.

Carlson, K. T. "The People's Lake." Environment, 17, 2 (1975): 16-20+.

Chevalier, M. and T. J. Cartwright. "Public Involvement in Planning: The Delaware River Case." In W. R. D. Sewell and I. Burton (eds.), Perceptions and Attitudes in Resources Management. Ottawa, Canada: Information Canada, 1971.

Clarke, F. J. "Interdisciplinary Planning to Meet Environmental Needs." Engineering Issues, 98, PP4 (1972): 497-503.

Clement, T. M. Jr., Lopez, G., and P. T. Mountain. Engineering a Victory for Our Environment: A Citizens' Guide to the U. S. Army Corps of Engineers. EPA Report CPE-R-7000054. Institute for the Study of Health and Society, Washington, DC, 1972. 420 p.

Connor, D. M. "Public Participation." In D. W. Hendricks et al. (eds.), Citizen Participation in Environmental Design and Public Projects. Fort Collins, CO: Water Resource Publications, 1975, pp. 575-605.

Conservation Foundation. "Developing the Nation's Water Resources -- A Study of Public Planning." CF Letter, 1-71 (January 1971): 1-16.

Cook, H. N. "Nourishing Public Participation." Water Spectrum, 3, 3 (1971): 7-11.

Copp, H. D. More Responsive Water Planning Is Possible. Bulletin No. 330. Engineering Extension Service, Washington State University, Pullman, WA, March 1973. 81 p.

Cormick, G. W. and J. McCarthy. Environmental Mediation: Flood Control, Recreation and Development in the Snoqualmie River Valley. Social Science Institute, Washington University, St. Louis, MO, 1974.

Cornell University. Study of Water Resource Public Decision Making. Report No. PB219 593/1. National Technical Information Service, Springfield, VA, December 1971. 45 p.

Creighton, J. L. Public Involvement Manual: Involving the Public in Water and Power Resources Decisions. U. S. Department of the Interior, Water and Power Resources Service, Washington, DC, January 1980. 333 p.

Creighton, J. L. "The Use of Values: Public Participation in the Planning Process." In G. A. Daneke et al. (eds.), Public Involvement and Social Impact Assessment. Boulder, CO: Westview Press, 1983, pp. 143-160.

Creighton, J. L., Priscoli, J. D., and C. M. Dunning. Public Involvement Techniques: A Reader of Ten Years Experience at the Institute for Water Resources. Report 82-R1. Institute for Water Resources, U. S. Army Corps of Engineers, Fort Belvoir, VA, 1983.

Crisp, H. W. "Successful Citizen Participation Methods for Wastewater Collection and Treatment Programs." Water Science and Technology, 13, 6 (1981): 1-9.

Crusberg, C. C. et al. "The Water Quality Resource Study Group: An Interdisciplinary Community Effort in Worcester, Massachusetts." Environmental Professional, 5, 2 (1983): 162-167.

Curran, T. "Water Resources Management in the Public Interest." Water Resources Bulletin, 7, 1 (1971): 33-39.

Curran, T. P. and T. W. King Jr. "NEPA and the State's Role in Water Resources Management." Water Resources Bulletin, 10, 1 (1974): 127-136.

Dahlgren, C. W. Public Participation in Planning: A Multi-Media Course. Center for Advanced Planning, Institute for Water Resources, U. S. Army Corps of Engineers, Alexandria, VA, 1972.

Daneke, G. A. "Public Involvement in Natural Resources Development: A Review of Water Resource Planning." Environmental Affairs, 6, 1 (1977): 11-31.

Daneke, G. A. and J. D. Priscoli. "Social Assessment and Resource Policy: Lessons from Water Planning." Natural Resources Journal, 19 (April 1979): 359-375.

David, E. L. Public Participation in Decision Making. Sea Grant Technical Report No. 26. School of Natural Resources, University of Michigan, Ann Arbor, MI, March 1972. 13 p.

Davis, A. C. "Information Response and Interaction-Dialogue Aspects of Public Participation." In J. M. Stewart (ed.), Proceedings: Conference on Public Participation in Water Resources Planning and Management, June 1974. Raleigh, NC: Water Resources Research Institute, University of North Carolina, 1974, pp. 19-50.

Davis, A. C. Public Participation in Water Pollution Control Policy and Decision Making. Report No. 88. Water Resources Research Institute, University of North Carolina, Raleigh, NC, December 1973. 66 p.

Davis, A. C., Anderson, J., and R. Gough. Alternative Information and Interaction Approaches to Public Participation in Water Resources Decisionmaking: A State-of-the-Arts Report. Report No. 106. Water Resources Research Institute, University of North Carolina, Raleigh, NC, 1975. 40 p.

Day, H. J. et al. "River Clean-Up Plan Developed with Citizens and Industry." Civil Engineering-ASCE, 50, 3 (1980): 78-81.

Diamant, R. Citizen's Guide to River Conservation. Washington, DC: Conservation Foundation, 1984. 124 p.

Dodge, B. H. "Achieving Public Involvement in the Corps of Engineers, Water Resources Planning." Water Resources Bulletin, 9, 3 (1973): 448-454.

Doerksen, H. R. and J. C. Pierce. "Citizen Influence in Water Policy Decisions: Context, Constraints, and Alternatives." Water Resources Bulletin, 11, 5 (1975): 959-964.

Dreyfus, D. A. "Competing Values in Water Development." Journal of Hydraulics Division ASCE, 99, 9 (1973): 1599-1604.

Dunn, D. F. Jr. "Public Participation in Environmental Design of Flood Control Channels." Paper presented at the ASCE Water Engineering Meeting, Atlanta, January 1972.

Dworsky, L. B., Allee, D. J., and S. C. Csallandy (eds.). Social and Economic Aspects of Water Resources Development. Ithaca, NY: Water Resources and Marine Science Center, Cornell University, 1972.

Dysart, B. C. "Education of Planners and Managers for Effective Public Participation." In J. M. Stewart (ed.), Proceedings: Conference on Public Participation in Water Resources Planning and Management, June 1974. Raleigh, NC: Water Resources Research Institute, University of North Carolina, 1974, pp. 77-127.

Dysart, B. C. Public Participation in Water and Waste-Water Planning. Department of Environmental Systems Engineering, Clemson University, Clemson, SC, 1975. 33 p.

Eaton, D. J. "Developing Regional Water Systems in the Netherlands." American Water Works Association Journal, 77, 6 (1985): 70-72.

Edgmon, T. D. "A Systems Resource Approach to Citizen Participation: The Case of the Corps of Engineers." Water Resources Bulletin, 15, 5 (1979): 1341-1352.

Edson, L. J. "Project ZAP." Field and Stream, 77 (March 1973): 16+.

Edwards, P. R. "A Public Involvement Strategy." Water Spectrum, 6, 3 (1974): 34-40.

Ellis, R. A. and J. F. Disinger. "Project Outcomes Correlate with Public Participation Variables." Journal of the Water Pollution Control Federation, 53, 11 (1981): 1564-1567.

Ertel, M. O. "Identification of Training Needs for Public Participation Responsibilities." Water Resources Bulletin, 16, 2 (1980): 300-304.

Entel, M. O. The Role of Citizen Advisory Groups in Water Resources Planning. Water Resources Research Institute, University of Massachusetts, Amherst, MA, July 1974.

Ertel, M. O. "The Role of Citizen Advisory Groups in Water Resources Planning." Water Resources Bulletin, 15 (December 1979): 1515-1523.

Ertel, M. O. "A Survey Research Evaluation of Citizen Participation Strategies." Water Resources Research, 15, 4 (1979): 757-762.

Esogbue, A. O. "A Fuzzy-Sets Model for Measuring the Effectiveness of Public Participation in Water Resources Planning." Water Resources Bulletin, 18, 3 (1982): 451-456.

Estrin, D. "Public Hearings: Comments on Their Use and Effectiveness." In P. Bonner and R. Shimizu (eds.), Proceedings of a Workshop on Public Participation. Windsor, Ontario, Canada: International Joint Commission, Great Lakes Research Advisory Board, 1975, pp. 45-50.

Ferrara, T. C. and K. M. Romstad. "Public Participation in Urban Water Planning." Journal of the Urban Planning and Development Division ASCE, (December 1971): 179-190.

Field, D. R., Barron, J. C., and B. F. Long. Water and Community Development: Social and Economic Perspectives. Ann Arbor, MI: Ann Arbor Science Publishers,1974. 302 p.

"Fishbowl Planning in Practice." Civil Engineering, 42, 9 (1972): 55.

Flanigan, F. H. "Case History of Citizen Participation in the EPA Chesapeake Bay Program." In Eastern Water and Energy Conference, Pittsburgh, May 1982: Proceedings. American Society of Civil Engineers, 1982, pp. 212-217.

Fohs, L. H. "Eliciting Public Participation." American Water Works Association Journal, 73, 5 (1981): 246-250.

Foley, C. O. (ed.). Techniques and Strategies for Public Involvement in the Water Resources Planning Process: Workshop Proceedings. Board of Engineers for Rivers and Harbors, U. S. Army Corps of Engineers, May 1971.

Fox, I. K. "Policy Problems in the Field of Water Resources." In A. Kneese and S. C. Smith (eds.), Water Research. Baltimore: Johns Hopkins Press, 1966, pp. 271-289.

Friedlander, J. M. and L. Cecil. "Converting the Boneyard from a Filthy Drainage Ditch to a Community Asset." In 3rd National Conference on Water Reuse, Cincinnati, OH, June 1976: Proceedings, pp. 298-304.

Froehlich, D. S. "Citizen Groups and Environmental Goals." Journal of Water Resources Planning and Management Division ASCE, 107, 1 (1981): 113-119.

Fulton, J. K. Development and Evaluation of Citizen Participation Techniques for Inland Lake and Shoreland Management. Ann Arbor, MI: Huron River Watershed Council, 1971.

Fusco, S. M. "Public Participation in Environmental Statements." Journal of Water Resource Planning and Management Division ASCE, 106, 1 (1980) 123-129.

Gannon, J. E. and M. S. Gold. "Grass-Roots Water Quality Protection." Water Spectrum, 13, 3 (1981): 18-23.

Gillette, E. "The Making of a Wild and Scenic River." Sierra Club Bulletin, 60, 8 (1975): 15-19.

Glasser, R., Manty, D., and G. Nehman. "Public Participation in Water Resources Planning." Paper presented at the International Water Resources Association Conference, UNESCO, Paris and Strasbourg, France, March 1975.

Godschalk, D. R. and B. Stiftel. "Making Waves: Public Participation in State Water Planning." Journal of Applied Behavioral Science, 17, 4 (1981): 597-614.

Godschalk, D. R. and B. Stiftel. Public Participation in Statewide 208 Water Quality Planning in North Carolina: An Evaluation. Report No. 155. Water Resources Research Institute, University of North Carolina, Raleigh, NC, 1980.

Goldman, S. J. et al. "Achieving Local Support for Surface Runoff Management in the San Francisco Bay Area." In Stormwater Management Alternatives Conference, Wilmington, October 1979: Proceedings, pp. 255-272.

Gordon, W. A Citizen's Handbook on Groundwater Protection. Natural Resources Defense Council, New York, 1984.

Greater Egypt Regional Planning and Development Commission. Areawide Waste Treatment and Water Quality Management Planning: Public Participation Activities. Carbondale, IL, 1980.

Grima, A. P. "Analyzing Public Inputs to Environmental Planning: A Summary and Discussion of Public Involvement in Great Lakes Management." In G. A. Daneke et al. (eds.), Public Involvement and Social Impact Assessment. Boulder, CO: Westview Press, 1983, pp. 111-119.

Grima, A. P. "Public Participation in Great Lakes Management: An Overview." In R. McCalla (ed.), Coastal Studies in Geography. Occasional Papers in Geography No. 4. St. Mary's University, Halifax, Canada, 1980, pp. 62-80.

Grima, A. P. "Shaping Water Quality Decisions: An Evaluation of a Public Consultation Programme." Water International, 8, 3 (1983): 120-126.

Grima, A. P. "The Utilization of Public Input in Water Quality Management: A Case Study and Discussion." In W. R. D. Sewell and M. L. Barker (eds.), Water Problems and Policies. Department of Geography, University of Victoria, Victoria, Canada, 1980, 173-186.

Grima, A. P. and C. Wilson-Hodges. "Regulation of Great Lakes Water Levels: The Public Speaks Out." Journal of Great Lakes Research, 3, 3-4 (1977): 240-257.

Groat, G. L. "Planning and Selecting Sites for Water Storage Facilities." Water and Sewage Works, 124, 9 (1977): 111-116.

Hampe, G. D. "Correlates of Public Participation in Public Meetings of the Corps of Engineers." Paper presented at the 12th Annual American Water Resources Conference, Chicago, IL, September 20-21, 1976.

Hanchey, J. R. Effective Public Participation in Federal Water Resources Planning. U. S. Army Corps of Engineers, New Orleans, LA, 1970.

Hanchey, J. R. Public Involvement in the Corps of Engineers Planning Process. IWR Research Report 75-R4. Institute for Water Resources, U. S. Army Corps of Engineers, Fort Belvoir, VA, October 1975. 44 p.

Harris, D. H. "The Human Dimensions of Water Resources Planning." Human Factors, 19, 3 (1977): 241-251.

Harris, E. S. "To Clean a Harbor." In Citizens Advisory Committee on Environmental Quality, Citizens Make the Difference: Case Studies of Environmental Action. Washington, DC, January 1973, pp. 27-34.

Haveman, R. H. Water Resources Investment and the Public Interest. Nashville, TN: Vanderbilt University Press, 1965.

Havlick, S. W. "The Construction of Trust: An Experiment in Expanding Democratic Processes in Water Resource Planning." Water Spectrum, 1, 2 (1970): 13-19.

Heilman, C. B. "Join Forces with John Q. Public." Water and Wastes Engineering, 16, 7 (1979): 26-.

Hendee, J. C. et al. "Methods for Acquiring Public Input." In J. C. Pierce and H. R. Doerksen (eds.), Water Politics and Public Involvement. Ann Arbor, MI: Ann Arbor Science Publishing Inc., 1976, pp. 125-144.

Herz, M. J. "The Use of Citizen Volunteer Groups for Marine Environmental Monitoring and Surveillance." In Ocean 75 Conference, San Diego, September 1975: Proceedings, IEEE and Marine Technology Society, pp. 697-699.

Hickman, G. L. "Incorporating the Environmental Quality Dimension in Planning River Management." In 40th North American Wildlife and Natural Resources Conference, Pittsburgh, PA, March 1975: Proceedings, pp. 264-272.

Hoelscher, J. "Public Participation at the State and Local Level: Where the Action Is!" In Eastern Water and Energy Conference, Pittsburgh, PA, May 1982: Proceedings, American Society of Civil Engineers, pp. 225-230.

"How to Save a River." Senior Scholastic, 105 (January 16, 1973): 4-7.

Hrezo, M. S. and W. J. Howe. Social Feasibility as an Alternative Approach to Water Resource Planning. Bulletin No. 149. Virginia Polytechnic Institute and State University Water Resources Research Center, Blacksburg, VA, 1985. 59 p.

Huang, J. "Toward the Goal of Direct Water Reuse: What Should We Do Next?" In Water Reuse Symposium, Washington, DC, March 1979: Proceedings, Vol. 1, American Water Works Association Research Foundation, pp. 260-268.

Hudspeth, T. R. Citizen Participation in Revitalization of the Burlington, Vermont Waterfront. Environmental Program, University of Vermont, Burlington, VT, 1982. 267 p.

Hudspeth, T. R. "Visual Preference as a Tool for Facilitating Citizen Participation in Urban Waterfront Revitalization." Journal of Environmental Management, 23, 4 (1986): 373-385.

Ibsen, C. A. and J. Ballweg. Public Perception of Water Resource Problems. Bulletin 29. Water Resources Research Center, Virginia Polytechnic Institute, Blacksburg, VA, 1969.

Ingram, H. "The Changing Decision Rules in the Politics of Water Development." Water Resources Bulletin, 8, 6 (1972): 1177-1188.

Ingram, H. "Patterns of Politics in Water Resources Development." Natural Resources Journal, 11, 1 (1971): 102-118.

Janisse, M. P., Perlman, D., and R. P. Perry. "Water Resource Management: A Psychological Perspective." In The Allocative Conflicts in Water Resources Management. Agassiz Center for Water Studies, University of Manitoba, Winnipeg, Canada, 1974, pp. 465-486.

Johnson, W. K. "Approaches for Developing Alternatives in Planning." Water Resources Bulletin, 10, 5 (1974): 1017-1022.

Kamieniecki, S. Public Representation in Environmental Policymaking: The Case of Water Quality Management. Boulder, CO: Westview Press, 1980.

Kasperson, R. E. "Political Behavior and the Decisionmaking Process in the Allocation of Water Resources Between Recreational and Municipal Use." Natural Resources Journal, 9, 2 (1969): 176-211.

Kauffman, K. G. "A Perspective on Public Involvement in Water Management Decision Making." Water Resources Management, 37, 5 (1977): 467-471.

Keene, J. and A. L. Strong. "The Brandywine Plan." Journal of the American Institute of Planners, 36, 1 (1970): 50-58.

Kelly, G. "Water: Searching for a Solution in Arizona." American Forests, 89, 2 (1983): 12-15.

Kicklighter, K. L. and R. Spitzer. "Public Participation in State NPDES Enforcement: Questionable Basis, Good Policy." Journal of Environmental Law, 6, 2 (1980): 185-215.

Klessig, L. L. "The Means and Ends of Public Participation." In Lake Restoration: Proceedings of a National Conference, August 1978, Minneapolis, MN. Office of Water Planning and Standards, U. S. Environmental Protection Agency, March 1979, pp. 27-31.

Klessig, L. L. and N. W. Bouwes. "Assessing the Socioeconomic Impacts of Lake Improvement Projects." Environmental Professional, 6, 3-4 (1984): 235-246.

Korsching, P. F. and P. J. Nowak. "Potential Contributions by Sociologists." In Water Resources Research: Problems and Potentials for Agriculture and Rural Communities. Soil Conservation Society of American Report, 1983, pp. 203-222.

Krauss, A. P. "Design Involvement Leads to Public Acceptance." Water and Wastes Engineering, 16, 11 (1979): 50-52.

Lane, P. H. "Nontechnical Problems in Urban Area Dam Construction." American Water Works Association Journal, 68, 3 (1976): 143-146.

League of Women Voters, Washington, DC. The following is a partial list of reports by the League on water issues in addition to those cited below:

    Lake Erie: Requiem or Reprieve?
    Man and the River.
    The Ohio River Basin.
    Red River of the North.
    So You'd Like to Do Something About Water Pollution.

League of Women Voters Education Fund. The Big Water Fight: Trials and Triumphs in Citizen Action Problems of Supply, Pollution, Floods, and Planning Across the U. S. A. Brattleboro, VT: Stephen Greene Press, 1966.

League of Women Voters. Seventh Land and Water Seminar: Citizens Seminar on Land and Water for Tomorrow in the Snake River Basin. Education Fund, Washington, DC, 1971. 53 p.

League of Women Voters. SOCs in Drinking Water: A Community Guide. Publication No. 532. Education Fund, Washington, DC, 1980. 4 p.

Leiffer, N. Public Involvement from a Public Perspective: An Approach to Public Involvement in Water Planning. Helena, MT: Department of Natural Resources and Conservation, February 1974.

Leitko, T. A. Issues, Interests and Power: Environmental Politics in the Community Setting. Report No. PB 291 338. National Technical Information Service, Springfield, VA, June 1977. 202 p.

Leopold, L. B. "Let's Sing 'Auld Lang Syne' for the Upper Brandywine." Natural History, 79, 6 (1970): 4-17.

Lombardo, P. "Appropriate Wastewater Management Planning for Small Communities." Compost Science / Land Utilization, 20, 6 (1979): 16-19.

Lord, W. B. "Water Resources Planning: Conflict Management." Water Spectrum, (Summer 1980): 1-10.

Lord, W. B. et al. Conflict Management in Federal Water Resources Planning. Institute of Behavioral Science, University of Colorado, Boulder, CO, 1978.

Lorenz, J. "Recreational Fishing." EPA Journal, 7 (May 1981): 30-32.

Lovrich, N. P. et al. "Policy Relevant Information and Public Attitudes: Is Public Ignorance a Barrier to Nonpoint Pollution Management?" Water Resources Bulletin, 22, 2 (1986): 229-236.

Ludtke, R. L. et al. Social and Economic Considerations for Water Resource Planning in the Park Subbasin, North Dakota. Research Report No. 2. University of North Dakota, Grand Forks, ND, February 1971.

MacDonald, D. V., Barney, K. P., and S. F. Jones. "Procedures for the Evaluation of Engineering Alternatives." Water Resources Bulletin, 13, 3 (1977): 583-598.

Males, R. M. Design of Prototype Mass Media Programs for Testing in the Lower James River Basin: Comprehensive Water Quality Management Study: State Water Control Board, Report PB 233 433/2WP, National Technical Information Service, Springfield, VA, February 1974. 29 p.

Mason, R. J. "Public Concerns and PLUARG: Selected Findings and Discussion." Journal of Great Lakes Research, 6, 3 (1980): 210-222.

Mattoon, J. "Public Affairs: An Essential Ingredient in Pollution Response." In Pollution Response Conference, St. Petersburg, FL, May 1979: Proceedings, U. S. Fish and Wildlife Service, pp. 146-150.

Mazmanian, D. A. Citizen Participation in Water Resources Planning. Washington, DC: Center for Responsive Governance, 1980.

Mazmanian, D. A. "Participatory Democracy in a Federal Agency." In J. Pierce and H. Doerksen (eds.), Water Politics and Public Involvement. Ann Arbor, MI: Ann Arbor Science Publishers Inc., 1976, pp. 201-223.

Mazmanian, D. A. and J. Nienaber. Can Organizations Change?: Environmental Protection, Citizen Participation, and the Corps of Engineers. Washington, DC: Brookings Institution, 1979. 220 p.

Mazmanian, D. A. and J. Nienaber. "Prospects for Public Participation in Federal Agencies: The Case of the Army Corps of Engineers." In J. Pierce and H. Doerksen (eds.), Water Politics and Public Involvement. Ann Arbor, MI: Ann Arbor Science Publishers Inc., 1976, pp. 225-247.

McCracken, C. Public Involvement in the Management of the Great Lakes. Unpublished B. A. thesis. Department of Geography, University of Toronto, Toronto, Canada, 1978. 72 p.

McGarry, R. S. "Public Involvement: Advantages and Disadvantages from the Viewpoint of an Engineer." In Eastern Water and Energy Conference, Pittsburgh, PA, May 1982: Proceedings, American Society of Civil Engineers, pp. 219-224.

McGrath, D. C. Jr. "Multidisciplinary Environmental Analysis: Jamaica Bay and Kennedy Airport." Journal of the American Institute of Planners, 37, 4 (1971): 243-252.

McKenzie, L. (ed.). The Grass Roots and Water Resources Management. Report No.10. Water Resources Center, Washington State University, Pullman, WA, July 1972. 156 p.

McNulty, H. "Public Support for Water Conservation: The League Experience." In Water Conservation and Municipal Wastewater Flow Reduction National Conference, Chicago, November 1978: Proceedings, U. S. Environmental Protection Agency, pp. 139-144.

Milbrath, L. W. An Extra Dimension of the Representation in Water Quality Planning: A Survey Study of Erie and Niagara Counties, New York, 1976. Occasional Paper No. 1. Environmental Studies Center, State University of New York, Buffalo, NY, January 1977.

Milbrath, L. W. "Incorporating the Views of the Uninterested but Impacted Public in Environmental Planning." Policy Studies Journal, 8, 6 (1980): 913-920.

Milbrath, L. W. "Using Environmental Beliefs and Perception to Predict Trade-Offs and Choices Among Water Quality Plan Alternatives." Socio-Economic Planning Sciences, 14, 3 (1980): 129-136.

Miller, W. H. "Environmental Impact Statements: Effect on Water Resources Projects." In American Water Works Association 95th Annual Conference, Minneapolis, MN, June 1975: Proceedings, pp. 26a-30a.

Mitchell, B. "Behavioral Aspects of Water Management: A Paradigm and a Case Study." Environment and Behavior, 3, 2 (1971): 135-154.

Monks, J. G. "Water Resource Decision Making: How Effective Is the Public Input?" In Institute of Environmental Sciences Conference, Anaheim, CA, April 1973: Proceedings, pp. 345-350.

Morley, C. G. "Public Participation: A Right to Decide." In The Allocative Conflicts in Water Resources Management. Agassiz Center for Water Studies, University of Manitoba, Winnipeg, Canada, 1974, pp. 509-524.

Nash, J. M. "The Fox: He Stalks the Wild Polluter." Business and Society Review, 11 (Autumn 1974): 11-13.

National Association of Counties Research Foundation. Community Action Program for Water Pollution Control. Washington DC: U. S. Government Printing Office, 1961.

Odell, R. The Saving of San Francisco Bay: A Report on Citizen Action and Regional Planning. Washington, DC: Conservation Foundation, 1972.

O'Mara, C. W. Getting in the Swim: How Citizens Can Influence Water Quality Planning -- Community Guide. Publication No. 188. League of Women Voters Education Fund, Washington, DC, 1977. 6 p.

Oregon State University, Water Resources Research Institute. Public Participation in Willamette Valley Environmental Decisions. Report No. PB 220 953/4. National Technical Information Service, Springfield, VA, April 1973. 152 p.

O'Reilly, D. "Dissension on Deck." Environmental Action, 10, 6 (1978): 4-8.

Organization for Economic Cooperation and Development. Water Management and the Environment. OECD Report 89771. Paris, 1973. 68 p.

O'Riordan, J. "The Public Involvement Program in the Okanagan Basin Study." Natural Resources Journal, 16, 1 (1976): 177-196.

Ortolano, L. "A Process for Federal Water Planning at the Field Level." Water Resources Bulletin, 10, 4 (1974): 766-778.

Ortolano, L. "Water Plan Ranking and the Public Interest." Journal of Water Resources Planning and Management Division ASCE, 102, 1 (1976): 35-48.

Ortolano, L. Water Resources Decision Making on the Basis of the Public Interest. IWR Report 75-1. Institute for Water Resources, U. S. Army Corps of Engineers, Fort Belvoir, VA, February 1975. 59 p.

Ortolano, L. and T. P. Wagner. Alternative Approaches to Water Resources Impact Evaluation. Draft Report. Institute for Water Resources, U. S. Army Corps of Engineers, Fort Belvoir, VA, 1973.

Ortolano, L. and T. P. Wagner. "Field Evaluation of Some Public Involvement Techniques." Water Resources Bulletin, 13, 6 (1977): 1131-1139.

Paluszek, J. L. "Water Quality and the Public Policy Process." Paper presented at the Water Pollution Control Federation 14th Annual Government Affairs Seminar, Washington, DC, March 1980. 17 p.

Pankowski, T. "Let's Revitalize Water Planning." Water Spectrum, 4, 1 (1972): 23-29.

Peavy, J. R. The Who of "To Whosoever They May Accrue": Identification of Publics In Water Resource Planning. Unpublished Special Problem Master paper, Georgia Institute of Technology, Atlanta, GA, 1974.

Petersen, M. S. "Morrison Creek Stream Group Basin." In C. R. Goldman (ed.), Environmental Quality and Water Development. San Francisco: W. H. Freeman and Co., 1973.

Phaler, K. "Water Quality Control in California: Citizen Participation in the Administrative Process." Ecology Law Quarterly, 1, 2 (1971): 400-425.

Phillips, K. J. "Citizen Participation in the York River Basin Study: Use of a Value Trade-Offs Questionnaire." Journal of Environmental Systems, 6, 3 (1977): 243-252.

Pierce, J. "Water Resource Preservation: Personal Value and Public Support." Environment and Behavior, 11 (1979): 147-161.

Pierce, J. C. and H. R. Doerksen. "Citizen Advisory Committees: The Impact of Recruitment on Representation and Responsiveness." In J. C. Pierce and H. R. Doerksen (eds.), Water Politics and Public Involvement. Ann Arbor, MI: Ann Arbor Science Publishing Inc., 1976, pp. 249-266.

Pierce, J. C. and H. R. Doerksen. Public Attitudes Toward Water Allocation in the State of Washington: Citizens, Interest Groups, and Agencies. Report PB 249 740. National Technical Information Service, Springfield, VA, November 1975. 170 p.

Pierce, J. C. and H. R. Doerksen (eds.). Water Politics and Public Involvement. Ann Arbor, MI: Ann Arbor Science Publishing Inc., 1976. 294 p.

Pierce, J. C., Lovrich, N. P. Jr., and A. K. Cook. The Allocation of Water to Instream Flows: Idaho Water Resources Management. Final Report. Office of Water Research and Technology, U. S. Department of the Interior, 1980.

Plumlee, J. P., Starling, J. D., and K. W. Kramer. "Citizen Participation in Water Quality Planning: A Case Study of Perceived Failure." Administration and Society, 16, 4 (1985); 455-473.

Potter, H. R. Participation in Water Resources Planning: Leader and Non-Leader Comparisons. Report PB80-156128, National Technical Information Service, Springfield, VA, February 1980. 40 p.

Potter, H. R. and H. J. Norville. Perceptions of Effective Public Participation in Water Resources Decision Making and Their Relationships to Levels of Participation. Technical Report No. 115. Water Resources Research Center, Purdue University, West Lafayette, IN, January 1979. 42 p.

"Preserving a Treasure." EPA Journal, 8 (September 10, 1982): 20-21.

Price, J. E. and L. Ortolano. "Bureau of Reclamation Planning: Environmental Factors." Journal of Water Resources Planning and Management Division ASCE, 107,1 (1981): 27-43.

Priscoli, J. D. "Beyond Public Hearings: Suggestive Techniques for Public Participation in a Transnational Resource Management Environment." In P. Bonner and R. Shimizu (eds.), Proceedings of a Workshop on Public Participation. Windsor, Ontario, Canada: International Joint Commission, Great Lakes Research Advisory Board, 1975, pp. 51-62.

Priscoli, J. D. "The Citizen Advisory Group as an Integrative Tool in Regional Water Resources Planning." In G. A. Daneke et al. (eds.), Public Involvement and Social Impact Assessment. Boulder, CO: Westview Press, 1983, pp. 79-87.

Priscoli, J. D. "Citizen Advisory Groups and Conflict Resolution in Regional Water Resources Planning." Water Resources Bulletin, 2, 6 (1975): 1233-1243.

Priscoli, J. D. "Integrating Social Analysis in Water Resources Planning: Some Emerging Trends in the Corps of Engineers." Water Resources Bulletin, 13 (October 1977): 953-958.

Priscoli, J. D. Public Participation in Level B Regional Water Resources Planning: A Preliminary View. Special Consulting Report. Water Resources Council, Washington, DC, Fall 1974.

Priscoli, J. D. Why the Federal and Regional Interest in Public Involvement in Water Resources Development. Working Paper 78-1. Institute for Water Resources, U. S. Army Corps of Engineers, Fort Belvoir, VA, January 1978.

Ragan Associates. The Water Pollution Control Act of 1972: Institutional Assessment -- Public Participation. Report PB 245 410. National Technical Information Service, Springfield, VA, October 1975. 278 p.

Ragan, J. The Nuts and Bolts of Public Participation in Water Quality Planning: Skills Workbook. Pacific Palisades, CA: James Ragan Associates, 1978.

Ragan, J. F. Jr. Public Participation in Water Resource Planning: An Evaluation of the Programs of 15 Corps of Engineers Districts. IWR Report 75-6. Institute for Water Resources, U. S. Army Corps of Engineers, Fort Belvoir, VA, 1975. 219 p.

Rastatter, C. L. (ed.). Municipal Wastewater Management: Public Involvement Activities Guide. Report No. EPA 430/9-79-005. Office of Water Program Operations, U. S. Environmental Protection Agency, Washington, DC, 1979.

Rastatter, C. L. (ed.). Municipal Wastewater Treatment: Citizen's Guide to Facility Planning. Washington, DC: U. S. Environmental Protection Agency, 1979. 263 p.

Reid, B. and G. Speth. Water Pollution Control Handbook: Citizens' Guide to the Federal Water Pollution Control Amendments of 1972. Project Clean Water, Natural Resources Defense Council, New York, NY, March 1973. 19 p.

Rickson, R. E. et al. Role of the Scientist/Technician in Water Policy Decisions at the Community Level: A Study in Purposive Communication. Bulletin 79. Water Resources Research Center, University of Minnesota, Minneapolis, MN, 1975. 51 p.

River Conservation Fund. Flowing Free: A Citizen's Guide for Protecting Wild and Scenic Rivers. Washington, DC, 1977. 76 p.

Robbins, R. L. "Organizing for Involvement: Citizen Participation Groups in Great Lakes Decisions." In B. Sadler (ed.), Involvement and Environment. Vol. 2. Edmonton, Canada: The Environment Council of Alberta, 1979, pp. 8-23.

Rosener, J. B. Citizen Participation in Southeast Florida: An Army Corps Experiment. Graduate School of Management, University of California, Irvine, CA, 1980.

Rosener, J. B. The Sanibel General Permit Process: An Evaluation. Institute for Water Resources, U. S. Army Corps of Engineers, Fort Belvoir, VA, August 1979.

Ross, C. R. "Decision-Making at Local, State, Federal, and International Levels." In C. R. Goldman et al. (eds.), Environmental Quality and Water Development. San Francisco: W. H. Freeman, 1973, pp. 398-412.

Ross, J. E., Elfring, C. A., and W. R. Clingan. Community Attitudes and Political Environments in Relation to Lake Harvesting Programs: The Life and Times of Lake Wingra. IES Report 109. Center for Biotic Systems, Institute for Environmental Studies, University of Wisconsin, Madison, WI, 1980. 58 p.

Ross, P. J. "Education of Publics for Participation in Water Resource Policy and Decision Making." In J. M. Stewart (ed.), Proceedings of the Conference on Public Participation in Water Resources Planning and Management. North Carolina Water Resource Research Institute, North Carolina State University, Raleigh, NC, June 1974, pp.129-164.

Ross, P. J., Spencer, B. G., and J. H. Peterson Jr. Public Participation in Water Resources Planning and Decision Making Through Information-Education Programs: A State-of-the-Arts Study. Water Resources Research Institute, Mississippi State University, Starkville, MS, 1974. 46 p.

Sargent, H. L. "Fishbowl Planning Immerses Pacific Northwest Citizens in Corps Planning." Civil Engineering, 42, 9 (1972): 54-57.

Sargent, H. L. (ed.). State Water Planning: How Can the Public Participate?: Proceeding of the Western Regional Extension Committee on Natural Resources and Environmental Policies, January 1971. Publication No. IV, Boise, ID.

Schafer, A. "Citizen Participation." In The Allocative Conflicts in Water Resources Management. Agassiz Center for Water Studies, University of Manitoba, Winnipeg, Canada, 1974, pp. 487-508.

Schierow, L. J. and G. Chesters. "Enhancing the Effectiveness of Public Participation in Defining Water Resource Policy." Water Resources Bulletin, 19, 1 (1983): 107-114.

Schlaht, T. F. Public Relations in Water Resources Planning. Professional Development Division, Board of Engineers for Rivers and Harbors, Washington, DC, May 1970.

Schmidtman, W. H. "The Role of the Concerned Citizen." In L. McKenzie (ed.). The Grass Roots and Water Resources Management. Report No. 10. Water Resources Center, Washington State University, Pullman, WA, July 1972.

Sefton, D. F. "Volunteer Lake Monitoring: Citizen Action to Improve Lakes." In 3rd Lake and Reservoir Management Conference, Knoxville, TN, October 1983: Proceedings, U. S. Environmental Protection Agency and North American Lake Management Society, pp. 473-477.

Segree, C. R. "Public Participation: Boon or Boondoggle?" Journal of the Water Pollution Control Federation, 51, 5 (1979): 880-883.

Sellevold, R. P. Case Study: Public Involvement in Planning. Seattle District Corps of Engineers, Seattle, WA, 1971.

Shepard, W. B. and D. J. Doubleday. Political Efficiency and Political Effectiveness in Water-Related Policy Areas. Water Resources Research Institute, Oregon State University, Corvallis, OR, 1977.

Sherman, R. H. "Achieving a Social Presence in Corps Planning." In Proceedings of the Social Scientists Conference, Vol.2: Flood Control Planning. Institute for Water Resources, U. S. Army Corps of Engineers, Fort Belvoir, VA, 1977, pp. 152-159.

Silberman, E. "Public Participation in Water Resource Development." Journal of Water Resources Planning and Management Division ASCE. 103, 1 (1977): 111-122.

Simison, H. E. Oregonians Restore the Willamette: Joint Citizen, State, and Federal Efforts Clean River Waters. U. S. Environmental Protection Agency, Washington, DC. 2 p.

Sinclair, G. W. and B. P. Hayley. The Public Involvement Program: Background Working Paper No. 2. Office of the Study Director, Okanagan Study Committee, March 1973.

Sinclair, M. An Evaluation of the I. J. C. Public Hearings. Canada Center for Inland Waters, Burlington, Ontario, Canada, 1974.

Sinclair, M. A Follow-Up Study to Evaluate the I. J. C.'s 1974 Hearings. Canada Center for Inland Waters, Burlington, Ontario, Canada, 1976.

Singg, R. N. and B. R. Webb. "Use of Delphi Methodology to Assess Goals and Social Impacts of a Watershed Project." Water Resources Bulletin, 15 (February 1979): 136-143.

Smith, C. Public Participation in Willamette Valley Environmental Decisions. Water Resources Research Institute, Oregon State University, Corvallis, OR, 1973.

Smith, D. F. "Changing Public Opinion: Problems and Prospects." In Proceedings of a Conference on Water Resources Planning and Public Opinion, March 1971, Water Resources Research Institute, University of Nebraska, pp. 49-59.

Stakhiv, E. Z. "Washington Metropolitan Area Water Supply Study: People, Planning, and Programs." In American Water Works Association 96th Annual Conference: Water Supply Management, Resources and Operations, New Orleans, June 1976, Vol. 1.

Starbird, E. A. "A River Restored: Oregon's Willamette." National Geographic,1414 (June 1972): 816-836.

Stokey, S. R. "Citizen Participation: Regional Experiences." Paper presented at the American Society of Civil Engineers Water Resources Engineering Meeting, Atlanta, January 1972.

Study Committee, Canada-British Columbia-Okanagan Basin Agreement. The Public Involvement Program. Preliminary Study Data Bulletin No. 8, June 1972.

Tabita, A. "Implications of Public Involvement in Water Resource Planning" Paper presented at the American Society of Civil Engineers Water Resources Engineering Meeting, Atlanta, January 1972.

Teniere-Buchot, P. F. "The Role of the Public in Water Management Decisions in France." Natural Resources Journal, 16, 1 (1976): 159-176.

Thelander, A. L. "Citizen Participation in Land and Water Use." Acta Sociologica, 24, 4 (1981): 321-329.

Thompson, P. "Brandywine Basin: Defeat of an Almost Pefect Plan." Science, 163 (March 14, 1969): 1180-1182.

Thomsen, A. L. Public Participation in Water and Land Management. Technical Report 57. Cornell University, Ithaca, NY, January 1973. 194 p.

Tinkham, L. A. "The Public's Role in Decision-Making for Federal Water Resources Development." Water Resources Bulletin, 10, 4 (1974): 691-696.

Toner, N. C. "Guidelines for Planning a Citizen Participation Program." In Water Conservation and Municipal Wastewater Flow Reduction National Conference, Chicago, November 1978: Proceedings, U. S. Environmental Protection Agency, pp. 112-122.

Tucker, R. C. "Planners as a 'Public' in Water Resources Public Participation Programs." Water Resources Bulletin, 8, 2 (1972): 257-265.

U. S. Army Corps of Engineers. Proceedings of the Social Scientists Conferences, Vol. 1: Social Aspects of Comprehensive Planning. Institute for Water Resources, Fort Belvoir, VA, December 1977. 287 p.

U. S. Army Corps of Engineers. Public Brochure: Alternatives and Their Pros and Cons, Small Boat Harbors Elliot Bay, Seattle Harbor. Seattle District, Seattle, WA. 57 p.

U. S. Army Corps of Engineers. Water Resources Policies and Authorities: Public Participation in Water Resources Planning. Circular No. 1165-2-100. Fort Belvoir, VA, May 1971.

U. S. Army Corps of Engineers. West Coast Deepwater Port Facilities Study, Appendix F: Public Participation. August 1973.

U. S. Army Engineers. Planning, Public Involvement: General Policies. Report No. ER-1105-2-800. Office of the Chief of Engineers, Washington, DC, January 1975.

U. S. Department of Energy. Public Information: Water Resources Planning and Management: Abstracts of Papers and Reports. Washington, DC, 1973.

U. S. Environmental Protection Agency. Engineering a Victory for Our Environment: A Citizens Guide to the U. S. Army Corps of Engineers. Washington, DC: U. S. Government Printing Office, 1972.

U. S. Environmental Protection Agency. The Metro Story: How Citizens Cleaned Up Lake Washington. Washington, DC, 1972. 2 p.

U. S. Environmental Protection Agency. Public Participation Handbook for Water Quality Management. Washington, DC, June 1976.

U. S. General Accounting Office. Federal, State, Local, and Public Roles in Constructing Waste Water Treatment Facilities. Report RED-65-45. Washington, DC, December 1975. 51 p.

U. S. Office of Water Research and Technology. Public Participation in Water Resource Development: A Bibliography. Report No. 76-205. Washington, DC, August 1976. 172 p.

Varma, C. V. "Public Participation of Water Users in Decision Making and Water Administration." In Water for Human Consumption. International Water Resources Association Report, Vol. 2. Dublin Ireland: Tycooly International Pub., 1982, pp. 523-532.

Vindasius, D. Evaluation of the Okanagan Public Involvement Programme. Water Planning and Management Branch, Environment Canada, Ottawa, Canada, 1975.

Vindasius, D. Public Participation Techniques and Methodologies: A Resume. Social Science Series No. 12. Water Planning and Management Branch, Inland Waters Directorate, Ottawa, Canada, 1974.

Vogt, S. F. Public Participation Handbook for Water Quality Management. Water Planning Division, U. S. Environmental Protection Agency, Washington, DC, 1976. 81 p.

Wagner, T. P. and L. Ortolano. "Analysis of New Techniques for Public Involvement in Water Planning." Water Resources Bulletin, 11, 2 (1975): 329-344.

Wagner, T. P. and L. Ortolano. Testing an Interative, Open Process for Water Resources Planning. IWR Report 76-2. Institute for Water Resources, U. S. Army Corps of Engineers, Fort Belvoir, VA, December 1976. 71 p.

Warner, K. P. Informational Public Participation in Water Resources Planning. Unpublished Ph.D. dissertation. University of Michigan, Ann Arbor, MI, 1972.

Warner, K. P. "Local Objectives as an Input in Evaluating Water Resources Plans and Projects." In G. Schramm and R. E. Burt Jr., An Analysis of Federal Water Planning and Evaluation Procedures. School of Natural Resources, University of Michigan, Ann Arbor, 1970, Appendix III.

Warner, K. P. Public Participation in Water Resource Development. National Water Commission, Arlington, VA, 1971.

Warner, K. P. A State-of-the-Arts Study of Public Participation in the Water Resources Planning Process. Report No. PB 204 245. National Technical Information Service, Springfield, VA, July 1971. 235 p.

Warriner, C. K. "Public Opinion and Collective Action: Formation of a Watershed District." Administrative Science Quarterly, 6, 3 (1961): 333-359.

Wengert, N. "Participation and the Administrative Process." In J. C. Pierce and H. R. Doerksen (eds.), Water Politics and Public Involvement. Ann Arbor, MI: Ann Arbor Science Publishing Inc., 1976, pp. 29-41.

Wengert, N. Public Participation and the 18 Major Steps in the Conception, Authorization, and Construction of Civil Works Projects. Memorandum. Center for Advanced Planning, Institute for Water Resources, U. S. Army Corps of Engineers, Fort Belvoir, VA, June 1970.

Wengert, N. "Public Participation in Water Planning: A Critique of Theory, Doctrine and Practice." Water Resources Bulletin, 7, 1 (1971): 26-32.

Wengert, N. Public Participation in Water Resources Development with a View to the Improvement of the Human Environment. Department of Political Science, Colorado State University, Fort Collins, CO, 1974. 68 p.

Wengert, N. "Where Can We Go with Public Participation in the Planning Process?" In D. J. Allee (ed.), The Role of Public Involvement in Water Resources Planning and Development. Water Resources and Marine Science Center, Cornell University, Ithaca, NY, 1974, pp. 109-126.

Wenrich, J. W. "Community Education for Participation in Water Resource Planning." In J. A. Straayer (ed.), Focus on Change: Intergovernmental Relations in Water Resources Planning. Policy Science Papers No. 1. Colorado State University, Fort Collins, CO, January 1970, pp. 235-246.

Westphal, J. M. and W. F. Halverson. "Assessing the Long-Term Effects of an Environmental Education Program: A Pragmatic Approach." Journal of Environmental Education, 17, 2 (1985-86): 26-30.

White, G. Strategies of American Water Management. Ann Arbor, MI: University of Michigan Press, 1971.

White, G. F. "Public Opinion in Planning Water Development." In C. R. Goldman et al. (eds.), Environmental Quality and Water Development. San Francisco: W. H. Freeman, 1973, pp. 157-169.

Widditsch, A. Public Workshops on the Puget Sound and Adjacent Waters Study: An Evaluation. IWR Report 72-2. Institute for Water Resources, U. S. Army Corps of Engineers, Alexandria, VA, June1972. 105 p.

Wilkinson, K. P. "Special Agency Program Accomplishment and Community Action Styles: The Case of Watershed Development." Rural Sociology, 34, 1 (1969): 29-42.

Wilkinson, K. P. and R. M. Singh. Generalized Participation of Voluntary Leaders in Local Watershed Projects. Water Resources Institute, Mississippi State University, Starkville, MS, 1969.

Willeke, G. E. "Citizen Participation: Here to Stay." Civil Engineering, 44, 1 (1974): 78-82.

Willeke, G. E. Identification of Publics in Water Resources Planning. Report No. ERC-1774. Department of City Planning, Environmental Resources Center, Georgia Institute of Technology, Atlanta, GA, 1974. 30 p.

Willeke, G. E. "Identification of Publics in Water Resources Planning." In J. C. Pierce and H. R. Doerksen (eds.), Water Politics and Public Involvement. Ann Arbor, MI: Ann Arbor Science Publishing Inc., 1976, pp. 43-62.

Willeke, G. E. "Identifying the Public in Water Resource Planning." Journal of Water Resources Planning and Management Division ASCE, 102, 1 (1976): 137-150.

Willeke, G. E. "Theory and Practice of Public Participation in Planning." Journal of Irrigation, Drainage Division ASCE, 100, CO1 (1974): 1-6.

Wilson, D. M. "Trees, Earth, Water and Ecological Upheaval: Logging Practices and Watershed Protection in California." California Law Review, 54, 2 (1966): 1117-1132.

Wilson, R. H. Towards a Philosophy of Planning: Attitudes of Federal Water Planners. Socio-economic Studies Series EPA-R5-73-015. U. S. Environmental Protection Agency, March 1973. 239 p.

Wojick, D. E. "Planning for Discourse." Water Spectrum, 10, 2 (1978): 17-23.

Wolff, R. D. Involving the Public and the Hierarchy in Corps of Engineers' Survey Investigation. Report EEP-45. Program in Engineering-Economic Planning,Stanford University, Stanford, CA, November 1971. 185 p. text and 130 p. appendices.

Wolman, G. M. "Selecting Alternatives in Water Resources Planning and the Politics of Agendas." Natural Resources Journal, 16 (October 1976): 773-789.

Wood, C. J. B. "Conflict in Resource Management and the Use of Threat: The Goldstream Controversy." Natural Resources Journal, 16, 1 (1976): 137-158.

Wood, W. L. Jr. Public Participation in the Alpine Lakes Controversy: The Coalignment of Interests. Unpublished M. S. thesis. Pennsylvania State University, University Park, PA, August 1980. 91 p.

Wrobel, D. D. "Public Participation Program Regulations for Facilities Planning." In Alternative Wastewater Treatment Systems Conference, Urbana, IL, June 1979: Proceedings. University of Illinois, pp. 27-32.

Weather Modification

Davis, R. J. "Options for Public Control of Atmospheric Management." Denver Journal of International Law and Policy, 10, 3 (1981): 523-535.

Farhar, B. C. "The Public Decides About Weather Modification." Environment and Behavior, 9, 3 (1977): 279-310.

Haas, J. E. "Social Aspects of Weather Modifications." American Meteorological Society Bulletin, 54, 7 (1973): 647-657.

Haas, J. E. "Weather Modification, The Public Will Decide." American Meteorological Society Bulletin, 54, 7 (1973): 658-660.

Haas, J. E., Boggs, K. S., and E. J. Bonner. "Science, Technology, and the Public: The Case of Planned Weather Modification." In W. R. Burch et al. (eds.), Social Behavior, Natural Resources, and the Environment. New York: Harper and Row, 1972, pp. 151-173.

Haas, J. E., Boggs, K. S., and E. J. Bonner. "Weather Modification and the Decision Process." Environment and Behavior, 3 (1971): 179-190.

Part IV

Environmental Mediation

Environmental Mediation

Abrams, N. E. and R. S. Berry. "Mediation: A Better Alternative to Science Courts." Bulletin of the Atomic Scientists, 33, 4 (1977): 50-53.

Aggerholm, D. A. "Can Environmental Mediation Make Things Happen?" In Beyond the Urban Fringe: Land Use Issues of Nonmetropolitan America. Washington, DC: Association of American Geographers, 1983, pp. 295-301.

Alexander, T. "A Promising Try at Environmental Detente for Coal." Fortune, 97, 3 (1978): 94-102.

Alheritiere, D. "Settlement of Public International Disputes in Shared Resources: Elements of a Comparative Study of International Instruments." Natural Resources Journal, 25, 3 (1985): 701-711.

Alm, A. et al. "American Bar Association Standing Committee Symposium: Siting of Hazardous Waste Facilities and Transportation of Hazardous Substances." Environmental Law Reporter, 15, 8 (1985): 10233-10261.

American Management Systems. "Issue Paper: The Potential Alternative Conflict-Management Techniques for Resolving Environmental Disputes Related to Energy Facilities." Paper prepared for the U. S. Department of Energy, Washington, DC, 1980.

American Management Systems. "The Potential of Mediation for Resolving Environmental Disputes Related to Energy Facilities." Paper prepared for the U. S. Department of Energy, Washington, DC, 1979.

Amy, D. J. "Environmental Mediation: An Alternative to Policy Stalemates." Policy Sciences, 15, 4 (1983): 345-365.

Amy, D. J. "The Politics of Environmental Mediation." Ecology Law Quarterly, 11, 1 (1983): 1-20.

Arnold, R. "Loggers vs. Environmentalists: Friends? or Foes?" Logging Management, (February 1978): 16-19.

Bacow, L. S. and J. R. Milkey. "Overcoming Local Opposition to Hazardous Waste Facilities: The Massachusetts Approach." Harvard Environmental Law Review, 6 (1982): 265-305.

Baldwin, P. Environmental Mediation: An Effective Alternative? Report of a conference held in Reston, VA, January 1978 by Resolve, Center for Environmental Conflict Resolution, Palo Alto, CA, 1978.

Ball, G., Sutton, M., and L. Brubaker. "Early Consultation in the EIR Process: New Opportunities for Environmental Professionals." Environmental Professional, 2, 1 (1980): 41-52.

Baur, E. J. "Mediating Environmental Disputes." Western Sociological Review, 8, 1 (1977): 16-24.

Bellman, H. S. "A Mediator Is a Mediator. . ." Environmental Consensus, (Spring 1980): 4-5.

Bellman, H. S. "Siting for a Sanitary Landfill for Eau Claire, Wisconsin." Environmental Professional, 2, 1 (1980): 56-57.

Bellman, H. S. and A. Sachs. " Parallels in Labor and Environmental Mediation." Working Paper of the Public Disputes Program, Program on Negotiation, Harvard Law School, Cambridge, MA, 1984.

Bellman, H. S., Cormick, G. W., and C. Sampson. Using Mediation When Siting Hazardous Waste Management Facilities: A Handbook. Report No. SW-944. Washington, DC: U. S. Government Printing Office, 1982.

Bellman, H. S. et al. "Environmental Conflict Resolution: Practitioners' Perspective of an Emerging Field." Environmental Consensus, (Winter 1981): 1-7.

Bernstein, J. Z. "Environmental Mediation." EPA Journal, 5 (November-December 1979): 30-31.

Bidol, P. Designing Environmental Conflict Management Approaches for State Natural Resource Agencies. School of Natural Resources, University of Michigan, Ann Arbor, MI, 1982.

Bidol, P. A. and J. R. Ehrmann. Environmental Conflict Management for State Agencies. Ann Arbor, MI: School of Natural Resources, University of Michigan, 1982.

Bingham, G. "Does Negotiation Hold Promise for Regulatory Reform?" Resolve, (Fall 1981): 1-8.

Bingham, G. "The Growth of the Environmental Dispute Resolution Field." In Resolving Environmental Disputes. Washington, DC: Conservation Foundation, 1986, pp. 13-63.

Bingham, G. "How Efficient Are Environmental Dispute Resolution Processes?" In Resolving Environmental Disputes. Washington, DC: Conservation Foundation, 1986, pp. 127-148.

Bingham, G. "How Successful Have Environmental Dispute Resolution Processes Been?" In Resolving Environmental Disputes. Washington, DC: Conservation Foundation, 1986, pp. 65-90.

Bingham, G. "Looking Ahead to the Next Decade." In Resolving Environmental Disputes. Washington, DC: Conservation Foundation, 1986, pp. 149-168.

Bingham, G. Resolving Environmental Disputes: A Decade of Experience. Washington, DC: Conservation Foundation, 1986. 284 p.

Bingham, G. Resolving Environmental Disputes: A Decade of Experience -- Executive Summary. Washington, DC: Conservation Foundation, 1985. 13 p.

Bingham, G. "Resolving Environmental Disputes: A Decade of Experience." Resolve, 17 (1986): entire issue.

Bingham, G. "What Factors Affect the Likelihood of Success?" In Resolving Environmental Disputes. Washington, DC: Conservation Foundation, 1986, pp. 91-126.

Bingham, G. and D. S. Miller. "Prospects for Resolving Hazardous Waste Siting Disputes through Negotiation." Natural Resources Lawyer, 17, 3 (1984): 473-490.

Bingham, G., Vaughn, B. and W. Gleason. Environmental Conflict Resolution: Annotated Bibliography. Washington, DC: Conservation Foundation, 1981.

Bosselman, F. P. "Buying Off the Neighbors: Negotiated Private Settlements of Development Disputes in Japan." Environmental Comment, (May 1977): 12-13.

Bowman, A. O. "Hazardous Waste Cleanup and Superfund Implementation in the Southeast." Policy Studies Journal, 14, 1 (1985): 100-110.

Buckle, L. G. and S. R. Thomas-Buckle. "Placing Environmental Mediation in Context: Lessons from 'Failed' Mediations." Environmental Impact Assessment Review, 6, 1 (1986): 55-70.

Burgess, H. "The Foothills Water Treatment Project: A Case Study of Environmental Mediation." Paper prepared for the U. S. Environmental Protection Agency by the Environmental Negotiations Project, MIT Laboratory of Architecture and Planning, Cambridge, MA, 1980.

Busterud, J. "Environmental Conflict Resolution." Environmental Science and Technology, 15, 2 (1981): 150-155.

Busterud, J. "Environmental Mediation: Bridging the Gap Between Energy Needs and Ecosystem." In Ecology and Coal Resource Development Conference, Grand Forks, ND, June 1978: Proceedings. International Congress for Energy and Ecosystem, 1978, Vol. 1, pp. 50-54.

Busterud, J. "Mediation: The State of the Art." Environmental Professional, 2, 1 (1980): 34-39.

Busterud, J. and G. Bingham. "Environmental Conflict Resolution Update." Environmental Professional, 2, 1 (1980): 131-132.

Busterud, J. and B. J. Vaughn. "Mediation or Litigation?" Solid Wastes Management, 22, 2 (1979): 24-29.

Carpenter, S. L. and W. J. D. Kennedy. "Conflict Anticipation: A Site-Specific Approach for Managing Environmental Conflicts." Paper presented to the Society of Mining Engineers of AIME, Tucson, AZ, October 1979.

Carpenter, S. L. and W. J. D. Kennedy. "Consensus Building: A Tool for Managing Energy-Environment Conflicts." Paper presented at the Management of Energy-Environment Conflicts Conference, Wye Plantation, MD, May 1980.

Carpenter, S. L. and W. J. D. Kennedy. "Environmental Conflict Management." Environmental Professional, 2, 1 (1980): 67-74.

Carpenter, S. L. and W. J. D. Kennedy. "Environmental Conflict Management in Western Communities." Paper presented at the Community Dispute Resolution Conference, Cherry Hill, NJ, June 1979.

Carpenter, S. L. and W. J. D. Kennedy. "Information Sharing and Conciliation: Tools for Environmental Conflict Management." Environmental Comment, (May 1977): 21-23.

Carpenter, S. L. and A. Sachs. "The Decision to Intervene." Working Paper of the Public Disputes Program, Program on Negotiation, Harvard Law School, Cambridge, MA, 1984.

Cifrino, D. "Tearing Down the Wall through Environmental Mediation." Conservation News, 43, 19 (1978): 8-11.

Clark, P. B. "Consensus Building: Mediating Energy, Environmental and Economic Conflict." Environmental Comment, (May 1977): 9-12.

Clark, P. B. "Mediating Energy, Environmental, and Economic Conflict Over Fuel Policy for Power Generation in New England." In L. M. Lake (ed.), Environmental Mediation: The Search for Consensus. Boulder, CO: Westview Press, 1980, pp. 173-204.

Clark, P. B. and W. M. Emrich. "New Tools for Resolving Environmental Disputes." Paper prepared by the American Arbitration Association for the Council on Environmental Quality and the Resource and Land Investigations Program, U. S. Department of the Interior, Washington, DC, 1980.

Clark, P. B. and D. B. Straus. "Computer Assisted Negotiations: Bigger Problems Need Better Tools." Environmental Professional, 2, 1 (1980): 75-87.

Clark-McGlennon Associates, Inc. Final Report on Phase One of Developing Methods for Environmental-Energy Dispute Settlement. American Arbitration Association, Washington, DC, 1978.

Clean Sites, Inc. "Sweeping Aside Startup Problems and Getting on with the Job." Chemical Week, 136 (June 5, 1985): 28-31.

Cohen, A. S., Cormick, G. W., and J. H. Lave. "Intervenor Roles: A Review." Crisis and Change, 3, 3 (1973):

Conservation Foundation. Second National Conference on Environmental Dispute Resolution, Washington, DC, October 1984: Proceedings. Washington, DC, 1984. 125 p.

Cormick, G. W. "Comparing Processes for the Resolution of Environmental Conflict: Intervention, Issues and Timing." Paper presented to the Society of Mining Engineers of AIME, Tucson, AZ, October 1979.

Cormick, G. W. "Environmental Mediation in the United States: Experience and Future Directions." Paper presented at the Annual Meeting of the American Association for the Advancement of Science, Toronto, Canada, 1981. 20 p.

Cormick, G. W. "The Ethics of Mediation: Some Unexplored Territory." Paper presented to the Society of Professionals in Dispute Resolution, New York, NY, October 1977.

Cormick, G. W. "How and When Should You Mediate Natural Resource Disputes?" Paper presented to Alternatives to Litigation seminar, Washington State Bar Association, Seattle, WA, July 1985.

Cormick, G. W. "Intervention and Self-Determination in Environmental Disputes: A Mediator's Perspective." Resolve, (Winter 1982): 1+.

Cormick, G. W. "Mediating Environmental Controversies: Perspectives and First Experience." Earth Law Journal, 2, 3 (1976): 215-224.

Cormick, G. W. "The Myth, the Reality, and the Future of Environmental Mediation." Environment, 24, 7 (1982): 14-17+.

Cormick, G. W. "Resolving Conflicts on the Uses of Range through Mediated Negotiations: Answers to the Ten Most Asked Questions." Paper presented to the National Range Conference, Oklahoma City, OK, November 1985.

Cormick, G. W. "Resolving Environmental Conflicts through Mediation: Experience, Process, and Potentials." Paper presented to the Annual Meeting of the American Sociological Association, San Francisco, September 1978.

Cormick, G. W. "Siting New Hazardous Waste Management Facilities Using Mediated Negotiations." Paper presented to the conference Meeting the New RCRA Requirements on Hazardous Waste, Alexandria, VA, October 1985.

Cormick, G. W. "The 'Theory' and Practice of Environmental Mediation." Environmental Professional, 2, 1 (1980): 24-33.

Cormick, G. W. and A. Knaster. "Mediation and Scientific Issues: Oil and Fishing Industries Negotiate." Environment, 28 (December 1986): 6-16.

Cormick, G. W. and J. McCarthy. Environmental Mediation: Flood Control, Recreation and Development in the Snoqualmie River Valley. Social Science Institute, Washington University, St. Louis, MO, 1974.

Cormick, G. W. and L. K. Patton. "Environmental Mediation: Defining the Process Through Experience." In L. M. Lake (ed.), Environmental Mediation: The Search for Consensus. Boulder, CO: Westview Press, 1980, pp. 76-97.

Cormick, G. W. and L. K. Patton. "Environmental Mediation: Potentials and Limitations." Environmental Comment, (May 1977): 13-16.

Craig, R. "The Keystone Process in Radioactive Waste Management." Environmental Consensus, (Winter 1980): 2-3.

Creighton, J. L. "A Tutorial: Acting as a Conflict Conciliator." Environmental Professional, 2, 1 (1980): 119-127.

Dash, R. "Which Party Are You?" Environmental Education Report, 8, 8 (1980): 4-6.

Dorcey, A. H. "Coastal Management as a Bargaining Process." Coastal Zone Management Journal, 11, 1-2 (1983): 13.

Dotson, A. B. "Who and How? Participation in Environmental Negotiation." Environmental Impact Assessment Review, 4, 2 (1983): 203-217.

Dryzek, J. S. and S. Hunter. "Environmental Mediation for International Problems." International Studies Quarterly, 31, 1 (1987): 87-102.

Duerksen, C. J. Responses to the Real Problems: Permit System Innovations for the 1980s. Conservation Foundation Report, Washington, DC, 1983.

Duffy, C. "State Hazardous Waste Facility Siting: Easing the Process through Local Cooperation and Preemption." Boston College Environmental Affairs Law Review, 11 (October 1984): 755-804.

Emrich, W. "New Approaches to Managing Environmental Conflict: How Can the Federal Government Use Them?" Paper prepared for the Council on Environmental Quality, Washington, DC, 1980.

Environmental Mediation International. Proceedings of the Environmental Mediation in Canada Seminar, Ottawa, Ontario, April 1983: Proceedings. 1983. 75 p.

Fanning, O. "The World's Newest Profession: The Environmental Mediator." Environment, 21, 7 (1979): 33-38.

Fetter, C. W. Jr. "Resolving Groundwater Contamination Issues Outside the Courts." Ground Water, 22, 2 (1984): 216-219.

Flack, J. E. and D. A. Summers. "Computer-Aided Conflict Resolution in Water Resource Planning: An Illustration." Water Resources Research, 7, 6 (1971): 1410-1414.

Fradin, D. M. The Moorhead Plant Dispute: Report of Minnesota's First Environmental Mediation. St. Paul, MN: Environmental Balance Association of Minnesota, 1976.

Goldbeck, W. "Mediation: An Instrument of Citizen Involvement." Arbitration Journal, 30, 4 (1975): 241-252.

Golten, R. J. "Confessions of an Environmental Litigator." Environmental Consensus, (Spring 1980): 1-2.

Golten, R. J. "Mediation: A 'Sellout' for Conservation Advocates or a Bargain?" Environmental Professional, 2, 1 (1980): 62-66.

Golten, R. J. and A. Sachs. "The Interplay of Environmental Litigation and Negotiation." Working Paper of the Public Disputes Program, Program on Negotiation, Harvard Law School, Cambridge, MA, 1984.

Greenberg, M. R. "Up-Front Environmental Mediation." Geographical Review, 67, 2 (1977): 235.

Greenberg, M. R. and D. B. Straus. "Up-Front Resolution of Environmental and Economic Disputes." Environmental Comment, (May 1977): 16-18.

Groves, D. L. "A Model for Conflict Resolution." International Journal of Environmental Studies, 22, 3-4 (1984): 173-181.

Gusman, S. "Selecting Participants for a Regulatory Negotiation." Environmental Impact Assessment Review, 4, 2 (1983): 195-202.

Gusman, S. and P. J. Harter. "Mediating Solutions to Environmental Risks." Annual Review of Public Health, 7 (1986): 293-312.

Gusman, S. V. and V. Huser. "Mediation in the Estuary." Coastal Zone Management Journal, 11, 4 (1984): 273-295.

Hair, J. D. "Winning through Mediation." Ecolibrium, 12, 4 (1983): 19.

Harlow, R. "Conflict Reduction in Environmental Policy." Journal of Conflict Resolution, 18, 3 (1974): 536-552.

Harter, P. J. "Negotiating Regulations: A Chance for Actual Participation." Environmental Forum, 1, 6 (1982): 8-11.

Harter, P. J. "Regulatory Negotiation: The Experience So Far." Resolve, (Winter 1984): 1+.

Haussman, F. C. Environmental Mediation: A Canadian Perspective. Environment Canada, Hull, Quebec, 1982.

Healy, R. G. Environmentalists and Developers: Can They Agree on Anything? Washington, DC: Conservation Foundation, 1977.

Hileman, B. "Environmental Dispute Resolution." Environmental Science and Technology, 17, 4 (1983): 165.

Huser, V. C. "The CREST Dispute: A Mediation Success." Environment, 24, 7 (1982): 18-20+.

Huser, V. C. "Environmental Mediation: Resolution of a Site-Specific Dispute with Area-Wide Policy Implications." Paper presented to the Society of Mining Engineers of AIME, Tucson, AZ, October 1979.

Huser, V. C. "Mediating Forestry Issues: This Three-Pronged Process Holds Great Promise in Resolving Resource Disputes, Including Turf Battles Over Forest Plans." American Forests, 92 (October 1986): 29-34.

Keystone Center. The Keystone Siting Process Handbook: A New Approach to Siting Hazardous Waste Management Facilities. Report LP-194. Texas Department of Water Resources, Austin, TX, January 1984. 52 p.

Keystone Center. An Overview of the Keystone Radioactive Waste Management Process: An Exercise in Problem Solving. Keystone, CO, 1980.

Keystone Center. Public Participation in Developing National Plans for Radioactive Waste Management. Keystone, CO, October 1980.

Keystone Center. Siting Non-Radioactive Hazardous Waste Facilities: An Overview. Final Report of the First Keystone Workshop on Managing Non-Radioactive Hazardous Wastes. Keystone Center, CO, 1980.

Keystone Center. Siting Waste Management Facilities in the Galveston Bay Area: A New Approach. Keystone, CO, November 1982. 50 p.

King, T. F. "Resolving Environmental Disputes: A Model from Historic Preservation." Social Impact Assessment, 83/84 (1983): 2-8.

Kinsey, D. N. "The Coastal Development Review Process in New Jersey: Avoiding Disputes and Resolving Conflicts." Environmental Comment, (May 1977): 19-20.

Kutay, K. Environmental Mediation: A Bibliographic Essay. School of Natural Resources, University of Michigan, Ann Arbor, MI, 1978.

Lake, L. M. "Characterizing Environmental Mediation." In L. M. Lake (ed.), Environmental Mediation: The Search for Consensus. Boulder, CO: Westview Press, 1980, pp. 58-75.

Lake, L. M. "Environmental Conflict and Decisionmaking." In L. M. Lake (ed.), Environmental Mediation: The Search for Consensus. Boulder, CO: Westview Press, 1980, pp. 1-31.

Lake, L. M. (ed.). Environmental Mediation: The Search for Consensus. Boulder, CO: Westview Press, 1980.

Lake, L. M. "Judicial Review: From Procedure to Substance." In L. M. Lake (ed.), Environmental Mediation: The Search for Consensus. Boulder, CO: Westview Press, 1980, pp. 32-57.

Lake, L. M. "Mediating Electric Power Plant Options for California: A Case Study in Conflict Avoidance." Paper presented at the Symposium on Environmental Mediation Case Studies held at the Annual Meeting of the American Association for the Advancement of Science, Denver, CO, 1977.

Lake, L. M. "Mediating Environmental Disputes." Ekistics, 44 (September 1977): 164-170.

Lake, L. M. "Mediating the West Side Highway Dispute in New York City." In L. M. Lake (ed.), Environmental Mediation: The Search for Consensus. Boulder, CO: Westview Press, 1980, pp. 205-234.

Lake, L. M. "Participatory Evaluations of Energy Options for California: A Case Study in Conflict Avoidance." In L. M. Lake (ed.), Environmental Mediation: The Search for Consensus. Boulder, CO: Westview Press, 1980, pp. 147-172.

Lake, L. M. "Public Choice Theory and Environmental Disputes: The West Side Highway Mediation Experiment." Paper presented at the Annual Meeting of the American Society for Public Administration, Chicago, IL, April 1975.

Lake, L. M. "Unifying the Concept of Third-Party Intervention in Environmental Disputes." Environmental Comment, (May 1977): 6-9.

Lambert, A. "Game Theory and Environmental Disputes." Environmental Management, 7, 5 (1983): 427-432.

Laue, J. and G. W. Cormick. "The Ethics of Intervention in Community Disputes." In G. Bermant et al. (eds.), The Ethics of Social Intervention. Washington, DC: Hemisphere Publishing, 1974.

Lee, K. N. "Defining Success in Environmental Dispute Resolution." Resolve, (Spring 1982): 1+.

Lentz, S. S. "The Labor Model for Mediation and Its Application to the Resolution of Environmental Disputes." Journal of Applied Behavioral Science, 22, 2 (1986): 127-139.

Lord, W. B. "Water Resources Planning: Conflict Management." Water Spectrum, (Summer 1980): 1-10.

Lord, W. B. et al. Conflict Management in Federal Water Resources Planning. Institute of Behavioral Science, University of Colorado, Boulder, CO, 1978.

Marcus, P. A. and W. M. Emrich (eds.). Working paper in Environmental Conflict Management. New York: American Arbitration Association, 1981.

McCarthy, J. E. "Learning from the Labor-Management Model." Environmental Consensus, (Summer 1980): 1-2.

McCarthy, J. E. "Resolving Environmental Conflicts." Environmental Science and Technology, 10, 1 (1976): 40-43.

McCarthy, J. E. and A. Shorett. "Mediation to Resolve Environmental Conflict: The Snohomish Experiment." Journal of Soil and Water Conservation, 31, 5 (1976): 212-213.

McCarthy, J. E. and A. Shorett. Negotiating Settlements: A Guide to Environmental Mediation. New York: American Arbitration Association, 1984.

McCloskey, M. "Environmental Conflicts: Why Aren't More Negotiated?" Paper presented to the Aspen Institute, Aspen, CO, July 1977.

McCrory, J. P. "Environmental Mediation: Another Piece for the Puzzle." Vermont Law Review, 6 (Spring 1981): 49-84.

Mernitz, S. "Geography and the Mediation of Environmental Disputes." Professional Geographer, 27, 4 (1975): 491-492.

Mernitz, S. Mediation of Environmental Disputes: A Sourcebook. New York: Praeger, 1980. 202 p.

Miller, A. and W. Cuff. "The Delphi Approach to the Mediation of Environmental Disputes." Environmental Management, 10, 3 (1986): 321-330.

Miller, W. H. "Movement Toward Environmental Peace." Industry Week, 196, 4 (1978): 20-22.

Moss, L. E. "Beyond Conflict: The Act of Environmental Mediation." Sierra, 66, 2 (1981): 40-45.

Murray, F. X. (ed.). Where We Agree: Summary and Synthesis. Report of the National Coal Policy Project. Boulder, CO: Westview Press, 1978.

National Conference of State Legislatures. Introduction to Environmental Conflict Management, A Legislative Perspective: Vol. I - The Process (53 p.); Vol. II - Institutionalizing Conflict Management: The Legislative Role (39 p. + 12 p. Appendices). Denver, CO, July 1984.

Nelkin, D. and M. Pollak. "Problems and Procedures in the Regulation of Technological Risk." In R. C. Schwing and W. A. Albers (eds.), Societal Risk Assessment: How Safe is Safe Enough? New York: Plenum Press, 1980, pp. 233-248 (discussion, pp. 248-253).

Nice, J. "Stalemates Spawn New Breed: The Eco-Mediators." High Country News, 11, 6 (1979): 6.

O'Connor, D. L. "Environmental Mediation: The State of the Art." Environmental Impact Assessment Review, 2 (October 1978): 9-17.

O'Connor, D. L. "Mediation: An Effective Way To Settle Hydro Licensing Disputes." Waterpower 83 Hydropower International Conference, Knoxville, TN, September 1983: Proceedings. Tennessee Valley Authority, 1984, Vol. 3, pp. 1174-1181.

O'Connor, D. L. Use of Mediation to Resolve the Dispute over Low-Head Hydroelectric Development at Swan Lake. Report of the Mediator to the Maine Office of Energy Resources, New England Environmental Mediation Project, Boston, MA, 1980.

O'Connor, D. L. and C. H. W. Foster. "Founding a Center for Environmental Mediation in New England." In North America Wildlife and Natural Resource 54th Conference, Miami Beach, FL, March 1980: Proceedings. Wildlife Management Institute, 1980, pp. 90-97.

O'Hare, M. "Not on My Block You Don't: Facility Siting and the Strategic Importance of Compensation." Public Policy, 25 (Fall 1977): 407-458.

Ognibene, P. J. "Environmental Negotiation." Electric Perspectives, (Fall 1983): 21-28.

Ozawa, C. P. and L. Susskind. "Mediating Science-Intensive Policy Disputes." Journal of Policy Analysis and Management, 5, 1 (1985): 23-39.

Patton, L. K. "Problems in Environmental Mediation: Human, Procedural, and Substantive." Environmental Comment, (November 1981): 7-10.

Patton, L. K. "Settling Environmental Disputes: The Experience with and Future of Environmental Mediation." Environmental Law, 14 (Spring 1984): 547-554.

Patton, L. K. and G. W. Cormick. "Mediation and the NEPA Process: The Interstate 90 Experience." Paper presented at the Environmental Impact Analysis Conference, University of Illinois, Champaign-Urbana, IL, May 1977.

Raiffa, H. "Environmental Conflict Resolution." In the Art and Science of Negotiation. Cambridge, MA: Harvard University Press, 1982, pp. 310-317.

Resolve. Environmental Mediation: An Effective Alternative? Center for Environmental Conflict Resolution, Palo Alto, CA, April 1978.

Resolve. Nuclear Waste Management Process Review Forum -- Executive Summary. Resolve-Center for Environmental Conflict Resolution, Palo Alto, CA, July 1980.

Resolve. Nuclear Waste Management Process Review Forum -- Final Report. Resolve-Center for Environmental Conflict Resolution, Palo Alto, CA, 1980.

Rich, L. A. "EPA Brings 'Reg-Neg' to RCRA." Chemical Week, 137 (November 13, 1985): 9-11.

Richman, R. and W. Gibson. "Environmental Conflict Resolution in Virginia." Environmental Consensus, (September 1979): 4-5.

Riesel, D. "Negotiation and Mediation of Environmental Disputes." Ohio State Journal on Dispute Resolution, 1, 1 (1985): 99-111.

Rivkin, M. D. "Negotiated Development: A Breakthrough in Environmental Controversies." Environmental Comment, (May 1977): 3-6.

Rivkin, M. D. Negotiated Development: A Breakthrough in Environmental Controversies (An Issue Report). Washington, DC: Conservation Foundation, 1977.

Rivkin, M. D. "Principles of Negotiated Development." Environmental Comment, (November 1981): 4-6.

Sadler, B. "Environmental Conflict Resolution in Canada?" Resolve, 18 (1986): 1+.

Sampson, C. "The Environmental Mediator." Environment, 21 (September 1979): 35.

Sampson, C. "The Mediator's Role in Environmental Disputes." Environmental Consensus, 2 (July 1979): 3.

Sampson, C. "The Roles of Environmental Professionals in Mediation." Environmental Professional, 2, 1 (1980): 53-55.

Schoenbrod, D. "Limits and Dangers of Environmental Mediation: A Review Essay." New York University Law Review, 58, 6 (1983): 1453-1476.

Sherman, H. D. "Colorado's Joint Review Process: More Involvement, Better Decisions, Less Delay." Environmental Consensus, (Fall 1980): 1+.

Shorett, A. J. "Environmental Mediation at the Port of Everett." Environmental Consensus, (December 1978): 3.

Shorett, A. J. "The Role of the Mediator in Environmental Disputes." Environmental Professional, 2, 1 (1980): 58-61.

Shrybman, S. "Environmental Mediation: A Boon to Canadian Environmentalists?" Resolve, 18 (1986): 2.

Shrybman, S. Environmental Mediation: Five Case Studies. Canadian Environmental Law Association, Toronto, Ontario, 1983.

Shrybman, S. Environmental Mediation: From Theory to Practice. Canadian Environmental Law Association, Toronto, Ontario, 1984.

Shrybman, S. Environmental Mediation: Three Case Assessments. Canadian Environmental Law Association, Toronto, Ontario, 1984.

Sorensen, J. H., Soderstrom, J. and S. A. Carnes. "Sweet for the Sour: Incentives in Environmental Mediation." Environmental Management, 8, 4 (1984): 287-294.

Stein, R. E. "Environmental Mediation of Transboundary Issues." Paper presented at the Annual Meeting of the American Pollution Control Association, Montreal, Quebec, June 1980.

Stein, R. E. and G. Grenville-Wood. Between Neighbors: How U. S. States and Canadian Provinces Settle Their Shared Environmental Problems. Environmental Mediation International, Ottawa, Ontario, n. d.

Stockholm, N. "Environmental Mediation: An Alternative to the Courtroom." Stanford Lawyer, 15, 1 (1980): 21-25.

Straus, D. B. "Managing Complexity: A New Look at Environmental Mediation." Environmental Science and Technology, 13, 6 (1979): 661-665.

Straus, D. B. "Mediating Environment, Energy and Economic Tradeoffs." Arbitration Journal, 32, 2 (1977): 96-110.

Straus, D. B. "Mediating Environmental and Economic Tradeoffs: A Case Study of the Search for Improved Tools for Facilitating the Process." Paper presented at the Symposium on Environmental Mediation Case Studies held at the Annual Meeting of the American Association for the Advancement of Science, Denver, CO, 1977.

Straus, D. B. "Mediating Environmental Disputes." Arbitration Journal, 33, 4 (1978): 5-8.

Straus, D. B. "Mediating Environmental, Energy, and Economic Tradeoffs: A Search for Improved Tools for Coastal Zone Planning." In L. M. Lake (ed.), Environmental Mediation: The Search for Consensus. Boulder, CO: Westview Press, 1980, pp. 123-146.

Straus, D. B. No Winners: Only Losers or Mutual Victories -- Mediating Environmental Disputes. New York: Arbitration Association, 1978.

Straus, D. B. and P. B. Clark. "Bigger Problems Need Better Tools: Guidelines to Identify, Manage and Resolve Environmental Disputes." Paper presented at the Annual Conference of the National Association of Environmental Professionals, Washington, DC, April 1980.

Straus, D. B. and M. R. Greenberg. Data Mediation of Environmental Disputes: Converting Facts from Weapons into Tools. New York: Research Institute, American Arbitration Association, 1978.

Stulberg, J. B. "The Theory and Practice of Mediation: A Reply to Professor Susskind." Vermont Law Review, 6 (Spring 1981): 85-117.

Sullivan, T. J. Resolving Development Disputes through Negotiation. New York: Plenum, 1984.

Susskind, L. E. "Environmental Mediating and the Accountability Problem." Vermont Law Review, 6 (Spring 1981): 1-47.

Susskind, L. E. "The Political Realities of Environmental Dispute Mediation." Paper presented to the American Arbitration Association, May 1978.

Susskind, L. E. "Resolving Environmental Disputes Through Ad Hocracy." Environmental Consensus, (Summer 1980): 3-5.

Susskind, L. E. "A Sharper Focus: Defining the Common Issues in Dispute Resolution." Environmental Impact Assessment Review, 6, 1 (1986): 51-54.

Susskind, L. E. The Uses of Negotiation and Mediation in Environmental Impact Assessment. Urban Studies and Planning, Massachusetts Institute of Technology, Cambridge, MA, January 1980. 27 p.

Susskind, L. E. "The Uses of Negotiation and Mediation in Public Policy Making." In F. Porter, F. A. Rossini, and C. P. Wolf (eds.), Integrated Impact Assessment. Boulder, CO: Westview Press, 1983, pp. 154-167.

Susskind, L. and S. McCreary. "Techniques for Resolving Coastal Resource Management Disputes Through Negotiation." American Planning Association Journal, 51, 3 (1985): 365-374.

Susskind, L. E. and A. Weinstein. "How To Resolve Environmental Disputes Out of Court." Technology Review, 85, 1 (1982): 38.

Susskind, L. E. and A. Weinstein. "Towards a Theory of Environmental Dispute Resolution." Boston College of Environmental Affairs Law Review, 9, 2 (1980-81): 311-357.

Susskind, L. E., Bacow, L. S. and M. Wheeler (eds.). Resolving Environmental Regulatory Disputes. Cambridge, MA: Schenckman, 1984.

Susskind, L. et al. Resolving Environmental Disputes: Approaches to Intervention, Negotiation, and Conflict Resolution. Laboratory of Architecture and Planning, Massachusetts Institute of Technology, Cambridge, MA, 1978.

Talbot, A. R. Environmental Mediation, Three Case Studies: The Island, the Highway, the Ferry Terminal. Seattle, WA: Institute for Environmental Mediation, 1981.

Talbot, A. R. Settling Things: Six Case Studies in Environmental Mediation. Washington, DC: Conservation Foundation, 1983. 101 p.

Thomas, H. D. "New England Task Force: Power Plants, People and the Environment." Environmental Consensus, (Fall 1980): 1+.

Tohn, E. "Mediating the Preparation of an Impact Report: Siting the Boston Harbor Wastewater Treatment Facility." Environmental Impact Assessment Review, 6, 1 (1986): 213-217.

Tremaine, J. R. and P. G. Yates. "Contract Zoning as a Negotiation Tool: Fairfax County, Virginia's 'Proffer Process.'" Environmental Comment, (May 1977): 23-24.

Tribe, L. H., Schelling, C. S., and J. Voss (eds.). When Values Conflict: Essays on Environmental Analysis, Discourse, and Decision. Cambridge, MA: Ballinger Publishing Co., 1976. 178 p.

U. S. General Accounting Office. Improving the Scientific and Technical Information Available to the Environmental Protection Agency in Its Decisionmaking Process. GAO Report CED-79-115. Washington, DC, September 1979. 68 p.

U. S. Senate. Committee on Labor and Human Resources. Proposed Asbestos Claims Facility: Hearings, March 19, 1985. 99th Congress, 1st Session. Washington, DC: U. S. Government Printing Office, 1985. 89 p.

Vaughn, B. J. "Environmental Mediation: Fighting Fair." Planning, 46, 8 (1980): 16-18.

Wald, P. M. "Negotiation of Environmental Disputes: A New Role for the Courts?" Columbia Journal of Environmental Law, 10, 1 (1985): 1-33.

Watson, J. L. and L. J. Danielson. "Environmental Mediation." Natural Resources Lawyer, 15, 4 (1983): 687-723.

Wehr, P. "Environmental Conciliation." In L. M. Lake (ed.), Environmental Mediation: The Search for Consensus. Boulder, CO: Westview Press, 1980, pp. 98-122.

Wehr, P. "Environmental Conflict Management: Problems, Theory and Method." In L. Kriesberg (ed.), Research in Social Movement, Conflict and Change. Vol. 2. Greenwich, CT: JAI Press, 1979, pp. 63-82.

Wehr, P. Environmental Peacemaking. Environmental Conciliation Project, Phase I - Preliminary Report. University of Colorado, Boulder, CO, June 1976. 62 p.

Wright, M. "Resolving Conflicts in Natural Resource Priorities: Some Experience in Developing Countries." In North America Wildlife and Natural Resource 54th Conference, Miami Beach, FL, March 1980: Proceedings. Wildlife Management Institute, 1980, pp. 71-82.

Yost, N. C. The Governance of Environmental Affairs -- Towards Consensus. Aspen Institute for Humanistic Studies, New York, 1982.

Yost, N. C. "New NEPA Regulations Stress Cooperation Rather than Conflict." Environmental Consensus, (March 1979): 1-2.

Part V

Science and Technology Decision Making

Science and Technology Decision Making

Ahmad, R. S. Community Participation, Technology Assessments, and Social Change. Battelle Columbus Laboratories, Washington Operations, Washington, DC, 1979.

Aikenhead, G. S. "Collective Decision-Making in the Social Context of Science." Science Education, 69, 4 (1985): 453-475.

Alford, R. Health Care Politics: Ideology and Interest Group Barriers to Reform. Chicago: University of Chicago Press, 1975.

Argyris, C. "Action Science and Intervention." Journal of Applied Behavior Analysis, 19, 2 (1983): 115-135.

Baehr, P. R. "Think Tanks - Who Needs Them? Advising a Government in a Democratic Society." Futures, 18, 3 (1986): 389-400.

Baker, J. J. W. "Three Modes of Protest Action." Bulletin of the Atomic Scientists, (February 1975): 8-15.

Ballard, S. C. and J. E. James. "Participatory Research and Utilization in the Technology Assessment Process: Issues and Recommendations." Knowledge, 4, 3 (1983): 409-428.

Bandyopadhyay, J. and V. Shiva. "The Legitimacy of People's Participation in the Formulation of Science and Technology Policy: Some Lessons from the Indian Experience." In J. C. Petersen (ed.), Citizen Participation in Science Policy. Amherst, MA: University of Massachusetts Press, 1984, pp. 96-106.

Baram, M. S. "Social Control of Science and Technology." Science, 172 (May 7, 1971): 535-539.

Barbour, I. G. "Democracy and Expertise in a Technological Society." National Forum: Phi Kappa Phi Journal, 63 (Winter 1983): 3-5.

Barbour, I. G. Technology, Environment, and Human Values. New York: Praeger, 1980.

Barbour, I. G. et al. Energy and Human Values. New York: Praeger, 1982. 239 p.

Bartels, D. "It's Good Enough for Science, But is it Good Enough for Social Action." Science, Technology and Human Values, 53 (Autumn 1985): 69-74.

Bazelon, D. L. "Coping with Technology Through the Legal Process." Cornell Law Review, 62, 5 (1977): 817-832.

Beckwith, J. "The Radical Science Movement in the United States." Monthly Review, 38, 3 (1986): 118.

Berg, M. R. et al. Factors Affecting Utilization of Technology Assessment Studies in Policy-Making. Center for Research on Utilization of Scientific Knowledge, Institute for Social Research, University of Michigan, Ann Arbor, MI, 1978.

Boyer, B. B. "Scientists, Citizens, and Bureaucrats: Notes on Bridging the Cultural Chasm." Abstracts of Papers of the American Chemical Society, 188 (August 1984): 12.

Bronfman, B. H. "Assessing the Validity of Public Involvement in Social Impact Assessment: The Community-Based Technology Assessment Program." In G. A. Daneke et al. (eds.), Public Involvement and Social Impact Assessment. Boulder, CO: Westview Press, 1983, pp. 215-225.

Bronfman, B. H., Carnes, S. A., and R. Ahmad. "Community Based Technology Assessment: Four Communities Plan Their Energy Future." In F. Porter, F. A. Rossini, and C. P. Wolf (eds.), Integrated Impact Assessment. Boulder, CO: Westview Press, 1983, pp. 202-218.

Bronfman, L. and T. Mattingly, Jr. "Critical Mass: Politics, Technology and the Public Interest." Nuclear Safety, 17 (1976): 539-549.

Butler, W. A. "The Environmental Defense Fund (EDF): Science and Law as Citizens' Weapons to Preserve the Environment." In Citizens' Advisory Committee on Environmental Quality, Citizens Make the Difference: Case Studies of Environmental Action. Washington, DC, January 1973, pp. 55-61.

Call, G. D. "Arsenic, ASARCO, and EPA-Cost-Benefit Analysis, Public Participation, and Polluter Games in the Regulation of Hazardous Air Pollutants." Ecology Law Quarterly, 12, 3 (1985):567-618.

Cambrosia, A. and P. Keating. "Studying a Biotechnology Research Centre: A Note on Local Socio-Political Issues." Social Studies of Science, 15, 4 (1985): 723-737.

Carpenter, R. "Information for Decisions in Environmental Policy." Science, 168 (1970): 1316-1322.

Carroll, J. D. "Participatory Technology." Science, 171 (February 19, 1971): 647-653.

Casper, B. M. "Technology Policy and Democracy." Science, 194 (October 1, 1976): 29-35.

Chakraborti, R. M. "The Nehru Science Centre: Public Participation in Science." Impact of Science on Society, 32, 4 (1982): 461-466.

Chavis, D. M., Stucky, P. E., and A. Wandersma. "Returning Basic Research to the Community: A Relationship Between Scientist and Citizen." American Psychologist, 38, 4 (1983): 424-434.

Checkoway, B. "Consumer and Health Planning Issues and Opportunities." In J. C. Petersen (ed.), Citizen Participation in Science Policy. Amherst, MA: University of Massachusetts Press, 1984, pp. 130-146.

Chubin, D. E. "Open Science and Closed Science: Tradeoff in a Democracy." Science, Technology, and Human Values, 51 (1985): 73-81.

Chubin, D. E. "Research Missions and the Public: Over-Selling and Buying the U. S. War on Cancer." In J. C. Petersen (ed.), Citizen Participation in Science Citizen Participation in Science and Technology Decision Making Policy. Amherst, MA: University of Massachusetts Press, 1984, pp. 109-129.

Chubin, D. E. and K. E. Studer. "The Politics of Cancer." Theory and Society, 6 (1978): 55-74.

Coates, J. F. "Why Public Participation Is Essential in Technology Assessment." Public Administration Review, 35 (January-February 1975): 67-69.

Coates, J. F. "Why Public Participation Is Essential in Technology Assessment." In G. Boyle et al. (eds.), The Politics of Technology. New York: Longman, Inc.,1977, pp. 186-188.

Coates, V. T. "Technology Assessment -- New Demands for Information." Chemical Engineering Progress, 70, 11 (1974): 41-45.

Commission of the European Communities. Science and European Public Opinion. Brussels, Belgium, 1977.

Crain, R. L., Katz, E., and D. B. Rosenthal. The Politics of Community Conflict: The Fluoridation Decision. New York: Bobbs-Merrill, 1969. 269 p.

Cronin, T. E. and N. C. Thomas. "Federal Advisory Processes: Advice and Discontent." Science, 171 (February 26, 1971): 771-779.

Culliton, B. J. "Science's Restive Public." Daedalus, 107 (1978): 147-156.

DiMento, J. "Citizen Environmental Litigation and Administrative Process." Duke Law Journal, 22 (1977): 409-452.

Dunlap, T. R. DDT: Scientists, Citizens, and Public Policy. Princeton, NJ: Princeton University Press, 1981. 304 p.

Dutton, D. "The Impact of Public Participation in Biomedical Policy: Evidence from Four Case Studies." In J. C. Petersen (ed.), Citizen Participation in Science Policy. Amherst, MA: University of Massachusetts Press, 1984, pp. 147-181.

Dutton, D. B. and J. L. Hochheimer. "Institutional Biosafety Committees and Public Participation: Assessing the Experiment." Nature, 297 (1982): 11-15.

Dylander, B. "Technology Assessment -- As Science and as Tool for Policy." Acta Sociologica, 23, 4 (1980): 217-237.

Eamon, W. "From the Secrets of Nature to Public Knowledge: The Origins of the Concept of Openness in Science." Minerva, 23, 3 (1985): 321-347.

Ebbin, S. and R. Kasper. Citizen Groups and the Nuclear Power Controversy: Uses of Scientific and Technological Information. Cambridge, MA: MIT Press, 1974.

Epstein, S. S. The Politics of Cancer. San Francisco: Sierra Club Books, 1979. 583 p.

Epstein, S. S., Monsour, W. J., and C. Nader (eds.). Science, Technology and the Public Interest: Information, Communications and Organizational Patterns. Jeannette, PA: Monsour Medical Foundation, 1977. 124 p.

Fawcett, S. "Macro-Engineering Projects in a Free Society." Technology in Society, 7, 4 (1985): 361-372.

Fernades, W. and R. Tandon (eds.). Participatory Research and Evaluation: Experiments in Research as a Process of Liberation. New Delhi: Indian Social Institute, 1981.

Friedman, R. S. "Representation in Regulatory Decision-Making: Scientific, Industrial, and Consumer Inputs to the F.D.A." Public Administration Review, 38, 3 (1978): 205-214.

Gershon, E. S. "Should Science be Stopped: The Case of Recombinant DNA Research." Public Interest, 71 (Spring 1983): 3-16.

Gianos, P. L. "Scientists and Policy Advisers: The Context of Influence." Western Political Quarterly, 27 (September 1974): 429-456.

Gibbons, J. H. and H. L. Gwin. "Technology and Governance." Technology in Society, 7, 4 (1985): 333-335.

Glenn, C. J. and J. D. Francis. "Communication and Science Policy Decision Making: A Case Study." Paper presented at the First National Symposium on Social Science in Resource Management, Corvallis, OR, May 1986.

Goodell, R. "Public Involvement in the DNA Research Controversy: The Case of Cambridge, Massachusetts." Newsletter on Science, Technology and Human Values, 27 (Spring 1979): 36-43.

Graham, L. R. "Comparing United States and Soviet Experiences: Science, Citizens, and the Policy-Making Process." Environment, 26, 7, (1984): 6-9+.

Gross, A. G. "Public Debates as Failed Social Dramas: The Recombinant DNA Controversy." Quarterly Journal of Speech, 70, 4 (1984): 397-409.

Haas, J. E., Boggs, K. S., and E. J. Bonner. "Science, Technology, and the Public: The Case of Planned Weather Modification." In W. R. Burch et al. (eds.), Social Behavior, Natural Resources, and the Environment. New York: Harper and Row, 1972, pp. 151-173.

Hadden, S. G. "Technical Information for Citizen Participation." Journal of Applied Behavioral Science, 17, 4 (1981): 537-549.

Havender, W. R. "The Science and Politics of Cyclamate." Public Interest, 71 (Spring 1983): 17-32.

Henderson, H. "Awakening from the Technological Trance." In H. Henderson, Creating Alternative Futures: The End of Economics. New York: Berkley Publishing Corp., 1978, pp. 303-326.

Henderson, H. "Technology Assessment." In H. Henderson, Creating Alternative Futures: The End of Economics. New York: Berkley Publishing Corp., 1978, pp. 327-338.

Hess, K. Community Technology. New York: Harper and Row, 1979.

Hollander, R. "Institutionalizing Public Service Science: Its Perils and Promise." In J. C. Petersen (ed.), Citizen Participation in Science Policy. Amherst, MA: University of Massachusetts Press, 1984, pp. 75-95.

Hollander, R. "The Science for Citizens Program and the Folly Island Workshop on Erosion Abatement." Environmental Impact Assessment Review, 1 (1980): 306-311.

Holman, H. R. and D. B. Dutton. "A Case for Public Participation in Science Policy Formation and Practice." Southern California Law Review, 51, 6 (1978): 1505-1534.

Horrobin, D. "In Praise of Non-Experts." New Scientist, 94 (June 24, 1982): 842-844.

Hutt, P. B. "Public Criticism of Health Science Policy." Daedalus, 107 (1978):157-169.

Kasperson, R. E. "6 Propositions on Public Participation and Their Relevance for Risk Communication." Risk Analysis, 6, 3 (1986): 275-281.

Kemeny, J. G. "Saving American Democracy: The Lessons of Three Mile Island." Technology Review, 82 (June-July 1980): 65-75.

Kennard, B. "Tomorrow's Technology: Who Decides?" In C. Bezold (ed.), Anticipatory Democracy: People in the Politics of the Future. New York: Vintage Books, 1978, pp. 183-189.

King, J. "A Science for the People." New Scientist, 74 (June 16, 1977): 634-636.

Kloman, E. H. "A Mini-Symposium: Public Participation in Technology Assessment." Public Administration Review, 35, 1 (1975): 67-81.

Kloman, E. H. "Public Participation in Technology Assessment." Public Administration Review, 34, 1 (1974): 51-61.

Kolata, G. "Freedom of Information Act: Problems at the FDA." Science, 189 (1975): 32-33.

Krimsky, S. "Beyond Technocracy: New Routes for Citizen Involvement in Social Risk Assessment." Journal of Voluntary Action Research, 11, 1 (1982): 8-23.

Krimsky, S. "Beyond Technocracy: New Routes for Citizen Involvement in Social Risk Assessment." In J. C. Petersen (ed.), Citizen Participation in Science Policy. Amherst, MA: University of Massachusetts Press, 1984, pp. 43-61.

Krimsky, S. "A Citizen Court in the Recombinant DNA Debate." Bulletin of the Atomic Scientists, 34, 8 (1978): 37-43.

Krimsky, S. "Citizen Participation in Scientific and Technological Decision-Making Part II." In S. Langton (ed.), Citizen Participation Perspectives: Proceedings of the National Conference on Citizen Participation, Washington, DC, September 28-October 1, 1978. Medford, MA: Lincoln Filene Center, 1979, pp. 181-186.

Krimsky, S. Genetic Alchemy: The Social History of the Recombinant DNA Debate. Cambridge, MA: MIT Press, 1982. 445 p.

Krimsky, S. " Paradigms and Politics: The Roots of Conflict Over Recombinant DNA Research." In R. P. Bareikis (ed.), Science and the Public Interest: Recombinant DNA Research: Proceedings of a Forum Held 10-12 November 1977, Indiana University. West Lafayette, IN: The Poynter Center, 1978, pp. 127-144.

Krimsky, S. Public Participation in the Formation of Science and Technology Policy. National Science Foundation, Washington, DC, 1979.

Krimsky, S. "The Role of the Citizen Court in the Recombinant DNA Debate." Bulletin of the Atomic Scientists, 34 (1978): 38-43.

Lakoff, S. A. "Scientists, Technologists, and Political Power." In I. Spiegel-Rosing and D. Price (eds.), Science, Technology and Society: A Cross-Disciplinary Perspective. Beverly Hills, CA: Sage Publications, 1977, pp. 355-391.

Lamson, R. W. "Citizen Participation in Scientific and Technological Decision-Making Part I." In S. Langton (ed.), Citizen Participation Perspectives: Proceedings of the National Conference on Citizen Participation, Washington, DC, September 28-October 1, 1978. Medford, MA: Lincoln Filene Center, 1979, pp. 179-180.

Lappe, M. and P. A. Martin. "The Place of the Public in the Conduct of Science." Southern California Law Review, 51 (1978): 535-554.

Leahy, P. and A. Mazur. "A Comparison of Movements Opposed to Nuclear Power, Fluoridation, and Abortion." Research in Social Movements, Conflicts and Change, 1 (1978): 143-154.

Levine, A. G. Love Canal: Science, Politics and People. Lexington, MA: Lexington Books, 1982.

Livingston, D. "Little Science Policy: A Research Agenda for the Study of Appropriate Technology and Decentralization." In J. Haberer (ed.), Science and Technology Policy: Perspective and Developments. Lexington, MA: D. C. Heath, 1977, pp. 99-108.

Livingston, D. "Little Science Policy: The Study of Appropriate Technology and Decentralization." Policy Studies Journal, 5 (Winter 1976): 185-192.

Livingston, D. "Science by the People: Public Participation in Research and Development." Paper presented at the Annual Meeting of the American Psychological Association, 1977. 6 p.

MacRae, D. Jr. "Technical Communities and Political Choice." Minerva, 14 (Spring 1976): 169-190.

Markle, G. E. and J. C. Petersen (eds.). Politics, Science, and Cancer: The Laetrile Phenomenon. Boulder, CO: Westview Press, 1980.

Markle, G. E., Petersen, J. C., and M. O. Wagenfeld. "Notes from the Cancer Underground: Participation in the Laetrile Movement. "Social Science and Medicine, 12 (1978): 31-37.

Mazmanian, D. A. "Citizens and the Assessment of Technology." Paper presented at the Annual Meetings of the American Political Science Association, Chicago, IL, August-September 1974.

Mazur, A. The Dynamics of Technical Controversy. Washington, DC: Communications Press, 1981. 150 p.

Mayo, D. G. "Increasing Public Participation in Controversies Involving Hazards: The Value of Metastatistical Rules." Science, Technology, and Human Values, 53 (1985): 55-68.

McCrae, D. "Science and the Formation of Policy in a Democracy." Minerva, 11 (1973): 228-242.

Mendelsohn, E. and P. Weingart. "The Social Assessment of Science: Issues and Perspectives." In E. Mendelsohn et al. (eds), The Social Assessment of Science: Conference Proceedings. Bielefeld, Germany: University of Bielefeld, 1978.

Miller, J. D. The American People and Science Policy: The Role of Public Attitudes in the Policy Process. New York: Pergamon Press, 1983. 145 p.

Miller, M. L. and R. P. Gale. "The Sociology of Science in Natural Resource Management Systems: Observations on Forestry and Marine Fisheries." Paper presented at the First National Symposium on Social Science in Resource Management, Corvallis, OR, May 1986.

Mitchell, J. "The Consumer Movement and Technological Change." In G. Boyle et al. (eds.), The Politics of Technology. New York: Longman, Inc., 1977, pp. 206-217.

Mottur, E. R. "Technology Assessment and Citizen Action." In R. Kasper (ed.), Technology Assessment: Understanding the Social Consequences of Technological Application. New York: Praeger, 1972.

Mullineaux, R. D. "Science and Public Understanding: How Scientists Influence Public Policy." Ecolibrium, 11, 2-3 (1982): 11-.

National Academy of Sciences. Technology: Processes of Assessment and Choice. Washington, DC: U. S. Government Printing Office, 1969.

Nelkin, D. (ed.). Controversy: The Politics of Technical Decisions. Beverly Hills, CA: Sage, 1979. 256 p.

Nelkin, D. "Discussion: Science and Technology in the Pits." In G. E. Markle and J. C. Petersen (eds.). Politics, Science, and Cancer: The Laetrile Phenomenon. Boulder, CO: Westview Press, 1980, pp. 181-184.

Nelkin, D. Evaluating Citizen Participation: Technological Decisionmaking. Center for Responsive Governance, Washington, DC, 1980. 28 p.

Nelkin, D. Nuclear Power and Its Critics: The Cayuga Lake Controversy. Science, Technology and Society Series No. 1. Ithaca, NY: Cornell University Press, 1971. 128 p.

Nelkin, D. "The Political Impact of Technical Expertise." Social Studies of Science, 5 (1975): 35-54.

Nelkin, D. "Science and Technology Policy and the Democratic Process." In J. C. Petersen (ed.), Citizen Participation in Science Policy. Amherst, MA: University of Massachusetts Press, 1984, pp. 18-39.

Nelkin, D. Science Textbook Controversies and the Politics of Equal Time. Cambridge, MA: MIT Press, 1977.

Nelkin, D. "Scientific Knowledge, Public Policy, and Democracy: A Review Essay." Knowledge: Creation, Diffusion, Utilization, 1, 1 (September 1979): 106-122.

Nelkin, D. Technological Decisions and Democracy: European Experiments in Public Participation. Beverly Hills, CA: Sage, 1977.

Nelkin, D. "Technology and Public Policy." In I. Spiegel-Rosing and D. Price (eds.), Science,
Technology and Society: A Cross-Disciplinary Perspective. Beverly Hills, CA: Sage
Publications, 1977, pp. 393-441.

Nelkin, D. "Thoughts on the Proposed Science Court." Newsletter on Science, Technology, and
Human Values, No. 18 (January 1977): 20-31.

Nelkin, D. and M. Pollak. "Consensus and Conflict Resolution: The Politics of Assessing Risk."
Science and Public Policy, (October 1979): 307-318.

Nelkin, D. and M. Pollak. "Ideology as Strategy: The Discourse of the Anti-Nuclear Movement in
France and Germany." Science, Technology and Human Values, 15 (1980): 3-13.

Nelkin, D. and M. Pollak. "Problems and Procedures in the Regulation of Technological Risk." In
R. C. Schwing and W. A. Albers (eds.), Societal Risk Assessment: How Safe Is Safe Enough?
New York: Plenum Press, 1980, pp. 233-248 (discussion pp. 248-253).

Nelkin, D. and M. Pollak. "Public Participation in Technological Decisions: Reality or Grand
Illusion?" Technology Review, 8, 8 (1979): 54-64.

Nelkin, D. and A. Rip. "Distributing Expertise: A Dutch Experiment in Public Interest Science."
Bulletin of the Atomic Scientists, (May 1979): 20-23+.

Nichols, K. G. "The De-Institutionalization of Technical Expertise." In H. Skoie (ed.), Scientific
Expertise and the Public: Conference Proceedings. Oslo: Institute for Studies in Research
and Higher Education, Norwegian Research Council for Science and the Humanities, 1979,
pp. 35-48.

Nichols, K. G. "Technology on Trial." OECD Observer, 98 (May 1979): 34-41.

Nichols, K. G. Technology on Trial: Public Participation in Decision-Making Related to Science
and Technology. Organization for Economic Cooperation and Development, Paris, 1979.
122 p.

Nobel, D. F. "Present Tense Technology." Democracy, 3 (Spring 1983): 8-24.

Nowotny, H. "Experts and Their Expertise: On the Changing Relationship Between Experts and
Their Public." Bulletin of Science, Technology, and Society, 1 (1981): 235-241.

Nowotny, H. and H. Hirsch. "The Consequences of Dissent: Sociological Reflections on the Controversy of the Low Dose Effects." Research Policy, 9 (1980): 278-294.

O'Brien, D. M. and D. A. Marchand (eds.). The Politics of Technology Assessment: Institutions,
Processes, and Policy Disputes. Lexington, MA: Lexington Books, 1982.

Orr, D. "Participation in the Age of Technology." Citizen Participation, 2 (November-December
1980): 15.

Otway, H. J. and D. von Winterfeldt. "Beyond Acceptable Risk: On the Social Acceptability of
Technologies." Policy Sciences, 14 (1982): 247-256.

Perry, R. W. et al. Community Stress and Social and Technological Change: A Framework for Interpreting the Behavior of Social Movements and Community Action Groups. Report No. B/HARC/411/80/034. Battelle Human Affairs Research Centers, Seattle, WA, June 1980. 150 p.

Petersen, J. C. (ed.). Citizen Participation in Science Policy. Amherst: University of Massachusetts Press, 1984. 241 p.

Petersen, J. C. (ed.). "Citizen Participation in Science Policy." Journal of Voluntary Action Research, 11 (January-March 1982): entire issue.

Petersen, J. C. "Citizen Participation in Science Policy." In J. C. Petersen (ed.), Citizen Participation in Science Policy. Amherst, MA: University of Massachusetts Press, 1984, pp. 1-17.

Petersen, J. C. "Science for Citizens: Death at an Early Age." Paper presented at the Conference on Citizen Participation and Technocracy in Public Decision Making, Cleveland, OH, 1983.

Petersen, J. C. and G. E. Markle. "Expansion of Conflict in Cancer Controversies." In L. Kriesberg (ed.), Research in Social Movements, Conflicts and Change. Greenwich, CT: JAI Press, 1981.

Petersen, J. C. and G. E. Markle. "The Laetrile Controversy." In D. Nelkin (ed.) Controversy: The Politics of Technical Decisions. Beverly Hills, CA: Sage, 1979. pp. 159-179.

Petersen, J. C. and G. E. Markle. "Politics and Science in the Laetrile Controversy." Social Studies of Science, 9 (1979): 139-166.

Pollak, M. "Public Participation." In H. Otway and M. Peltu (eds.), Regulating Industrial Risks: Science, Hazards and Public Protection. Boston: Butterworths, 1985, pp. 76-93.

Primack, J. and F. von Hippel. Advice and Dissent: Scientists in the Political Arena. New York: Basic Books, 1974. 299 p.

"Public Involvement in Science and Technology." Science and Public Policy, 4 (February 1977): 49-51.

Ravetz, J. R. "Criticisms of Science." In I. Spiegel-Rosing and D. deSolla Price (eds.), Science, Technology and Society: A Cross-Disciplinary Perspective. London: Sage, pp. 71-89.

Rayner, J. and D. Peerla. "To Spray or Not to Spray? Exclusive Concepts of Science and Nature in the Canadian Spruce Budworm Controversy." Paper presented at the First National Symposium on Social Science in Resource Management, Corvallis, OR, May 1986.

"Recombinant DNA: Not So Fast." Economist, 291 (May 26, 1984): 100+.

Rip, A. "Controversies as Informal Technology Assessment." Knowledge: Creation, Diffusion, Utilization, 8, 2 (1986): 349-371.

Rip, A. "Societal Processes of Technology Assessment." In H. A. Becker and A. L. Porter (eds.), Impact Assessment Today. Vol. 1. Utrecht: Van Arkel, 1986, pp. 415-433.

Rossini, F. A. and A. L. Porter. "Public Participation and Professionalism in Impact Assessment." In J. C. Petersen (ed.), Citizen Participation in Science Policy. Amherst, MA: University of Massachusetts Press, 1984, pp. 62-74.

Salter, L. "The Role of the Public in Scientific Determination of Policy: The Canadian Inquiry Process." University of Toronto Law Journal, 31 (Fall 1981): 343-362.

Schrum, W. "The Organizational Context of Public Interest Science." Technology in Society, 6, 4 (1984): 299-312.

Sklair, L. "Science, Technology and Democracy." In G. Boyle et al. (eds.), The Politics of Technology. New York: Longman, Inc., 1977, pp. 172-185.

Skoie, H. (ed.). Scientific Expertise and the Public: Conference Proceedings. Oslo: Institute for Studies in Research and Higher Education, Norwegian Research Council for Science and the Humanities, 1979. 228 p.

Stevens, C. H. "A State That Listens to Citizens and Science." New Scientist, 49 (February 11, 1971): 298-300.

Strickland, S. Politics, Science, and Dread Disease. Cambridge, MA: Harvard University Press, 1972.

Studer, K. E. and D. E. Chubin. The Cancer Mission: Social Contexts of Biomedical Research. Beverly Hills, CA: Sage, 1980.

Troyer, R. J. and G. E. Markle. Cigarettes: The Battle Over Smoking. New Brunswick, NJ: Rutgers University Press, 1983.

U. S. Congress. Office of Technology Assessment. "Public Participation and Public Confidence in the Superfund Program." In Superfund Strategy. Report No. OTA -ITE-252. Washington, DC, April 1985, pp. 257-274.

von Hippel, F. and J. Primack. "Public Interest Science." Science, 177 (September 29, 1972): 1166-1171.

von Winterfeldt, D. and W. Edwards. "Patterns of Conflict about Risky Technologies." Risk Analysis, 4, 1 (1984): 55-68.

Wade, N. "Freedom of Information." Science, 175 (1972): 493-502.

Wenk, E. "Scientists, Engineers, and Citizens." Science, 206 (1979): 771.

Wenk, E. Jr. "Technology Assessment in Public Policy: A New Instrument for Social Management of Technology." IEEE Proceedings, 63, 3 (1975): 371-379.

Wenk, E. Jr. Tradeoffs: Imperatives of Choice in a High-Tech World. Baltimore, MD: Johns Hopkins University Press, 1986. 272 p.

Wicklein, J. "How Sweden Keeps Its Computers Honest: A New Law Helps the Citizen Fight Back." Progressive, 44 (November 1980): 34-38.

Wolstenholme, G. "Public Confidence in Scientific Research: The British Response to Genetic Engineering." Technology in Society, 6, 1 (1984): 9-16.

Wynne, B. "Redefining the Issues of Risk and Public Acceptance: The Social Viability of Technology." Futures, 15, 1 (1983): 13.

Wynne, B. "The Rhetoric of Consensus Politics: A Critical Review of Technology Assessment." Research Policy, 4 (1975): 108-158.

Yellin, J. "Science, Technology, and Administrative Government: Institutional Designs for Environmental Decision Making." Yale Journal, 92, 7 (1983): 1300.

About the Authors

FREDERICK FRANKENA received a Ph.D. from Michigan State University in 1983, specializing in the social and environmental impact of technology and the politics of technical expertise. He has published articles and presented papers at national and international conferences on topics related to citizen participation in environmental affairs.

JOANN KOELLN FRANKENA is a librarian who graduated from the University of Minnesota with an M.L.S. degree in 1974. A native of Minnesota, she worked for the Duluth Public Library for 10 years before assuming her present position as Head of Information Services at the Library of Michigan.

The literature of environmental studies is both vast and diverse. The authors' complementary skills and interests have served to increase the breadth and completeness of this bibliography.